International Series on Computer, Entertainment and Media Technology

Series Editor
Newton Lee, Institute for Education, Research, and Scholarships
Los Angeles, USA

The International Series on Computer, Entertainment and Media Technology presents forward-looking ideas, cutting-edge research, and in-depth case studies across a wide spectrum of computer, entertainment and media technology. The series covers a range of content from professional to academic. Computer Technology includes artificial intelligence, databases, computer networks, computer hardware, software engineering, cybersecurity, human computer interaction, programming languages, bioinformatics, telecommunication, mobile apps, and quality assurance. Entertainment Technology includes computer games, electronic toys, scenery fabrication, theatrical property, costume, lighting, sound, video, music, show control, animation, animatronics, interactive environments, computer simulation, visual effects, augmented reality, and virtual reality. Media Technology includes art media, print media, digital media, electronic media, big data, asset management, signal processing, data recording, data storage, data transmission, media psychology, wearable devices, robotics, and physical computing.

Jane Thomason

Infinite Playgrounds

Gaming as the Architecture of Tomorrow

Jane Thomason
UCL Centre for Blockchain Technologies
London, UK

ISSN 2364-947X ISSN 2364-9488 (electronic)
International Series on Computer, Entertainment and Media Technology
ISBN 978-3-032-08526-9 ISBN 978-3-032-08527-6 (eBook)
https://doi.org/10.1007/978-3-032-08527-6

© The Editor(s) (if applicable) and The Author(s), under exclusive license to Springer Nature Switzerland AG 2026

This work is subject to copyright. All rights are solely and exclusively licensed by the Publisher, whether the whole or part of the material is concerned, specifically the rights of translation, reprinting, reuse of illustrations, recitation, broadcasting, reproduction on microfilms or in any other physical way, and transmission or information storage and retrieval, electronic adaptation, computer software, or by similar or dissimilar methodology now known or hereafter developed.
The use of general descriptive names, registered names, trademarks, service marks, etc. in this publication does not imply, even in the absence of a specific statement, that such names are exempt from the relevant protective laws and regulations and therefore free for general use.
The publisher, the authors and the editors are safe to assume that the advice and information in this book are believed to be true and accurate at the date of publication. Neither the publisher nor the authors or the editors give a warranty, expressed or implied, with respect to the material contained herein or for any errors or omissions that may have been made. The publisher remains neutral with regard to jurisdictional claims in published maps and institutional affiliations.

This Springer imprint is published by the registered company Springer Nature Switzerland AG
The registered company address is: Gewerbestrasse 11, 6330 Cham, Switzerland

If disposing of this product, please recycle the paper.

Foreword

When I founded SiGMA, I envisioned more than a platform for networking and deal-making. I wanted to help shape an ecosystem that inspires trust, fosters innovation, and operates with integrity. The journey since then has reinforced a simple truth: growth without responsibility is not progress—it is risk.

The gaming industry sits at a fascinating crossroads. Our technologies reach millions, our events draw leaders from every corner of the globe, and our influence can drive economies forward. Yet with such reach comes an undeniable obligation: to protect players, uphold fair play, and ensure that our innovations never come at the expense of the vulnerable.

Once a wild, ungoverned terrain, the gaming sector has grown into a powerful global movement. At SiGMA, we've watched it fuel economies, inspire cultural shifts, and influence the frameworks that guide governance.

"Infinite Playgrounds" offers a tantalising glimpse into this extraordinary transformation. From Web3 economies and immersive experiences to AI agents and digital identity, gaming is becoming the proving ground for how humans and machines will coexist in the coming decades.

Our summits serve as a meeting ground for the architects of tomorrow: a bridge between the regulators and policy makers and the boots on the ground. In-depth conversations on innovation, regulation, and responsible disruption are examined throughout this book with the same depth and vision.

Witnessing the gaming sector emerge as a catalyst for new ecosystems of growth, particularly within emerging markets, is nothing short of inspirational. Across the globe—from Colombo to Manila—young people are stepping into digital economies that just a few years ago had barely been dreamt of gateways to financial empowerment, educational opportunity, and the creation of businesses that transcend borders; these have been games worth playing.

But with opportunity comes responsibility. Responsible gaming is not merely an operational requirement—it is our moral compass. It demands we create systems that protect those that are vulnerable, educate our communities, and embrace tools that identify and mitigate harm before it escalates. It is about embedding safety into the very DNA of our industry so that entertainment never becomes exploitation.

As gaming technologies integrate deeper into our lives—touching everything from health to governance—questions of ethics, inclusion, and impact become critical. This book doesn't shy away from those questions, and that's what makes it such a valuable read.

Regulation, too, is often misunderstood. Some see it as an obstacle; I see it as the architecture of trust. Sound, transparent, and adaptive regulation provides the framework that allows creativity to flourish responsibly. It levels the playing field, rewards compliance, and deters bad actors. Without it, we do not have a sustainable industry, we have chaos.

What inspires me most is how regulation and innovation can, in fact, fuel each other. By collaborating with governments, aligning with international standards, and committing to ethical conduct, we not only safeguard our players but also create fertile ground for investment, growth, and legitimacy.

This book is a testament to what is possible when industry converges with purpose. It reminds us that our work extends far beyond the boardroom and the expo floor. We have the chance—and the responsibility—to build an industry that is not only prosperous, but principled.

I hope as you turn these pages, you see the same opportunity I do: to lead with integrity, to innovate with conscience, and to leave behind a legacy of trust, fairness, and positive impact.

I congratulate Dr Thomason on a timely and important contribution. The digital future is being written right now—and gaming is holding the pen.

Founder, SiGMA Group Eman Pulis,
Valetta, Malta

Preface

The world is changing at a pace few could have imagined. Technologies once confined to the realm of science fiction are rapidly reshaping how we live, work, learn, connect, and play. Of all the digital frontiers, gaming stands as one of the most dynamic, immersive, and transformative forces of our time. No longer simply a pastime for the young or tech-savvy, gaming has evolved into a global infrastructure that spans education, finance, governance, mental health, and even geopolitics.

As I've travelled the world, from blockchain summits in Singapore to innovation hubs in Africa and Web3 forums in Europe, I've witnessed the extraordinary convergence of technologies, AI, metaverse, blockchain, immersive reality, all accelerating through gaming. It is not just that games are becoming more intelligent or immersive; it is that the very architecture of our digital society is being prototyped, stress-tested, and reimagined inside virtual worlds.

This book, *Infinite Playgrounds: Gaming as the Architecture of Tomorrow*, is a call to attention. It explores how gaming is no longer on the periphery of digital transformation, it *is* the catalyst. It explores how emerging markets are leapfrogging legacy systems, how tokenized economies are building new models of value and identity, and how the gamification of life is blurring boundaries between the physical and the virtual, the real, and the imagined.

Gaming is becoming our new classroom, marketplace, workplace, and even therapist's chair. But with this power comes responsibility. We must design for inclusion, safety, mental well-being, and for ethical innovation. We must ensure that the new digital realms we build empower the many, not the few.

This book is written for the policy shapers, educators, investors, parents, players, and for anyone curious about where we go next. It reflects a deep belief that the future is not something we wait for. It's something we build. And in this future, gaming is not just about play, it is about possibility.

Let us build it wisely.

London, UK   Jane Thomason

Competing Interests There are no competing interests to declare.

Acknowledgments

No book is ever written alone, and this work is the result of a collective journey across time zones, events, disciplines, and digital frontiers.
To my family and dearest friends, thank you for your love, patience, and belief in my relentless drive to understand, explain, and shape the future. Your support allows me to stay curious, courageous, and committed. My son Jock was the one who sparked this journey: "Mum, you have to learn about Blockchain, it's going to change everything." He was right. My daughter Georgia has been an extraordinary companion in this journey, rapidly carving her own path in technology and science while sharing her experiences and allowing me to walk alongside her. To her wonderful Block.one family, Serg Metelin, Jay Chang, Brian Mehler, Winnie Liu, and Abby Blumer, who have also become my family, thank you for the adventures, innovation, and shared dreams. To my granddaughter Florence, who inspires me to strive to make the world she will live in better.

Loretta Joseph has been an unwavering source of inspiration and a true powerhouse in the world of emerging technology and policy. Her fearless advocacy, trailblazing regulatory work, and global influence have opened doors for countless people seeking to build a more inclusive and ethical digital future. Loretta's ability to cut through complexity with clarity and conviction is matched only by her warmth, loyalty, and generosity of spirit. Beyond her professional brilliance, she has been a close friend and steadfast ally throughout my journey, offering encouragement, laughter, and wisdom at every turn. I am deeply grateful for her companionship and her tireless dedication to making the world better through technology and humanity.

To the global community of thinkers, builders, gamers, entrepreneurs, and visionaries who are actively co-creating this new digital frontier. Your work, insights, and courage to experiment at the edge have inspired every chapter of this book.

To AIBC SIGMA, from whose events, I have learned much of what I share in the book and a special thanks to Olga Yaroshevsky who has welcomed me and given me a voice since 2021.

To the contributors and case study collaborators from across Asia, Africa, Europe, the Americas, and the Middle East, thank you for lending your voices, stories, and innovations to make this a truly global work. You have helped ground theory in practice and vision in reality.

A special thank you to Oksana Khodak who worked tirelessly on the Technical Compendium and Case Studies. Your dedication was instrumental in bringing this book to life.

I extend deep appreciation to the extraordinary women in tech who have shaped and strengthened this path and to the men who have been powerful allies, thank you for your support and shared vision. There are many founders, researchers, and designers whom I've connected with cannot be named individually, but please know your efforts, ideas, and shared purpose live on in the pages of this book.

To the young people of today, the coders, creators, streamers, and dreamers—you are not just the gamers of tomorrow. You are the architects of our digital future. This book is, in many ways, written for you.

Much of the knowledge in this book does not come from traditional academic texts or published papers; it has been gathered through lived experience, direct engagement, and immersion in the rapidly evolving world of innovation. The learning has been from on-the-ground events and interactions, shared in real time by innovators building the future. It has been drawn from countless hours spent at conferences and summits, listening to panels, engaging in deep conversations with founders, developers, investors, and visionaries. Insights have come from walking the exhibition floors, exploring cutting-edge prototypes, and witnessing firsthand the creative energy that fuels the gaming and deep tech ecosystems. These are the voices and ideas that often remain undocumented, yet they are shaping the frontiers of what's possible. This book seeks to bring together the raw, emergent knowledge that lives in the minds of innovators and on the stages of global events, where tomorrow is being imagined today.

The future of gaming is not just about entertainment. It is about equity, imagination, innovation, and collective purpose. I hope this book contributes, in some small way, to that unfolding journey.

With heartfelt thanks,
Dr. Jane Thomason

The author used ChatGPT, a language model developed by OpenAI, for language editing, research assistance, generating draft text, citation checking, and summarizing related literature during the preparation of this manuscript. The final content was reviewed and edited by the author, who takes full responsibility for its accuracy and integrity.

Contents

1	**The Evolution of Gaming**	1
	Introduction	1
	The Changing Shape of Gaming	4
	Economic Trends and Market Size	5
	Technological Advancements	6
	Artificial Intelligence (AI) and Machine Learning in Games	6
	Virtual and Augmented Reality (VR/AR)	6
	Cloud Gaming	7
	Quantum Computing and Next-Gen Processing	7
	Gaming Today	8
	Global Gaming Innovation	9
	The Industry Ecosystem and Job Creation	11
	Gamification in Key Industries	12
	The Convergence of Gaming and Social Platforms	13
	Evolving Game Genres and Mechanics	13
	Esports—The New Competitive Frontier	15
	Regulation and Ethical Challenges	17
	Overview of the Book	18
	Cross-Chapter Insights	18
	Case Studies	19
	Tencent Games	19
	Fortnite (Epic Games)	20
	References	22
2	**Web3, Digital Property Rights, and the NextGen Internet**	23
	Introduction to Web3	23
	Decentralized Finance (DeFi)	24
	Non-Fungible Tokens (NFTs)	24
	Distributed Autonomous Organizations (DAOs)	25
	Decentralized Cloud Storage	26
	Web4 and Web5: Next-Generation Internet Paradigms	26

	The Evolving Web3 Landscape..................................	27
	Digital Property Rights..	29
	Regulation for Next Gen Gaming..............................	29
	Conclusion	31
	Cross-Chapter Insights	32
	Case Studies	32
	The Sandbox—Building the Metaverse, One Block at a Time...	32
	Star Atlas—Building the First Massive Web3 AAA Game	34
	References...	36
3	**Digital Assets and Tokenization**..............................	39
	Introduction..	39
	Tokenization	40
	Token Standards	40
	Tokenization and In-Game Economies...........................	41
	Tokenization and eSports	42
	Tokenization and Secondary Markets............................	43
	The Regulatory Horizon	44
	A Model Law for Responsible Innovation	46
	Conclusion	47
	Cross-Chapter Insights	47
	Case Studies	48
	Axie Infinity—Play-to-Earn and the Rise of Digital Microeconomies	48
	Steam and Epic Store—Competing Gateways to the Digital Gaming Marketplace.................................	49
	Yield Guild Games (YGG)—Turning Play-to-Earn into a Global Talent Guild.......................................	51
	References...	52
4	**Building the New Gaming Economy**	55
	Introduction..	55
	New Economic Models.......................................	56
	GameFi: The Fusion of Gaming and Decentralized Finance	56
	Play-to-Earn Games	57
	Play-and-Own (PandO).....................................	58
	Create-to-Earn..	58
	Watch-to-Earn/Engage-to-Earn...............................	59
	Economic Opportunity in Esports...............................	59
	Metaverse and New Economic Opportunities......................	60
	Virtual Real Estate in Gaming	62
	Digital Fashion and Collectables	63
	Legal and Commercial Complexities	64

	Health and Education	64
	Gaming in e-Commerce	64
	Human Work in the Gaming Economy	65
	Global Access and Economic Inclusion	65
	Cultural and Economic Implications	66
	AI and Blockchain Convergence: The Intelligent Infrastructure of the Future of Gaming	67
	Blockchain: Ownership, Identity, and Interoperability	67
	Decentralized AI Agents: Autonomy in a Tokenized World	68
	Gaming as the New School	68
	Post-Quantum Horizons: The Coming Security Challenge	69
	Conclusion	69
	Cross-Chapter Insights	70
	Case Studies	71
	EVE Online—ISK and the Emergence of Spacefaring Mega-Economies	71
	Twitch—Streaming as a Platform Economy	73
	Alethea AI—Train-to-Earn and the Dawn of Intelligent NFTs	75
	YouTube Gaming—The Rise of Game Streaming and Creator Economies	76
	References	78
5	**Bridging the Digital Divide Through Play**	**79**
	Emerging Markets: The Future Growth Engine of Gaming	79
	Gaming as a Gateway to Digital Inclusion	84
	Telco and Private Sector Partnerships	86
	Scalable Models for the Next Billion	88
	Risks and Challenges	91
	Conclusion	92
	Cross-Chapter Insights	92
	Case Studies	93
	Mobile Legends: Bang Bang—Mobile Esports (MLBB) at Scale	93
	References	95
6	**Gamifying Life, Learning, Health, and Consumer Behaviors**	**97**
	Introduction	97
	Gamification and Serious Games in Health Care	98
	Digital Therapeutics and Clinical Applications	98
	Tokenizing Wellness: Health as a Digital Asset	99
	Gamified Mental Health and Emotional Wellness	100
	Immersive Medicine and Metaverse Therapies	101
	Rehabilitation, Physical Fitness, and Pain Management	101

	Cognitive Training and Social Therapy	102
	Health Education and Workforce Training	102
	Future Outlook: Phygital Well-Being	103
	MetaEducation: Global, Gamified, and Generative	103
	Gamification and Serious Games in Education	105
	What Will Learning Look Like in 2050?	105
	The Silver Metaverse: Gaming and Later Life	107
	New Economies of Purpose	109
	Silver Esports and Competitive Longevity	109
	Gaming Meets Hospitality and Travel	110
	Tokenized Loyalty Becomes a Game Economy	111
	Gamification and the Future of Mobility	112
	The Gamified Showroom	113
	Driving Entertainment: The Car as a Game Console	113
	Gamification of Product Development	114
	Repair and Maintenance with XR	114
	Community, Loyalty, and the Token Economy	114
	Gaming Meets Mobility in the Metaverse	115
	A Playbook for Social Impact	115
	Cross-Cultural Applications of Gamification	116
	Limitations and Constraints	116
	Conclusion	117
	Cross-Chapter Insights	117
	Case Studies	118
	Minecraft: Education Edition	118
	Sea Hero Quest—Gaming for Cognitive Science	120
	References	121
7	**Gaming and Ethics: Safeguarding the Future of Digital Play**	125
	Introduction	126
	Ethical Design	127
	Game Design Ethics: Mechanics, Monetization, and Manipulation	127
	Online Toxicity, Harassment, and Moderation Challenges	128
	Bias and Inclusion in AI and NPC Design	128
	Equity, Access, and Inclusive Representation	128
	ESG, Sustainability, and the Ethical Game Company	129
	Environmental Responsibility in Gaming	129
	Social Impact and Inclusion	129
	Gaming, Mental Health, and Navigating a Digital Childhood	130
	The Psychological Impact of Gaming	130
	Governance, Regulation, and the Metaverse	131
	Monetization Ethics and Fair Play	131

	Regulatory Responses to Ethical and Legal Challenges in Gaming	132
	How to Approach Ethics in Gaming	135
	Who Sets the Rules?	136
	Ethics-By-Design Checklist for Developers	137
	Ethics in the Metaverse—The Next Frontier for Gaming	137
	Identity, Avatars, and Moral Agency	138
	Data Ethics: Surveillance at Scale	138
	Monetization and Economic Justice	139
	Mental Health and Well-being	139
	Child Safety and Content Moderation	139
	Conclusion	140
	Cross-Chapter Insights	142
	References	142
8	**AI and Adaptive Worlds**	143
	Introduction	143
	AI as the New Architect of Game Worlds	144
	Procedural Content Generation and World-Building	145
	Intelligent NPCs and Emotional Adaptation	145
	Voice AI and Conversational Interactivity	145
	Human-AI Collaboration in Storytelling	146
	Challenges and Gaps	147
	The Ethics and Regulation of Addictive Game Design	148
	Monetization Ethics and Fair Play	149
	Moderation, Harassment, and Community Health	150
	Selected Regulatory Responses	151
	Conclusion	152
	Cross-Chapter Insight	153
	Case Studies	153
	Case Study: AI Dungeon by Latitude—Decentralized Storage in AI-Driven Narrative Gaming	153
	References	155
9	**Neural Gaming and the Brain–Computer Interface Frontier**	157
	The Mind as the Controller	157
	Accessibility and Inclusion	162
	Cognitive Enhancement and Neurofeedback	163
	AI-BCI Integration	164
	Ethical Challenges	164
	Data Privacy: Who Owns Neural Data, and How Is It Stored or Shared?	164
	Consent: Are Users Fully Informed of What Is Being Captured and How It's Used?	165

	Psychological Effects: Could Deep Immersion or Real-Time Feedback Cause Harm?..............................	165
	Bias and Equity: Are BCIs Designed Inclusively, or Do They Favor Certain Brainwave Patterns or Demographics?........	166
	Conclusion: The Neural Horizon of Play........................	166
	Cross Chapter Insights.......................................	167
	Case Studies..	167
	Neurable—Brain–Computer Interfaces and the Rise of Neural Gaming Identity................................	167
	NexMind—Brain-to-Computer Control in Immersive Gaming Interfaces..	169
	References..	170
10	**The Gamer's Edge: Skills for the Digital Century**...............	173
	Introduction: Gaming as a Skills Incubator......................	173
	Impact of AI and Automation..................................	174
	Human Work in the Gaming Economy...........................	175
	Skilling for AI and Immersive Technologies.....................	177
	The Uberization of Education and Skills Development...........	178
	Learning by Doing: Education as an Immersive Experience.......	179
	Learn-to-Earn: Turning Education into Economic Opportunity.....	179
	Tokenized Skills and Portable Digital Identity..................	180
	Reimagining Skills Training in the Digital Age.................	180
	The Reinvention of Universities and Colleges....................	181
	Immersive and Decentralized Education.........................	182
	Esports as Leadership Lab.....................................	183
	Serious Games for Workforce Training..........................	183
	Global Access and Economic Inclusion..........................	185
	Navigating the Digital Skills Journey...........................	186
	Parenting Challenges......................................	186
	Gaming as a Blueprint for Future Readiness.....................	187
	Cross-Chapter Insights.......................................	188
	Case Study...	188
	Roblox—A Universe of User-Generated Worlds and Digital Creativity..	188
	Discord: From Gamer Chat to Digital Third Place...............	190
	Reddit—The Front Page of the Internet and the Rise of Decentralized Communities..............................	191
	References..	193

11	**Infinite Playgrounds: Gaming and the Architecture of Tomorrow**	195
	Gaming at a Turning Point	195
	From Player to Creator	196
	From Centralized Control to Decentralized Ownership	196
	From Content Consumption to Skill Accumulation	196
	From Physical Workspaces to Gamified Virtual Labor	197
	From Educational Institutions to Learning Ecosystems	197
	From Attention Economies to Trust Economies	197
	From Entertainment to Civic Infrastructure	197
	A Vision for the Future	198
	What Is the Future We Want to Build Through Gaming?	198

Technical Companion 199

Glossary of Terms 247

References 251

Chapter 1
The Evolution of Gaming

Abstract The chapter lays the groundwork for the foundational thesis that gaming is: (i) becoming a foundational layer of economic and social systems; (ii) empowering digital inclusion and new job markets; and (iii) creating ethical and governance challenges as it evolves into a mass influence tool. The chapter traces the evolution of gaming from arcades and home consoles to become a $300 billion global powerhouse, shaping culture, commerce, and technology. It examines how gaming expanded across generations, geographies, and devices to become one of the most dynamic industries of the twenty-first century. Readers will explore the explosion of mobile gaming, particularly in Asia, where mobile-first adoption has redefined access and engagement. The chapter also charts the rapid growth of Esports, now rivalling traditional sports in viewership and sponsorship. By uncovering gaming's socio-economic impact and technological underpinnings, the chapter lays the groundwork for understanding how gaming has evolved beyond entertainment to become a foundational layer of our digital future, fueling economies, driving innovation, and transforming social interaction.

Keywords Gaming evolution · Digital infrastructure · Esports · Mobile gaming · Web3 · Blockchain · Gamification · Virtual reality · Augmented reality · Artificial intelligence · Global gaming markets · Digital identity · Gaming economy · Social gaming platforms · Inclusive narratives · Game-based learning · Job creation in gaming

Introduction

This book focuses on video games and Esports, not on iGaming or gambling. It explores the cultural, economic, and technological evolution of gaming as an interactive, skill-based, and increasingly immersive form of digital entertainment and social engagement. This book explores competitive Esports, game development, digital assets, gamification, and the use of games in education, health, and future job skills. It highlights how video games are transforming society, while addressing the ethical, technological, and policy challenges that accompany this rapidly growing sector.

This chapter traces the evolution of gaming, examining how it expanded across generations, geographies, and devices to become one of the most dynamic industries of the twenty-first century. Readers will explore the journey from the rise of consoles to the explosion of mobile gaming, particularly in Asia, where mobile-first adoption has redefined access and engagement. The chapter also charts the growth of Esports, now rivalling traditional sports in viewership and sponsorship. It also charts the convergence of gaming and social platforms, like Discord and Reddit. This chapter lays the groundwork for understanding how gaming has evolved beyond entertainment to become a foundational layer of our digital future, fueling economies, driving innovation, and transforming how people connect and play. Aside from entertainment, gaming has provided stress relief, mood enhancement, and social connection. It has also improved decision-making, multitasking, problem-solving, strategic planning, and adaptive thinking. The future of gaming is not just entertainment, it's a new economy.

Gaming is now the architecture of a new civilization. This metaphor reflects the increasingly foundational role gaming playing across technological, cultural, and economic dimensions. With over 3.5 billion players globally (nearly half the world's population), gaming has become the most pervasive form of media consumption, outpacing both film and music in global revenues (Newzoo 2023). With a market valuation near $400 billion (projections of total gaming industry revenue, inclusive of software, hardware, Esports, in-game spending, and emerging Web3 sectors), gaming is reshaping healthcare, education, governance, commerce, and even aging (PwC 2023).

In countries like South Korea and Saudi Arabia, gaming is not only a national pastime, but a strategic industry supported by public investment and policy frameworks. Major game platforms now serve as environments for social interaction, digital commerce, skill acquisition, and education. These developments position gaming as a central pillar in the architecture of digital life. In the digital future, gaming will define identity, community, and economy. Games are becoming platforms where players build worlds, govern economies, and shape their destinies. In Web3 environments, players are citizens, who own assets, vote on changes, and earn income. These games are effectively digital nations with currencies, identities, and laws, powered by blockchain and governed by decentralized autonomous organizations (DAOs).

Mobile platforms are a game-changer. Half of all gaming now happens on smartphones, making it the primary gateway for players across Southeast Asia, Latin America, and Africa. As broadband expands and mobile penetration deepens, these regions are poised to become the next billion-user gaming markets. Asia sits at the heart of this, with 62 of the top 100 global gaming companies based on the region, and countries like the Philippines officially declaring gaming a national growth sector. The Middle East, too, is rising rapidly. With revenue per gamer in Saudi Arabia nine times higher than in China, and with a growing young population, the region is aiming to become a global gaming hub (Newzoo 2023).

Networked infrastructure, in this context, refers to the convergence of software, hardware, data flows, and social interactions that constitute the backbone of digital society (Plantin et al. 2018). If gaming is framed as a form of networked infrastructure, it offers coherence to the argument that gaming has transcended its entertainment roots. As global connectivity increasingly relies on digital platforms that facilitate commerce, identity, and governance, gaming environments now function as socio-technical systems that mirror real-world structures. Platforms like Fortnite, Roblox, and Axie Infinity are programmable, interoperable ecosystems that host economic transactions, community formation, and skill development. These platforms illustrate how gaming architectures now support broader participation in the digital economy, effectively functioning as infrastructures of engagement and inclusion in underserved or digitally emergent regions.

Esports is another growing gaming-related phenomenon. Streaming platforms have become arenas where young people watch, play, and compete in Twitch streams and TikTok clips. AI is generating emotionally intelligent storylines and coaching players with real-time feedback. This means non-player characters (NPCs) are able to improvise, evolve, and interact like sentient beings.

For younger generations, Gen Z and Gen Alpha, gaming is life. Their identities, friendships, creative expressions, and even professional reputations are forged in virtual spaces. This generation will collaborate inside shared digital worlds with AI teammates and interoperable avatars.

But the power of gaming goes beyond games. It is healing trauma, treating anxiety, and rehabilitating cognition. Games are being designed for post-traumatic stress therapy, mental health support, and movement gamification. Seniors are exploring new worlds from their living rooms, engaging in gamified memory training, socializing with digital companions, and preserving legacy through avatar-based storytelling.

Gaming also exploring new interfaces between humans and machine, where brain–computer interfaces (BCIs) are turning thoughts into actions. In the future, players will control games with electrical signals from their minds, creating feedback loops where digital environments adapt in real time to emotion, attention, and cognition.

As this world takes shape, new jobs are emerging across storytelling, behavioral science, world-building, digital ethics, and experience design. Gamers are becoming entrepreneurs, strategists, healers, and educators. The skills most needed in this new world, such as empathy, creativity, and critical thinking, are those that games can nurture. Gaming is the scaffold of the future digital society, where people will learn, heal, socialize, and work. The next decade belongs to those who can imagine, design, and build these new worlds.

The Changing Shape of Gaming

Gaming has undergone a remarkable transformation over the past five decades. What began with simple arcade machines and home consoles has evolved into a multi-platform, multi-generational cultural force, embedded in global economies, social interaction, and technological advancement.

Each generation has experienced gaming through a different lens. In the 1980s and 90 s, Gen X and early Millennials grew up with consoles like the Nintendo Entertainment System and Sega Genesis, where pixelated graphics and side-scrolling adventures defined childhood entertainment. These early systems introduced the concept of gaming as a shared family or living room activity. By the early 2000s, gaming had shifted again to online multiplayer modes. The emergence of PC gaming brought new social dynamics. For Gen Z, gaming is not just a recreational activity but a digital lifestyle, central to how they play, learn, and connect. Today, Gen Alpha is growing up in immersive, always-on virtual environments that blend entertainment with education, creation, and socialization.

Geography has also shaped gaming's trajectory. While early innovations were largely concentrated in the US and Japan, regions like South Korea, China, and Southeast Asia have since redefined the global gaming landscape. South Korea's pioneering Esports scene laid the foundation for professional competitive gaming, while China's mobile-first population turned smartphones into primary gaming devices, fueling a surge in hyper-casual and free-to-play games. Similarly, in Africa and Latin America, mobile gaming is driving digital inclusion, offering affordable entertainment, economic opportunity, and even educational engagement in low-infrastructure environments.

The shift across devices has been equally fast paced. From arcade cabinets and cartridge-based consoles to high-powered gaming PCs, smartphones, VR headsets, and cloud-based streaming platforms, gaming has become platform-agnostic and ubiquitous. Players know game anytime, anywhere, on phones during commutes, in VR for fitness, or on Twitch for community. Innovations in cloud computing have further blurred the boundaries between hardware and content, enabling complex, high-fidelity games to run on lightweight devices and opening access to a broader global audience.

This cross-generational, cross-cultural, and cross-platform evolution has elevated gaming from entertainment to infrastructure, one that now influences commerce, communication, education, mental health, and digital identity, it is the digital heartbeat of a global generation.

Economic Trends and Market Size

In 2023, the global gaming market (inclusive of consoles, PC, and mobile) was estimated at around $247 billion (GlobeNewswire 2023a). By 2030, conservative analyses project the market to reach roughly $370 billion (GlobeNewswire 2023a). For example, a comprehensive industry report pegs the market at $371.5 billion in 2030 (up from $247.2B in 2023) (GlobeNewswire 2023a). However, other forecasts anticipate much higher growth, Fortune Business Insights projects the market could surge to $665.7 billion by 2030 (Fortune Business Insights 2024). The consensus is that gaming will see strong revenue expansion, even the slower-growth scenario would mean the industry adding well over $100 billion in annual revenue within a decade, outpacing most other media sectors. Extending further to 2035, one study forecasts a market size of about $350 billion by 2035 (Market Research Future 2024a), while more bullish analysts might expect half a trillion or more by that time.

Several factors are driving this growth: the increasing global population of gamers, higher monetization per player (through new revenue streams), and the penetration of games into new markets and demographics. Notably, mobile gaming continues to be the largest segment by revenue. Mobile games are widespread and lucrative, especially in Asia; the mobile segment was valued around $80–90 billion in the early 2020s and is projected to exceed $120 billion by 2035, remaining "a dominant force in the industry" due to smartphone ubiquity and a steady influx of new players (Market Research Future 2024a). Console and PC gaming will also grow, though a bit slower; consoles are projected to roughly double from ~$50 billion in 2024 to ~$100 billion in 2035 and PC gaming similarly rising to around $80 billion by 2035 (Market Research Future 2024a). Regionally, the Asia-Pacific market, led by China, is enormous and still expanding. Asia-Pacific already comprised about 50% of global game revenues in 2022 (Fortune Business Insights 2024) and is expected to maintain leadership due to its vast gamer base and mobile-first culture. North America and Europe will also see growth but at a slower pace. In emerging markets, improving internet access and cheaper smartphones are unlocking new gamer populations, contributing to global growth. In summary, by 2025–2035, the economic footprint of gaming will be bigger than ever, rivaling or surpassing traditional film, music, and sport sectors in size (Market Research Future 2024a).

Underlying the market growth are evolving revenue models in the game industry. The traditional model of one-time game purchases has shifted toward continuous monetization and services. In-game purchases generate a huge share of revenue, especially in free-to-play titles. However, new models like subscription services and streaming platforms are becoming a staple of gaming. The success of services like Xbox Game Pass, PlayStation Plus, and NVIDIA GeForce Now points to a future where gamers subscribe to large libraries of games much like they do for Netflix (but interactive). Subscription models provide recurring revenue for companies and lower the cost barrier for players, and by 2035 many players may primarily access games through all-you-can-play subscriptions or cloud rentals rather than individual purchases.

User-Generated Content (UGC) with platforms like Roblox and Minecraft already showing the profitability of letting players build and monetize content, and this community-driven content creation will likely become a pillar of game monetization. At the same time, advertising and brand partnerships in games are growing, especially as free-to-play and metaverse-like experiences proliferate. Brands sponsor in-game events or place virtual billboards in popular games, contributing to revenue. Dynamic in-game ads tailored to players will be common, especially in VR/AR settings where virtual product placement can mirror real-world advertising.

Technological Advancements

Key technological advancements underpinning the gaming transformation are described in detail in the *Technical Companion*. This section highlights the most important categories.

Artificial Intelligence (AI) and Machine Learning in Games

AI will reshape game development and gameplay over the next decade. Advances in generative AI are enabling games to create content, characters, and entire worlds. AI-driven NPCs are expected to engage players with more human-like dialogue and adapt to player behavior, enhancing immersion and player agency. Game studios are already experimenting with AI tools for level design, quality assurance, and game balancing, accelerating the development process. AI and machine learning will enable hyper-personalization and emergent gameplay in the gaming experiences of 2025–2035.

Virtual and Augmented Reality (VR/AR)

VR/AR technologies will make immersive gaming more accessible worldwide. The VR gaming market is projected to grow; one analysis estimates an increase from about $15 billion in 2024 to $65.5 billion by 2030, representing approximately 28% annual growth (Market Research Future 2024b). Lighter, more affordable VR headsets and AR glasses are expected by the late 2020s, enabling longer play sessions and more comfort. These technologies will blur the line between game and reality, as hardware improves, VR games will offer higher resolution displays, wider fields of view, and tactile haptic feedback, making experiences more lifelike and social. Augmented reality gaming is also set to expand beyond early successes like

Pokémon GO. With the anticipated advent of consumer AR glasses, AR games could move from smartphone screens to the direct field of vision, creating interactive game layers on city streets, classrooms, and homes. Integration of AI with AR/VR will further boost immersion as AI-driven AR avatars will enhance interaction and personalization.

Cloud Gaming

High-speed networks and cloud computing infrastructure will make cloud gaming mainstream in the coming decade. In cloud gaming, the heavy processing is done on remote servers, and video footage is streamed to players' devices. This allows high-end games to be played on modest hardware like phones, tablets, or smart TVs. Advancements in telecom infrastructure, particularly 5G's low-latency, high-bandwidth capabilities, are making lag-free, high-definition game streaming feasible. This will improve gaming access globally, where a player with only a smart TV or basic laptop could stream the latest AAA game directly from a data center. Cloud edge computing, which deploys servers closer to users, will further reduce latency, a critical factor for fast paced competitive games. Over the next decade, major platform holders like Microsoft, Sony and Tencent are likely to expand their cloud offerings and subscription libraries, making gaming into a service accessible on any screen. By 2035, subscriptions to cloud gaming platforms could provide access to vast catalogs of games run on high-performance servers. This shift will also impact game design, as titles begin to leverage scalable cloud resources. In sum, cloud gaming is poised to remove hardware barriers, making high-quality games universally accessible and reshaping the distribution models of the global game industry (GlobeNewswire 2023b).

Quantum Computing and Next-Gen Processing

Quantum computing holds long-term potential to impact gaming by the 2030s in specialized ways. Quantum computers leverage quantum mechanics to perform certain computations far faster than classical computers. By 2035, developers will use quantum cloud services to tackle complex problems in game development (VentureBeat 2024). Noisy Intermediate-Scale Quantum computers could be used to generate unpredictable, rich game content or to train AI models in ways classical computers cannot (VentureBeat 2024). This may lead to tools that allow game worlds to be far more dynamic. If quantum computing continues to advance, gaming will stand to benefit as an early adopter of breakthroughs in simulation and optimization (PatentPC 2023). It may even be possible to develop hybrid cloud architectures where certain game computations are offloaded to quantum co-processors for enhanced simulation or real-time problem-solving. While quantum computing in gaming will likely remain behind-the-scenes, its integration could result in games with unprecedented complexity and realism.

Gaming Today

Nearly 40% of the global population are active gamers, engaging across mobile phones, consoles, PCs, and increasingly, cloud platforms and virtual environments. The ecosystem includes AAA studios, indie developers, Esports leagues, content creators, influencers, and modders, and millions of fans who interact through Twitch, YouTube Gaming, and Discord communities. Gaming is no longer just an entertainment medium; it is an economic engine, a cultural force, and a new frontier for digital identity and ownership.

Mobile gaming now represents over 50% of global gaming revenue, due to widespread smartphone penetration and free-to-play monetization models. These models have allowed billions to engage without expensive hardware. Mobile gaming has been a significant driver of this expansion, with over 60% of gamers playing on smartphones. Accessibility, convenience, and casual game formats have made mobile the entry point for billions, particularly in emerging markets. More than 70% of players engage with games socially, whether through co-op play, virtual guilds, or online communities. Gaming has become a shared digital space where identity, interaction, and creativity converge in real time.

Games like Genshin Impact, Free Fire, and Clash of Clans dominate app store charts and generate billions through in-game purchases, skins, and battle passes. The rise of hyper-casual games, social multiplayer titles, and mobile Esports is reshaping player behavior and expectations. Cloud gaming also extends AAA experiences to mobile, further blurring the lines between platforms.

The image of the typical gamer has undergone a transformation from adolescent males to the modern gamer who is diverse, connected, and everywhere. Nearly half of all gamers globally today are women, and the average age of a gamer is 34. Gaming has become an intergenerational activity, embraced not only by Gen Z and Millennials, but also increasingly by Boomers and Gen X, whose participation is growing rapidly. This shift reflects a broader cultural normalization of gaming.

This evolution in audience and behavior has paralleled a reshaping of gaming's economic model. Where revenue once depended heavily on upfront game sales and console hardware, today's gaming economy is powered by multiple, complementary streams. Microtransactions, such as skins, cosmetic upgrades, and in-game currencies have become a cornerstone of monetization, particularly in free-to-play environments. Subscription services like Xbox Game Pass and PlayStation Plus offer vast libraries of games for a monthly fee, introducing users to new content while generating recurring revenue. Battle passes and season passes provide structured content updates and incentives for ongoing engagement. Cloud gaming platforms such as NVIDIA GeForce NOW and Xbox Cloud Gaming are removing hardware barriers entirely, offering access to high-performance games via the internet.

New frontiers in monetization are emerging through blockchain, with NFTs and digital collectables being explored as mechanisms for player ownership and secondary market trading. Esports, now a billion-dollar industry in its own right, is pioneering sponsorship deals, tournament prize pools, and streaming rights contributing to a growing ecosystem of professional and semi-professional players.

The leading companies that shape gaming's future include, Sony, with its PlayStation ecosystem and blockbuster titles, Tencent and NetEase have defined China's mobile-first dominance and expanded their influence globally through acquisitions and licensing deals. Microsoft, through its acquisition of Activision Blizzard, is betting heavily on subscriptions and cross-platform integration. Nintendo continues to leverage its IP and hybrid hardware strategy. Others like Electronic Arts, Epic Games, Take-Two Interactive, and Sweden's Embracer Group are pushing innovation in sports simulation, live services, open-world experiences, and global publishing reach. miHoYo, the Chinese developer behind *Genshin Impact*, exemplifies the rising influence of anime-style RPGs and cross-platform global fandom.

Together, these companies are building ecosystems that define how people gather and play and how digital value is created and exchanged. The convergence of demographic expansion, technological accessibility, and sophisticated monetization has made gaming not only the most resilient entertainment sector but also a blueprint for the future of digital engagement.

Global Gaming Innovation

Gaming innovation is a global phenomenon, with key hubs emerging across different continents. In Asia, Japan, South Korea, and China remain at the forefront of hardware and software innovation. Companies like Nintendo, Sony, Tencent, and NetEase are pioneering new genres, business models, and technologies. South Korea's dominance in Esports and China's leadership in mobile gaming is particularly notable.

In North America, the United States and Canada are home to major studios of Electronic Arts, Activision Blizzard, Epic Games, and indie developers pushing the boundaries of storytelling, graphics, and online infrastructure. Silicon Valley's tech ecosystem supports advances in AI, cloud gaming, and VR/AR.

Europe's UK, Sweden, Finland, and Poland are recognized for creative indie studios and technical excellence. CD Projekt Red (Poland), Supercell (Finland), and Mojang (Sweden) have produced globally influential titles. London and Berlin are also centers for VR/AR startups.

Asia dominates the global gaming industry and accounts for nearly 50% of global gaming revenue, driven by massive user bases in China, Japan, South Korea, and Southeast Asia. China alone contributes over $50 billion annually, despite periodic regulatory crackdowns and is home to global giants like Tencent and NetEase.

Mobile gaming dominates in Asia, particularly in markets like the Philippines, India, and Indonesia, where low-cost smartphones and fast mobile networks make mobile the primary gateway to gaming. Titles like Honour of Kings, PUBG Mobile, and Mobile Legends: Bang Bang attracts tens of millions of daily active users. Southeast Asia is also emerging as a hotbed for mobile Esports, with cities like Jakarta, Manila, and Kuala Lumpur hosting large-scale competitive events.

Emerging markets are playing an increasingly important role in the future of gaming. Regions such as Southeast Asia, Latin America, the Middle East, and Africa are experiencing rapid growth in both player base and revenue. For example, Southeast Asia is projected to surpass $7 billion in gaming revenue by 2025, driven by mobile gaming and Esports. In India, the mobile game Ludo King has surpassed 800 million downloads, reflecting the country's massive and growing audience. Brazil and Mexico are leading Latin America's gaming growth, with local studios producing culturally relevant content and international companies investing in regional infrastructure. The Middle East, particularly Saudi Arabia and the United Arab Emirates, is investing heavily in Esports and gaming events, aiming to become a global hub for competitive gaming. These markets are characterized by high mobile penetration, youthful populations, and increasing internet access, making them fertile ground for innovation and new business models.

Gaming has become a truly global cultural force, and this trend will only deepen by 2035. As of mid-decade, roughly 40% of the world's population plays video games in some form (Plarium 2024)—a number that will grow as mobile and cloud gaming reach new demographics. This ubiquity means games are now a mainstream medium for social interaction and cultural expression worldwide. Online gaming platforms allow players from different countries to meet and collaborate in virtual worlds, forming transnational communities. By 2030, the global Esports audience alone is expected to reach around 640 million people, with mega-tournaments drawing viewership on par with traditional sporting events. For example, by 2025, the Esports fanbase (both dedicated and occasional viewers) is projected at 640 million, a figure led by regions like Asia-Pacific. These massive, shared experiences—watching a championship or participating in a Metaverse concert within a game—are forging a collective gaming culture that transcends borders. In many ways, games have become social hubs: surveys show players spend significant time in-game socializing (chatting, hanging out) beyond just completing game objectives (Plarium 2024). By 2035, we can expect virtual communities to be even more robust, with in-game events that reflect real-world cultural diversity. Games will also continue to reflect local cultures. We anticipate more games developed in Asia, Africa, and Latin America gaining global popularity, bringing unique mythologies, art styles, and perspectives into the worldwide gaming canon. This cultural exchange is two ways not only do games export culture, but they also absorb it. Research has shown that video games have a direct impact on cultural transmission, spreading knowledge, values, and narratives across societies (Rauschnabel et al. 2022). In the next decade, the line between gaming and other cultural forms such as music, cinema, art, will blur, as cross-media collaborations become the norm (like games spawning TV series and movies). Ultimately, by 2035, gaming will be ingrained in global culture as a common language for storytelling and social connection shared by billions.

The Industry Ecosystem and Job Creation

The expansion of gaming will spur significant job creation and economic activity across multiple connected sectors. Game development studios will need more talent—not only programmers and artists, but also AI specialists, data analysts, and narrative designers—to craft the next generation of complex, AI-driven and immersive games. As games embrace more advanced technologies such as VR and AI, interdisciplinary expertise will be in demand. This is discussed at length in Chap. 10.

The gaming workforce is growing worldwide; for instance, the number of people employed in the video game industry in the US grew over 8% annually between 2019 and 2024 (IBISWorld 2024), and this trend is expected to continue globally. By 2030, some estimates suggest the global industry could support well over one- to two-million direct jobs and many more in related occupations.

New types of jobs are also emerging community managers, Esports coaches, streamers, professional gamers, content creators, and virtual economy entrepreneurs. The rise of Esports is creating career paths for pro players, team staff, tournament organizers, and broadcast crews. The Esports market, though smaller in revenue compared to traditional gaming, is booming—from about $2–3 billion in the mid-2020s, it is forecast to reach $7.4 billion by 2030 (GlobeNewswire 2023c). This growth will generate more salaried roles for players, coaches, analysts, and production professionals in the Esports ecosystem.

Streaming and video content creation around games (on platforms like Twitch and YouTube) have already become viable careers for thousands of people. Over seven million people stream on Twitch each month as of 2023 (Backlinko 2023), and top streamers earn multi-million-dollar incomes through ads, subscriptions, and sponsorships. By 2035, interactive live streaming and fan-driven content will be an even larger cottage industry, offering livelihoods for a new generation of entertainers who build communities around gameplay.

Governments in countries such as South Korea, Poland, and Canada actively invest in gaming as a strategic growth sector, recognizing its potential for economic impact and soft power. The gaming ecosystem of developers, publishers, platform operators, hardware vendors, content creators, and competitive leagues will be a cornerstone of the digital economy.

Gamification in Key Industries

The application of game design elements in non-gaming contexts has become a powerful tool across various industries, driving engagement, motivation, and behavioral change. As gaming technologies and psychology become more sophisticated, gamification is expected to play an even greater role in shaping the future of work, education, health, and beyond.

In education, gamification is transforming learning environments by making education more interactive and rewarding. Platforms like Kahoot! and Duolingo use points, badges, leaderboards, and progress tracking to motivate students and reinforce learning. Educational games such as Minecraft Education Edition allow students to explore subjects like history, mathematics, and coding in immersive, collaborative settings. Research shows that gamified learning can improve retention, engagement, and problem-solving skills.

In healthcare, gamification is used to encourage healthy behaviors, improve patient outcomes, and support medical training. Apps like Zombies, Run! turn exercise into an adventure, while platforms such as MySugr gamify diabetes management by rewarding users for tracking their blood sugar. In rehabilitation, games like Re-Mission help young cancer patients adhere to treatment regimens. Medical professionals use simulation games and VR-based training modules to practice procedures and decision-making in risk-free environments.

Businesses are leveraging gamification to enhance employee training, productivity, and engagement. Platforms like Salesforce Trailhead and Microsoft Learn use badges, points, and progress bars to guide employees through learning paths. Companies such as Deloitte have reported increased participation and completion rates in leadership training programs after introducing gamified elements. Gamification is also used in project management tools (e.g., Asana, Trello) to motivate teams and celebrate milestones.

Brands use gamification to build loyalty and increase customer engagement. Starbucks' Rewards program, for example, incorporates points, levels, and challenges to incentivize repeat purchases. Nike's Nike Run Club app uses achievements and social sharing to foster a community of active users. Gamified marketing campaigns, such as McDonald's Monopoly, have proven effective in driving sales and customer interaction.

Governments and NGOs are adopting gamification to promote civic engagement and positive social behaviors. Apps like Recyclebank reward users for eco-friendly actions, while platforms such as Foldit crowdsource scientific problem-solving through puzzle games. In Singapore, the government's Healthy 365 app uses gamified challenges to encourage citizens to adopt healthier lifestyles.

As AI, and data analytics advance, gamification will become more personalized and immersive. Adaptive gamified systems could tailor challenges and rewards to individual users, maximizing motivation and learning. The integration of gamification with wearable devices and IoT will further blur the lines between digital and real-world achievements.

The Convergence of Gaming and Social Platforms

In the digital age, the relationship between gaming and social interaction has evolved into a powerful convergence, where the boundaries between game platforms and social networks are increasingly blurred. Today, gamers gather, chat, create, and form identities in persistent, interconnected digital spaces.

At the forefront of this convergence are platforms like Discord and Reddit, which have become essential hubs for modern gaming culture (See Case Study). Discord, originally launched as a voice and chat tool for multiplayer games, has grown into a full-fledged communication ecosystem with over 150 million monthly users. Gamers use it to coordinate in-game strategies, stream content, organize tournaments, and even co-create new gaming communities. Its "servers" now function as tailored spaces where users gather based on shared interests, often extending far beyond gameplay into areas like music, education, mental health, and creator economy collaboration.

Reddit has become the forum of record for nearly every major game franchise and niche gaming interest. Subreddits like r/gaming, r/leagueoflegends, and r/gamedev enable players and developers to share updates, memes, reviews, and technical insights. This crowdsourced ecosystem of feedback and cultural exchange empowers players to shape narratives, advocate for features, and hold studios accountable, effectively giving rise to a co-created culture of gaming.

Major social platforms like Twitch, YouTube Gaming, and TikTok have turned gaming into a spectator sport and a creative medium. Gaming is not only played, but also performed, consumed, and reinterpreted. Influencers and streamers build entire careers broadcasting their gameplay, sharing commentary, and engaging with audiences in real time. The "watch-and-play" loop has become central to how younger generations experience gaming, often spending as much time watching others play as they do play themselves.

This fusion of gaming and social platforms is shaping how identities are formed online. Gamers adopt personas, build followings, and participate in digital economies within these shared spaces. Clans, guilds, and fan groups now span continents, time zones, and languages and provide a persistent sense of belonging.

Ultimately, the convergence of gaming and social platforms has redefined what it means to be a gamer. It's no longer a solitary activity, but a deeply social experience woven into the fabric of digital life. In this new paradigm, games are on the stage—but the community is the story.

Evolving Game Genres and Mechanics

Game design is also innovating in terms of mechanics and genre-blending. The coming decade will likely see more hybrid game genres that defy traditional categories, for example, games that combine real-time strategy, role-playing, and user-generated content (UGC) into a single experience. Sandbox and open-world design will continue to thrive, giving players large toolsets to create their own fun within a game's framework, as seen in *Minecraft* and *Roblox*, which are expected to inspire successors (Newzoo 2023). Procedural content generation will not only apply to narrative but also to level design, puzzles, and even music—ensuring that games can provide fresh content continuously, which is crucial for subscription-based and live service games (McRae 2021). UGC integration will likely be standard; many games will ship with robust editors or creation modes, essentially inviting players to design quests, maps, or cosmetic items that can be shared, with creators potentially earning revenue.

Another major shift is the trend toward transmedia convergence in storytelling. Game franchises are no longer isolated, they extend into movies, series, comics, and more. Popular stories from books or television are increasingly adapted into games. This has been demonstrated by *The Witcher* franchise, which began as a Polish fantasy novel series, became a successful game trilogy, and was later adapted into a Netflix series (TweakTown 2020).

This transmedia trend will likely accelerate as creators can keep audiences engaged between game releases and attract newcomers from one format to another. In the future, some game narratives might intentionally leave plot threads to be resolved in TV series seasons or films, requiring cross-platform engagement for full understanding.

Convergence with other media introduces new design possibilities. There will be more cinematic storytelling techniques in games and films, and series will adopt interactive elements. Games might incorporate live-action footage or real-time rendered graphics indistinguishable from film by 2035, further blurring the lines between mediums. Transmedia also encourages trans platform play, with each platform offering a unique narrative layer. Designers will be tasked with crafting seamless narrative transitions across formats to maintain story continuity and audience engagement.

The content of game narratives is also broadening. As mentioned, representation of different genders, ethnicities, and worldviews in games is improving and will likely continue to do so, driven both by social expectations and by the increasingly diverse development teams. Games in 2025–2035 will tell stories exploring the lives of characters in non-Western cultures or addressing themes of mental health, identity, and social justice. Already, indie games have led the way in tackling serious themes with empathy, creativity, and titles that deal with topics like grief, coming-of-age, and queer identity. The industry recognizes that players want stories that reflect their own experiences and values. Thus, narrative design will likely prioritize branching perspectives, letting players choose between multiple protagonists of different backgrounds or shifting viewpoint during the story to show a more holistic picture.

Procedural storytelling with AI means that conversations with NPCs might not be fully scripted but generated in response to player prompts. This could make game worlds feel more alive and self-consistent, enhancing the world-building. Players effectively become storytellers too when they share emergent experiences with others; these player stories become part of the broader narrative tapestry of a game's community. Games like EVE Online have shown how player-driven narratives (corporation wars, heists, etc.) can become legendary; future games might lean into that by providing the tools and freedom for players to create history in the game world that persists and is recognized officially by the game's lore. The concept of an "interactive narrative" will extend beyond just the game—players might influence a story that spans comics, alternate reality games (ARG), and interactive episodes on streaming services as part of one narrative arc. The convergence of storytelling methods will push games to innovate narrative delivery, making storytelling a truly interactive, cross-platform experience where the player's engagement can shape the game.

Esports—The New Competitive Frontier

Esports have rapidly matured into a global industry with over 500 million fans and thousands of professional athletes. Major events like the League of Legends World Championship, The International (Dota 2), and CS: GO Majors fill stadiums and generate millions of live stream views. In 2023, Saudi Arabia's Gamers8 hosted 12 Esports titles with a record $45 million prize pool, highlighting Esports' growing geopolitical significance.

China, South Korea, and now the Middle East dominate the competitive scenes. Meanwhile, North America and Europe are home to high-value teams and franchised leagues. Esports clubs like Team Liquid, FaZe Clan, and T1 are becoming multimedia brands, blending sports, entertainment, and influencer marketing.

From billion-dollar prize pools to university scholarships, competitive gaming is rewriting what it means to be an athlete in the digital age. Esports are building the stadiums of the future digitally. From virtual arenas to global fan bases connected through streaming, Esports redefine live entertainment. This isn't just gaming. It's a new era of sport.

Asia is the epicenter of Esports innovation. Esports create jobs, new media formats, and cross-border entertainment empires from South Korea to the Philippines. Esports have emerged as a thriving global industry projected to be worth over $6.75 billion by 2030 (Marr 2023). More than a cultural phenomenon, Esports are fast becoming a cornerstone of the future of live entertainment, transforming how people compete, spectate, socialize, and even redefine athleticism in the digital age.

At its core, Esports replicate many of the dynamics of traditional sports: elite performance, team structures, fans, sponsorships, and league-based formats. Yet it differs fundamentally in its digital foundation. The competition is conducted entirely within video game environments, and the ecosystem includes unique stakeholders, most notably game publishers and licensing partners who control the intellectual property. This means Esports isn't just a new version of sport, it's a new genre of entertainment altogether.

Unlike traditional sports, where the game remains relatively static over time, Esports are fluid. A patch update or game mechanic tweak can redefine competitive strategies overnight. Professional players must master rapid reflexes, memorize complex game mechanics, and commit to rigorous training schedules of 70–80 h per week, mirroring the dedication of Olympians. Teams now hire nutritionists, psychologists, and tactical coaches, embedding high-performance systems into this digital sport (Schudey et al. 2023).

The Esports ecosystem is vast and dynamic, comprising game developers, event organizers, media platforms, brands, and fans. Esports tournaments attract tens of thousands of in-person spectators and millions of online viewers. The 2021 International (Dota 2) boasted a prize pool of $40 million—comparable to Wimbledon's $50 million—and top events such as League of Legends Worlds regularly surpass 100 million hours watched.

Despite this, the Esports' audience still represents just 15% of the total global gaming population, estimated at three billion. This untapped potential—especially across mobile gaming markets in Asia and the Middle East—signals enormous room for growth. Mobile Esports titles like Mobile Legends: Bang Bang and PUBG Mobile are surging in popularity, with Southeast Asia leading adoption (Schudey et al. 2023).

Nowhere is the Esports acceleration more apparent than in the Middle East. Saudi Arabia's Gamers8 has become the world's largest independent Esports festival, offering over $45 million in prizes and drawing global talent. The UAE is also investing heavily, hosting global tournaments like BLAST Premier and supporting local clubs such as Nigma Galaxy. These efforts not only showcase regional commitment to Esports but also position the Middle East as a future powerhouse in the global Esports' economy (Schudey et al. 2023).

The Esports business model is still maturing. Unlike traditional sports, which generate revenue through media rights and merchandising, Esports clubs often rely on sponsorships and prize money. Media rights monetization remains underdeveloped, and revenue flows can be inconsistent. Powerful game publishers control the IP, which introduces risks for third-party event organizers and clubs.

Regulatory frameworks are also undeveloped. Few governments recognize Esports as an official sport, and players often lack healthcare, pensions, or career pathways. This has prompted federations in countries like Japan, China, and South Korea to introduce support mechanisms including minimum salaries, real estate benefits, and legal services for athletes (Schudey et al. 2023).

Esports clubs are no longer just competitive teams; they are evolving into full-fledged entertainment brands. Teams like FaZe Clan, G2, and Team Liquid have diversified into media, merchandise, content creation, and NFT drops. Some clubs now field multiple game rosters, attract celebrity investors, and boast tens of millions of followers across Twitch, Instagram, and YouTube. In 2022, the top 10 Esports clubs were collectively valued at over $3 billion (Schudey et al. 2023).

Yet, sustainability is a challenge. FaZe Clan's IPO at a $725 million valuation dropped dramatically in the following year, underscoring the need for more sustainable business models. Many clubs are now following the lead of top content creators by developing mobile apps, branded merchandise, and interactive fan experiences to diversify revenue.

Governments and multilateral institutions are taking note. France and China have officially recognized Esports athletes. The Olympic Council of Asia included Esports titles in its 2022 Asian Games. Yet the lack of standardized global rules and career protections continues to hinder mainstream legitimacy. As Esports become more culturally significant, a global regulatory dialogue will be essential (Schudey et al. 2023).

Institutions such as the International Esports Federation and regional summits like the UAE's Games for Change and Saudi Arabia's Next World Forum are beginning to lay the groundwork. However, unlike physical sports, which enjoy universally accepted rules and federations, Esports must navigate the complexities of IP ownership and genre diversity.

Esports is more than a game, it is a medium where sport, entertainment, fandom, and technology converge. As generative AI, VR, and metaverse mature, Esports stand to become a fully immersive and participatory form of live entertainment. Esports content has the potential to reshape the future of how people consume sport-like competition through Twitch, YouTube, and interactive experiences (Marr 2023).

With its young, tech-savvy, and loyal fanbase, Esports offer an unparalleled opportunity for brands, media companies, and governments to engage the next generation. While challenges remain in regulation, monetization, and governance, the trajectory is clear. Esports are not a subculture—it is becoming the cultural and commercial infrastructure of global entertainment.

The sports industry is undergoing a seismic shift, driven by data, digital engagement, and the globalization of fandom. Consumption habits are changing—fans now follow players more than teams, and data-driven experiences are unlocking new ways to interact. Clubs are becoming media and tech businesses, leveraging AI agents, virtual reality, and gamified marketing campaigns to attract and retain fans. The rise of VR stadiums and metaverse-based events allows global access to local experiences. Ownership of sports data is becoming critical, not just for clubs, but for fans too, who are being targeted with real-time offers and personalized engagement. Web3 technologies enable community economies and digital property rights, while partnerships with gaming and gambling platforms blur the lines between fandom, entertainment, and monetization.

Regulation and Ethical Challenges

As the gaming industry expands, data privacy, consumer protection, community health, and addiction management are under growing regulatory and ethical scrutiny. Modern games collect extensive personal and behavioral data, prompting the enforcement of regulations like the GDPR and COPPA, with further demands expected by 2035, including privacy-by-design development and limitations on data retention. High-profile cases, such as Epic Games' $520 million FTC settlement, highlight the consequences of privacy breaches and deceptive design practices. Simultaneously, governments and platforms are cracking down on toxic behavior in online communities, leveraging AI moderation tools like ToxMod and legal mandates under acts like the EU's Digital Services Act. By 2030, real-time content moderation, reputation tracking, and advanced parental controls will become standard, ensuring safer and more inclusive environments. Additionally, the recognition of gaming disorder by the WHO has spurred international action to address addiction, especially among minors. Nations like China have introduced curfews and identity verification, while developers are implementing wellness features and rethinking exploitative mechanics such as loot boxes. Policies will continue to evolve, shaping a more transparent, ethical, and player-focused gaming ecosystem.

Overview of the Book

This book presents a bold reimagining of gaming—not merely as entertainment, but as a driver of innovation, inclusion, and global infrastructure. It is designed to speak to a growing audience of game developers, policymakers, educators, investors, and parents who are seeking clarity and direction on the future of digital society. Structured in three parts, the book explores how gaming is: (i) becoming a foundational layer of economic and social systems; (ii) empowering digital inclusion and new job markets; and (iii) creating ethical and governance challenges as it evolves into a mass influence tool.

"Technical Companion." The Technical Companion to *"Infinite Playgrounds: Gaming and the Architecture of Tomorrow"* offers a comprehensive, systems-level exploration of the technological foundations shaping the next era of interactive digital experiences. Organized into five key parts, the compendium demystifies the core infrastructure of Web3 gaming; blockchain technology, smart contracts, token standards, and decentralized storage and examines the tools, languages, and platforms enabling development and deployment of immersive, asset-driven environments. The Companion maps the expanding ecosystem of developer tools, NFT marketplaces, wallet integrations, and cross-chain interoperability protocols, highlighting their role in powering user-owned economies and game-based digital identities. It explores governance frameworks, creator monetization platforms, and compliance technologies that underpin secure, ethical, and scalable gaming ecosystems. It considers critical risks such as security vulnerabilities, sustainability, and market concentration. The Technical Companion provides practical insight for builders, educators, regulators, and innovators. This companion equips readers to understand, evaluate, and participate in the technologies driving gaming's evolution into a decentralized, inclusive, and economically significant digital frontier.

Cross-Chapter Insights

Chapter 1 lays the foundation for understanding scale, monetization, and global influence. These themes reappear in *Steam and Epic Games Store* (Chap. 3), which shape the commercial infrastructure of digital gaming, and in *Mobile Legends:*

Bang Bang (Chap. 5), which localizes mass gaming for mobile-first users. The creator economies discussed in *Roblox* and *Fortnite Creative* (Chap. 10) further build on the transformation of players into producers, a theme rooted in the transition from centralized to participatory platforms.

Case Studies

Tencent Games

Game/Platform Name: Tencent Games
Developer/Publisher: Tencent (led by Ma Huateng, commonly known as Pony Ma, the co-founder, Chairman, and CEO)
Year Released: 2003
Genre: Video game publishing and development platform
Technology Stack: Proprietary tools like QuickSilverX Engine (game engine), Dawn Global Illumination Baking System (high-fidelity lighting), Superman Animation Pipeline (character animation), Giner Game AI Engine (3D environments), MotorNerve Animation System (character locomotion), Anti-cheat Expert (ACE), Game Multimedia Engine (speech-to-text, noise suppression, low-latency chat). Tencent Games is a global publisher and developer of video games including PUBG MOBILE, Call of Duty Mobile, and League of Legends, played in over 200 countries. As a pioneer in cloud gaming, Tencent has created infrastructure allowing high-end gameplay without high-end hardware. It has set industry standards in mobile game optimization and real-time performance, with innovative anti-cheat systems ensuring fair play.

Innovation

Cloud gaming service enabling high-end gameplay without premium hardware
    AI-based matchmaking and game personalization
    AI for game testing and NPC behavior
    Pioneering mobile performance in games like Honor of Kings and PUBG mobile
    Anti-cheat systems safeguarding game integrity

Impact

User Adoption and Demographics
Hundreds of millions of users across 200+ countries. WeGame platform exceeds 200 million active users and 4.5 billion downloads. Honor of Kings alone has over 100 million daily active users.

Economic Value Generated
Honor of Kings has generated over $1.1 billion in mobile revenue as of 2025. PUBG Mobile and The Battle of the Golden Shower generated $769.7 M and $210.45 M respectively. Tencent's gaming sector grew 13% in Q1 2025, and its US$636.42 B market cap places it second globally after Microsoft.

Cultural/Social Influence
Tencent normalized gaming in China, elevating it to cultural mainstream. It introduced Chinese narratives globally and built one of the largest Esports ecosystems.

Geographic Reach
China, US, Canada, LATAM, and Europe.

Challenges and Controversies

Global Political Tensions
Concerns over Chinese investments in U.S. studios led to scrutiny and India banned several Tencent titles over national security fears.

Data Privacy and Surveillance
Tencent apps are regulated by Chinese authorities, raising concerns about surveillance and data use abroad.

Monetization Controversies
Games reliant on in-app purchases have triggered criticism for promoting pay-to-win dynamics and deepening economic divides.

Lessons and Legacy

Tencent demonstrates the success of platform-based ecosystems blending gaming, communication, and media. However, its centralized structure poses regulatory and ethical concerns.

Fortnite (Epic Games)

Game/Platform Name: Fortnite
  Developer/Publisher: Epic Games
  Year Released: 2017
  Genre: Online video game (Survival, Battle Royale, Sandbox)
  Technology Stack: Unreal Engine (UE5/UE4), C++, Blueprints, Python, JavaScript/TypeScript, Verse, Epic Online Services, AWS, PlayFab, Kubernetes, PostgreSQL, Redis, NoSQL

Case Studies

Fortnite is a multiplayer shooter where 100 players compete on an island, building structures and collecting resources. Known for rapid gameplay, building mechanics, and vibrant graphics, it also hosts live concerts and cross-brand integrations, making it a defining title in the Metaverse era.

Innovation

Mainstreamed Battle Royale as a genre
    Introducing real-time building mechanics
    Hosted interactive live virtual events (e.g., Ariana Grande concert)
    Cross-IP skins and branded content (Marvel, Star Wars, NBA)
    User-generated content ecosystem and creator tools

Impact

User Adoption and Demographics
By end-2024, Fortnite had 250 M active players and 650 M total accounts. A record 44.7 M accessed the game in a single day; 62% of users are 18–24 years old.

Economic Value Generated
Fortnite generated $1.15 M in May 2025. Lifetime mobile revenue before the bank exceeded $1.1B.

Cultural/Social Influence
Fortnite shaped livestreaming culture, youth identity, and digital concerts. It became symbolic of gaming's convergence with pop culture and virtual socializing.

Geographic Reach
Predominantly US and Europe, with growing global adoption.

Challenges and Controversies

Monetization Tensions
Epic bypassed app store fees, triggering legal battles and temporary bans. In 2025, the game returned to major mobile platforms.

Inappropriate Content
Critics allege the game promotes gun violence and aggression.

Addictive Design
Legal scrutiny arose over compulsive mechanics. A $126 M refund was issued to players misled by purchase mechanics.

Lessons and Legacy

Fortnite introduced Metaverse-style interaction into mainstream gaming. It blurred lines between play, commerce, and culture, and validated user-generated economies.

References

Backlinko. (2023). *Twitch user statistics*. https://backlinko.com/twitch-users
Fortune Business Insights. (2024). Video Game Market Size. https://www.fortunebusinessinsights.com/
GlobeNewswire. (2023a). *Cloud gaming market forecast to reach $48.1B by 2030*. https://www.globenewswire.com/news-release/2023/10/02/2735546/0/en/Cloud-Gaming-Market-Size-to-Reach-USD-48-19-Billion-by-2030.html
GlobeNewswire. (2023b). Gaming market reports and forecasts. https://www.globenewswire.com/
GlobeNewswire. (2023c). *Esports market forecast is to reach $7.4B by 2030*. https://www.globenewswire.com/news-release/2023/09/14/2734212/0/en/Esports-Market.html
IBISWorld. (2024). *Video game industry employment trends in the U.S.* https://www.ibisworld.com
Market Research Future. (2024a). Global Gaming Market Forecast 2035. https://www.marketresearchfuture.com/
Market Research Future. (2024b). *Virtual reality gaming market research report 2024–2030*. https://www.marketresearchfuture.com/reports/virtual-reality-gaming-market-1794
Marr, B. (2023, December 4). *Game on! The top 10 video game trends in 2024*. Forbes. https://www.forbes.com/sites/bernardmarr/2023/12/04/game-on-the-top-10-video-game-trends-in-2024/
McRae, E. (2021). *Procedural storytelling: Game narrative beyond the script*. Edwin McRae Game Writing. https://edmcrae.com/procedural-narrative
Newzoo. (2023). *Global games market report*. https://newzoo.com/insights/trend-reports/global-games-market-report-2023
PatentPC. (2023). *Noisy Intermediate-Scale Quantum (NISQ) technology and its potential for gaming innovation*. https://www.patentpc.com/nisq-quantum-gaming
Plarium. (2024). *Gaming as a global phenomenon: Stats and insights*. https://www.plarium.com/en/blog/gamingstatistics/
Plantin, J.-C., Lagoze, C., Edwards, P. N., and Sandvig, C. (2018). Infrastructure studies meet platform studies in the age of Google and Facebook. *New Media and Society, 20*(1), 293–310. https://doi.org/10.1177/1461444816661553.
PwC. (2023). *Global Entertainment and Media Outlook 2023–2027*. PricewaterhouseCoopers. https://www.pwc.com/gx/en/industries/tmt/media/outlook.html
Rauschnabel, P. A., He, J., & Ro, Y. K. (2022). Antecedents to the adoption of augmented reality smart glasses: A closer look at privacy risks. *Technological Forecasting and Social Change*, 174, 121260. https://doi.org/10.1016/j.techfore.2021.121260
Schudey, A., Kasperovich, P., Ikram, A., Panhans, D., and Matviets, L. (2023). *Let the game begin: How Esports is shaping the future of live entertainment*. Boston Consulting Group. https://www.bcg.com/publications/2023/how-Esports-is-shaping-future-of-live-entertainment
TweakTown. (2020, January 22). *The Witcher 3 sales spike 554% after Netflix show's launch*. https://www.tweaktown.com/news/69895/witcher-3-sales-spike-554-after-netflix-shows-launch/index.html
VentureBeat. (2024). *Quantum computing's impact on gaming: The future of game development by 2035*. https://venturebeat.com/quantum-computing-gaming-2035

Chapter 2
Web3, Digital Property Rights, and the NextGen Internet

Abstract *"Web3, Digital Property Rights and the NextGen Internet"* describes how Web3 is changing the gaming industry by shifting power from platforms to players. This chapter explores how blockchain technology is enabling the formation of new gaming business models built around ownership, transparency, and decentralization. Readers will be introduced to Play-to-Earn (P2E) and Play-and-Own frameworks, where players are rewarded with real value for their time, skill, and creativity. The chapter also explains the role of Non-Fungible Tokens (NFTs) in establishing digital property rights and how Decentralized Autonomous Organizations (DAOs) allow communities to govern and co-create game worlds. It explains how through smart contracts and token economies, players can now become stakeholders, own in-game assets, influence development, and participate in revenue streams. With case studies and real-world examples, this chapter reveals how Web3 is not just reshaping games but transforming players into digital entrepreneurs in a rapidly growing participatory economy.

Keywords Web3 · digital property rights · Non-Fungible Tokens (NFTs) · Play-to-Earn (P2E) gaming · Decentralized Autonomous Organizations (DAOs) · Smart contracts · Decentralized finance (DeFi) · Digital asset ownership · Tokenized economies · Decentralized governance · Self-sovereign identity · Regulation of Web3 gaming · Blockchain in gaming · Web4 and Web5 · Creator economies

Introduction to Web3

This chapter explores how blockchain technology enables new gaming business models built around ownership, transparency, and decentralization. The chapter also explains the role of NFTs in establishing digital property rights and how DAOs allow communities to govern and co-create game worlds. Readers will be introduced to P2E frameworks, where players are rewarded with real value for their time, skill, and creativity. The chapter also explores some of the darker sides of P2E games, including economic unsustainability and player exploitation.

Web1 enabled the static sharing of information through protocols, Web2 introduced interactivity and user-generated content but with centralized control over user data. In response, Web3 incorporated blockchain and smart contracts to enable decentralization, digital ownership, and peer-to-peer value exchange (Zhou et al. 2022).

Web3 will do for value what the internet has done for information (Tomaino 2021). It will decentralize, remove asymmetries, and allow peer-to-peer transactions. The "Internet of Value" is a world where value moves and is exchanged on a P2P basis. The fundamental tenets of Web3 are sovereignty and self-custody of the user's digital property. Innovations in self-sovereign identity and verifiable claims, in particular, enable individuals to identify themselves, conduct transactions, and attest to facts about themselves without disclosing the underlying or related data (Burke 2021).

Web3, underpinned by decentralization, transparency, and increased user utility, has created the basis for the Internet as it will exist in the future. Web3 deploys tools including DeFi, NFTs, decentralized governance, decentralized cloud services, and self-sovereign Identity to provide this peer-to-peer utility (Burke 2021).

Decentralized Finance (DeFi)

DeFi enables anyone to interact directly with peers without intermediaries, which improves efficiency, transparency, and access, with a mobile phone. DeFi enables traditional financial services peer-to-peer (Burke 2021).

Non-Fungible Tokens (NFTs)

Digital assets represent tangible things like collectables, tickets, art, virtual land, music, and gaming items. NFTs will be the gateway to digital consumption. Physical items can be represented as NFTs that can be redeemed in the real world without intermediaries, to solve the problem of digital to physical redemption (Burke 2021). NFTs confer (i) ownership benefits, (ii) in-game functionality (e.g., skins, items, and avatars), (iii) brand and community engagement; and smart contract automation features.

NFTs are the gateway to digital property rights in Web3 gaming as a primary means of value exchange. NFTs are coded with smart contracts that govern ownership verification and transferability management of the NFTs. NFTs can also link the NFT to other digital assets. NFTs authenticate digital assets by attaching to images on JPEG files, particularly MP3s, GIFs, videos, or other digital assets, and certify their authenticity and ownership (McDonell 2021). NFTs essentially are the vehicle to mediate the exchange of digital collectables. NFT focus has moved away from speculative tokens to utility-based NFTs, such as skins with real-time in-game utility and rarity; cross-game avatars usable across multiple virtual worlds; crafting resources tied to player-generated content and dynamic NFTs that evolve with player achievements.

The role of NFTs in gaming is to enable any form of in-game element to be tokenized and exchanged with other gamers. This challenges traditional gaming, where in-game elements or collectables are purchased but are non-transferable. NFTs in gaming offer authentic ownership and transferable ownership in the gaming experience. NFTs also facilitate game trading, which might boost their value since NFT objects can vary in their rarity. A smart NFT could provide a complete history of previous ownership, usage, and trades, giving creators essential data. The Smart NFTs will grant access to skins, tournament entrances, hidden levels, weapons, and content. Alethea AI (see case study) is the creator of the "intelligent NFTs," or iNFTs. Alethea is building its token economy based on train-to-earn.

Distributed Autonomous Organizations (DAOs)

DAOs are the predominant DeFi governance mechanism (Beck and Asher 2021). Shuttleworth (2021) defines a Decentralized Autonomous Organization as "A community-led entity with no central authority. It is fully autonomous and transparent: smart contracts lay the foundational rules, execute the agreed-upon decisions, and at any point, proposals, voting, and even the very code itself can be publicly audited." DAOs incorporate (i) smart contracts operate and govern the organization; (ii) computer code writes and executes smart contracts; (iii) monitoring and enforcing smart contracts is by computer algorithms; (iv) all participants agree in advance to abide by the code of the smart contracts, as a result, the mechanisms for dispute resolution can be weak (Morrison et al. 2020).

Rozas et al. (2021) outline blockchain-based tools for shared governance, including: (i) tokenization; (ii) self-enforcement and formalization of rules; (iii) autonomous automation; decentralization of power over the infrastructure; increased transparency and codification of trust.

DAOs offer token holders governance rights, enabling players to vote on game changes and development funding (Hassan et al. 2021). Users get voting rights and can influence how it operates by investing in DAO. Once a DAO operates, all the decisions and specifications on spending its funds are made when a consensus is reached. Everyone with a stake in a DAO is entitled to make proposals regarding its future. To prevent the network from being spammed with proposals, a monetary deposit could be required to create one. Subsequently, the stakeholders vote on the proposal. The majority need to have an agreement to perform any action. The percentage required to reach that majority can be specified in its code and varies depending on the DAO.

Each DAO has rules which are encoded in smart contracts. DAOs oversee the allocation of resources tied to the projects they are associated with. The community defines the rules by which a DAO operates and encodes them in smart contracts. These are transparent and publicly available so that anyone can understand the protocol operation. DAOs generally receive funding through token issuance, where the protocol sells tokens to raise funds for the DAO treasury. While there are variations in DAO governance and quorum requirements, the only way to change the rules is through member voting.

Zwitter and Hazenberg (2020) describe DAO governance with two governance components, internal and external. Internal governance, with non-hierarchical management and democratic features, where voting rights are based on several parameters, such as the ownership of tokens, can be capped at certain levels. The second component is external governance, which relies on server clusters and individual nodes for the functioning of the network and decision-making. Because this is the underpinning infrastructure, and they control more nodes and server capacity, developers and miners wield the greatest influence.

DAOs are emerging as powerful governance tools in gaming, offering players a direct stake in shaping the virtual worlds they inhabit. By replacing centralized control with community-driven decision-making, DAOs enable gamers to vote on game updates, economic policies, and ecosystem rules, effectively turning players into co-creators and stakeholders. This aligns with the rise of play-to-earn and Metaverse models, where digital ownership and participatory governance become integral to gameplay. From managing in-game treasuries to funding new features, DAOs are changing games into self-governing economies, with new relationships between developers and communities.

Decentralized Cloud Storage

Decentralized cloud allows people with excess resources, e.g., hard drive storage or computing capacity, to rent their resources for a fee. No single entity controls the platform, and multiple providers compete to store user data.

Web4 and Web5: Next-Generation Internet Paradigms

The evolution of the internet has been marked by successive waves of technological and conceptual development. Web4 is emerging as the next phase, characterized by hyper-personalization, pervasive computing, and advanced human–machine interaction. It integrates the Internet of Things (IoT), agentic AI, and natural language interfaces to facilitate seamless experiences across physical and digital realms (Almeida 2017). Approaches to defining Web4 include: (1) the expansion of ubiquitous computing and context-aware devices (Bschacher 2013), (2) personalization of web experiences based on individual identity (Polanska 2014), and (3) the rise of agent-centric communication powered by natural language processing (Nath et al. 2015). The emergence of transformer-based AI, including generative models and voice interfaces, has further enabled these visions. In gaming, Web4 technologies are enabling real-time voice-based interaction, adaptive storytelling, and integration with smart devices, creating immersive, responsive, and personalized gameplay environments.

Web5, conceptualized by Jack Dorsey, represents a distinct evolution focused on self-sovereign identity and decentralized data storage (TBD 2023). Web5 seeks to restore user control over identity and data through decentralized identifiers (DIDs), verifiable credentials, and decentralized web nodes (Namcious 2022). These technologies allow for secure, user-owned identities and portable digital footprints across platforms. In gaming, Web5 offers the potential for persistent, player-controlled identities, transferable game progress, and cross-game avatars—without reliance on token economies. While still in its early stages, Web5 proposes a user-centric internet architecture that decouples identity from platform ownership, laying the groundwork for more equitable and privacy-preserving digital ecosystems.

The Evolving Web3 Landscape

As Gen Z and Gen Alpha players increasingly value personalization, expression, and agency, the fusion of blockchain and gaming offers a compelling new paradigm. Play-to-Earn is not dead, it's evolving. The early hype exposed weaknesses but also unlocked new visions of what gaming economies can be. The next era of Web3 games will be built on fun, fairness, and digital ownership, not just on the promise of income. For developers, investors, and players alike, the challenge is clear: create games worth playing, economies worth participating in, and ecosystems that can endure beyond hype cycles.

In the long run, tokenized in-game economies will blur the line between gaming, work, and creative entrepreneurship. Players will own their digital labor, co-create the value of game worlds, form DAOs to govern game economies, and earn income through participation, not just purchases. Games like Gods Unchained, Illuvium, and Big Time are exploring more sustainable ecosystems, and mainstream publishers like Ubisoft, Square Enix, and Epic Games are experimenting with Web3 features, but with cautious optimism.

"Perspectives in Play" (YGG 2024) offers a comprehensive overview of the evolving landscape of Web3 gaming. The report examines strategic shifts, emerging technologies, and the future trajectory of blockchain gaming.

- *Transition to Fun-First Gaming: A* significant shift is observed from the traditional P2E models to games that prioritize engaging and enjoyable experiences. Blockchain technology is increasingly being utilized as a tool to enhance gameplay rather than being the central focus. This evolution is supported by the grow-

ing involvement of professionals from traditional gaming backgrounds, with over 52.5% of industry professionals now originating from the gaming sector.
- *Emphasis on Digital Asset Ownership:* The concept of true ownership of in-game assets remains a cornerstone of blockchain gaming. Approximately 71.1% of respondents identify digital asset ownership as the most significant benefit of blockchain integration in games. Innovations such as dynamic NFTs, soulbound tokens, and token-gating mechanisms are enhancing player engagement and personalization.
- *Integration of SocialFi and Community Engagement:* The integration of social finance elements is fostering deeper community involvement. Features like memecoins and community-driven governance models are creating more inclusive and dynamic gaming ecosystems, aligning with the broader vision of decentralized and player-centric game development.
- *Emergence of Decentralized Esports:* The report highlights the potential of decentralized systems to reshape the Esports landscape. By leveraging blockchain technology, decentralized Esports aim to offer fairer, more transparent ecosystems with features like instant prize pool payments and advanced anti-cheat mechanisms, enhancing trust and efficiency.
- *Global Expansion and Regional Growth:* Blockchain gaming is witnessing robust growth in regions such as South America, the Middle East, and Africa. Factors contributing to this expansion include regulatory clarity, significant investments in Web3 initiatives, and a surge in local developer communities.
- *Addressing Industry Challenges:* Despite the positive developments, the industry faces challenges like onboarding complexities and user experience hurdles. Persistent misconceptions about blockchain games being scams continue to hinder adoption. The report emphasizes the need for improved education and user-friendly interfaces to overcome these barriers.
- *The Rise of Purpose-Driven Gaming Economies:* The P2E space is still grappling with regulation, especially in areas where gaming intersects with finance and securities law. Some jurisdictions treat tokens as regulated assets, while others lack clear frameworks. This uncertainty has delayed institutional investment and discouraged mainstream game developers.

The future of P2E lies not in speculative profit but in empowerment, creativity, and ownership. Emerging trends include: (i) Interoperable gaming assets useable across multiple games or Metaverses, (ii) creator economies where creators and designers are paid royalties, (iii) DAO-led game development with community governance and co-creation, and impact games where earnings contribute to real-world causes (e.g., carbon offsets, education). This will require developers to prioritize user experience, seamless onboarding, and education.

Digital Property Rights

Web3 creates the possibility of digital property rights or the legal and practical ability of individuals or entities to own, control, transfer, and derive value from digital assets, data, and virtual goods in the online or digital environment. Blockchain is the technology that underpins digital property rights. Blockchain prevents fraud, makes in-game purchases easier, allows secure exchange and storage of in-game assets, enables interoperability for players' profiles, and allows players to collaborate with developers to improve a game. Core components of digital property rights are:

- *Ownership*. The right to claim legal possession of a digital asset (e.g., domain names, NFTs, digital art, in-game items, data, software).
- *Control and Use*. The right to access, modify, use, or restrict others from using the digital property.
- *Transferability*. The ability to sell, trade, license, or otherwise transfer the digital sset to another party.
- *Exclusivity*. The right to exclude others from access or use, often enforced by encryption, permissions, or smart contracts.
- *Economic Rights*. The right to monetize the asset, receive royalties, or earn revenue from its use or resale.

Digital property rights will be fundamental to the digital economy and will open economic opportunities to the ecosystem.

Regulation for Next Gen Gaming

The convergence of gaming with blockchain, digital assets, and decentralized finance presents further regulatory complexity. Crypto, NFT economies, and stablecoin wallets challenge existing oversight structures. Proactive jurisdictions like the Philippines and the UAE are responding by incorporating digital asset regulations into their financial frameworks. These efforts include defining standards for KYC/AML in tokenized environments, regulating fiat-to-crypto interfaces, and supporting the legal use of programmable money.

Regulatory approaches to gaming are diverse and uneven around the world. Excessively restrictive regulation risks pushing gaming activity into unregulated or illicit spaces. Drawing lessons from Europe and Latin America experts warn that punitive tax regimes and overly complex restrictions can inadvertently incentivize the growth of black markets. A sustainable regulatory model must strike a balance between safeguarding consumers and preserving innovation, offering clear, fair, and flexible pathways for compliance.

The Philippines has positioned itself as a leader through a comprehensive and agile licensing regime overseen by PAGCOR. Reforms such as tax reductions, the legal integration of e-wallets, and supplier accreditation have helped attract international gaming operators and promote compliance. In contrast, countries like Thailand, Sri Lanka, and Japan remain in regulatory flux due to political delays or cultural ambivalence. This regional fragmentation underscores the necessity for localized compliance strategies and culturally aligned operational models.

Security and digital trust are emerging as central regulatory concerns. Many gaming platforms invest less than 3% of revenue in cybersecurity, leaving systems vulnerable to fraud, data breaches, and identity theft. In contrast, the banking sector typically allocates 10–15% of revenue to cyber resilience. To ensure platform integrity, future regulations will likely mandate stronger standards, including encryption and penetration testing, to comply with international frameworks such as GDPR and ISO/IEC 27001. Accreditation is increasingly central to modern regulation.

The Philippines has mandated ongoing certification for B2B suppliers, game developers, affiliates, and payment providers. These requirements move beyond one-time registration toward continuous monitoring and accountability. Regulatory bodies are now exploring frameworks that incorporate ethical marketing practices, ESG metrics, and support for inclusive economic participation.

As artificial intelligence and gamification reshape user experiences, regulators face new challenges in behavioral oversight. AI-driven personalization may enhance engagement but also increase the risks of addiction or manipulation. Future frameworks are expected to include protections such as biometric age verification, ethical AI use, built-in cooldown mechanisms, and real-time data protection—all embedded within the user experience itself.

Some jurisdictions are also leveraging regulation as a tool for broader economic and civic development. The Philippines, for example, has implemented the Crypto Asset Service Provider framework to license exchanges, staking services, and token issuance. It has also integrated blockchain into public sector processes, including remittances, identity systems, and even digital education through gaming guilds. Similarly, the UAE and Saudi Arabia are investing in Esports infrastructure and Web3 ecosystems, aiming to lead in innovation while managing regulatory risks around tokenomics, influencer conduct, and responsible game design.

With the rise of currency-backed stablecoins and programmable in-game assets, gaming platforms are also functioning as financial ecosystems. This development necessitates a rethinking of financial regulation within gaming, especially concerning money laundering, capital controls, and financial inclusion. The Philippines' central bank is already piloting models in collaboration with fintech providers to ensure oversight and user safety.

Emerging technologies are also raising sovereignty and cybersecurity questions. Regulatory strategies are beginning to explore quantum-resistant cryptography, AI fraud detection, and decentralized identity as foundational components of future-proof systems.

Regulations and innovation are often seen as opposing forces. Since new blockchains offer faster transactions and new functionalities, it is important to ensure that these functionalities are not implemented at the expense of security. By its inherent properties, like immutability, transparency, and automation, blockchain enhances the ability to monitor, report, and ensure adherence to regulations and security standards. Mechanisms, like insurance through government-backed institutions, rarely apply to decentralized finance. This absence creates a challenging landscape, where the responsibility for due diligence rests on individuals who may lack the necessary expertise (Williams 2025). Companies like Chainalysis and TRM Labs help businesses provide regular checkups regarding compliance and risk management, as well as provide investigations in case of incidents (See Technical Compendium).

Conclusion

As gaming evolves into a technologically advanced and economically significant global sector, regulation becomes a strategic instrument shaping its future. The transformation of gaming into a platform for finance, identity, education, and digital infrastructure demands that regulatory frameworks be adaptive, forward-looking, and integrative. In this context, regulation is not a constraint on innovation but a potential enabler of sustainable growth and competitive advantage. Yet, there remains regulatory and legal uncertainty around NFTs and DAOs.

A paradigm shift is underway in regulatory philosophy. Instead of simply mitigating risk, modern frameworks aim to design for inclusive participation. This includes accrediting gaming DAOs, enabling data portability, supporting ethical AI development, and incentivizing access across gender, geography, and economic background. The goal is not only to regulate markets but to shape a more equitable digital society.

Web3 represents a fundamental shift in how value, ownership, and participation are structured in virtual worlds. As explored throughout this chapter, Web3 challenges the entrenched dynamics of platform dominance and passive consumption by introducing systems where players are co-creators, co-owners, and stakeholders.

NFTs, DAOs, smart contracts, and digital property rights are practical, enforceable, and monetizable. This enables new paradigms such as *Play-to-Earn*, *Play-and-Own*, and *Play-and-Create*, which reward creativity, time, and effort with tangible economic value. Yet, as the Play-to-Earn hype of 2021–2022 revealed, sustainable economies cannot be built on speculation alone. The crash of unsustainable token models and the exploitative dynamics in some gaming guilds highlighted the risks of gamifying labor without meaningful engagement, fairness, or fun.

Ultimately, the future of gaming will be determined as much by regulatory innovation and technological advancement. Jurisdictions that co-develop regulatory systems with industry stakeholders, civil society, and users will be best positioned to lead. Regulation is no longer reactive enforcement; it is a co-designed architecture that defines the boundaries and possibilities of play in the digital age. In doing so, it will underpin the role of gaming not just as entertainment, but as a driver of economic, educational, and civic transformation.

The rise of purpose-driven economies and DAO-governed games signals course correction. The future is now being built around hybrid models that combine blockchain-enabled ownership with compelling gameplay, strong communities, and long-term vision. As projects like *Axie Infinity*, *The Sandbox*, *Star Atlas*, and *Alethea AI* demonstrate, Web3 is evolving rapidly, from speculative earning to creative empowerment.

Web3 gaming sets the stage for a new kind of digital society, one where players may build careers, governance systems, and meaningful communities entirely within virtual environments. As this space matures, the challenge will be to ensure that these digital economies are not only decentralized and interoperable but also inclusive, ethical, and designed for lasting value.

Cross-Chapter Insights

The case studies of *The Sandbox* and *Star Atlas* introduce decentralized ownership, NFTs, and creator-first Metaverses. These innovations intersect with the economic experimentation of *Axie Infinity* (Chap. 3), which pioneered tradable digital assets, and with *Alethea AI* (Chap. 4), where tokenized avatars engage in AI-powered interactions. Tools enabling this property layer—such as *Moralis* and *Alchemy*—are further detailed in the Technical Companion. Themes of identity and user sovereignty also emerge in *Neurable* (Chap. 9), where ownership extends to brainwave-driven identities.

Case Studies

The Sandbox—Building the Metaverse, One Block at a Time

Game/Platform Name: The Sandbox
Developer/Publisher: Originalysis (founded by Sebastien Borget), now part of Animoca Brands
Year Released: 2012 (mobile), relaunched on blockchain in 2018
Genre: Metaverse/virtual real estate/play-to-earn
Technology Stack: Ethereum blockchain (now Polygon Layer 2), ERC-721/1155 NFTs, SAND token, VoxEdit, Game Maker

The Sandbox is a decentralized Metaverse where users can create, own, and monetize interactive 3D experiences on blockchain. Evolving from a 2D pixel-art game into a fully immersive, no-code Metaverse powered by NFTs, The Sandbox empowers users to become creators, developers, and digital entrepreneurs.

Innovation

Ownership of virtual land (LAND) as NFTs tradable on open markets
    No-code game creation via VoxEdit and Game Maker
    Thriving creator economy earning SAND tokens from experiences
    Migration to Polygon in 2022 for faster, greener transactions
    The Sandbox merges creator empowerment with digital property rights, making it a flagship in Metaverse innovation.

Impact

5.7 M+ registered users
    1000+ published games and experiences (GameBeast)
    166,464 LAND parcels
    400+ brand collaborations (e.g., Warner Music, Gucci, Snoop Dogg)
    Top creators earn 400,000+ SAND annually
    Game Jam contests with 2500+ entrants in 2024.
    The Sandbox has fueled the rise of a Web3-based creator economy.

Challenges and Controversies

Ethereum scalability issues led to migration to Polygon
    Onboarding friction from Web3 wallet setup and LAND buying complexity
    SAND token volatility affecting incomes and asset values
    Early-stage governance via The Sandbox DAO
    Balancing decentralization, usability, and creator equity remains key.

Lessons and Legacy

For Developers: Merge blockchain ownership tools with streamlined UX.
    For Players: True ownership and income potential depend on creativity and community engagement.
    For Policymakers: Virtual economies raise urgent issues around taxation, IP, and labor rights.

Future Outlook

The Sandbox DAO enables community-led governance 2024 launch
    Cross-platform interoperability to unify digital assets
    Expanded paid roles in design, events, education, and real estate (Metaverse Jobs)
    Rise of branded and educational Metaverse content
    The Sandbox is building core infrastructure for a creator-first digital economy.

The Sandbox DAO

The DAO invites users to shape Metaverse governance, including:
  Game and feature development
  Event structures and reward tiers
  Token-weighted voting rights based on LAND/NFT holdings
  This initiative exemplifies how blockchain enables user-led digital economies.

Star Atlas—Building the First Massive Web3 AAA Game

Game/Platform Name: Star Atlas
Developer/Publisher: ATMTA Inc.
Year Released: 2021
Genre: Space exploration MMO/Strategy/Play-to-Earn
Technology Stack: Solana blockchain, Unreal Engine 5, MetaGravity's HyperScale engine, DAO governance, NFT ownership, ATLAS and POLIS tokens

Star Atlas is a next-generation space strategy game that merges high-fidelity graphics with blockchain-based ownership. Built on Solana, it introduces a player-driven economy, decentralized governance, and large-scale multiplayer infrastructure. Star Atlas enables players to buy and trade ships, land, and resources, participate in faction warfare, and earn income through in-game activity—all while owning their digital assets.

Innovation

Combines cinematic 3D graphics via Unreal Engine 5 with on-chain economics
  NFT-based ownership of in-game assets
  Solana blockchain enables fast and low-cost DeFi and NFT operations
  MetaGravity's HyperScale engine supports thousands of players and bots in one world
  Powered by Aethir's decentralized GPU cloud
  Star Atlas pioneers AAA graphics fused with decentralized Web3 infrastructure.

Impact

First AAA-grade Web3-native game
  ATLAS token ranks among the top 20 gaming cryptos
  $1.8 M+ in NFT sales from the Golden Era campaign
  SAGE version logged 2.093 M transactions in 1 day

Case Studies 35

Active POLIS DAO governance and post-crash community recovery
Sets new standards in blockchain-based persistent MMO scalability

Challenges and Controversies

FTX collapse caused treasury loss and trust issues
   Roadmap delays and delivery concerns
   Technical strain from merging the AAA design with decentralized infra
   Market speculation impacting token and asset values
   Star Atlas is rebuilding trust through transparency, governance, and tech leadership.

Lessons and Legacy

For Developers: Multi-stakeholder coordination and scalable design are vital for AAA Web3 games.
   For Players: True digital ownership and governance come with economic risks.
   For Policymakers: Highlights emerging borderless digital economies and new asset/labor categories.

Future Outlook

1000+ live player support targeted for early 2024
   POLIS DAO governance expansion and community-led proposals
   Deepening Unreal Engine 5 integration with blockchain layers
   Real-time faction warfare and cross-chain economic hubs
   Star Atlas positions itself as a self-governing digital nation, a persistent, decentralized MMO universe.

Star Atlas DAO

The Star Atlas DAO allows players to vote on ecosystem changes, including economic rules, gameplay mechanics, and treasury usage. Operating fully on Solana, it uses locked POLIS tokens for on-chain proposal voting.

A unique component is the Star Atlas Foundation, acting as a legal intermediary to implement DAO decisions. The DAO is multi-tiered—universal, regional, factional, and guild-level—though only the universal DAO is currently live.

Guilds or DACs (Decentralized Autonomous Corporations) are collaborative groups pooling assets and coordinating strategies. Decision-making tools for DACs are being developed. These collectives already coordinate economic activity, warfare, and exploration.

Star Atlas Economy

Star Atlas offers a player-owned economy through NFT assets (ships, equipment, land) tokenized on Solana. Players earn ATLAS through mining, trading, and exploration, with token exchangeability via global crypto markets.

Creation tools include SDKs, APIs, and building documentation via the **Build Hub**. Although no-code tools are not yet public, the platform enables developer-built items with dynamic value based on market demand and player activity.

References

Almeida, F. L. (2017, November). Concept and dimensions of Web 4.0. International Journal of Computers & Technology, 16(7), 7040–7046. Retrieved from https://doi.org/10.24297/ijct.v16i7.6446

Beck, J., and Asher, M. (2021, February 3). Why Decentralized Autonomous Organizations (DAOs) Are Essential to DeFi. ConsenSys. https://consensys.net/blog/codefi/daos/

Bschacher, K. (2013). Web 4.0: The emergence of ubiquitous intelligence. In *Proceedings of the 2013 International Conference on Web Intelligence* (pp. 104–110). ACM.

Burke, J. (2021). The Web 3 Toolbox. Retrieved 14 July 2022, from https://outlierventures.io/research/the-web-3-toolbox/

Hassan, S., De Filippi, P., and Reijers, W. (2021). Decentralized autonomous organization. *Internet Policy Review, 10*(2). https://doi.org/10.14763/2021.2.1556

McDonell, S. (2021, March 12). *NFTs explained: Why people are spending millions on digital assets*. TIME. https://time.com/5947720/NFT-art/

Morrison, R., Mazey, N. C. H. L., Wingreen S. C. (2020) The DAO Controversy: The Case for a New Species of Corporate Governance? Frontiers in Blockchain, Volume 3—2020. https://www.frontiersin.org/journals/blockchain/articles/10.3389/fbloc.2020.00025

Namcious. (2022). Jack Dorsey's Web5 explained: A new version of the internet built on Bitcoin. *Decrypt*. https://decrypt.co

Nath, A., Dhar, T., and Basishtha, A. (2015). Towards Web 4.0: Concepts, technologies and challenges. *International Journal of Computer Science and Information Technologies, 6*(6), 5331–5334.

Polanska, M. (2014). Web 4.0: User-centric internet and the end of anonymity. *Journal of Internet Studies, 2*(1), 33–45.

Rozas D, Tenorio-Fornés A and Hassan S (2021) Analysis of the Potentials of Blockchain for the Governance of Global Digital Commons. Front. Blockchain 4:577680. https://doi.org/10.3389/fbloc.2021.577680

Shuttleworth, D. (2021, October 7). *What Is A DAO And How Do They Work?*. ConsenSys. https://consensys.net/blog/blockchain-explained/what-is-a-dao-and-how-do-they-work/

TBD. (2023). *Web5: The decentralized web platform*. https://www.tbd.website

Tomaino, N. (2021). The Web3 playbook: Using tokens to bootstrap new networks. The Generalist. https://www.readthegeneralist.com/briefing/web3

Williams, B. (2025). Decentralized Identities: Exploring Blockchain Solutions for Secure Authentication. Barrett Williams. Retrieved from https://www.google.com.ua/books/edition/Decentralized_Identities/Uz9CEQAAQBAJ?hl=en&gbpv=0

Yield Guild Games (2024) Perspectives in Play. https://storage.googleapis.com/external_communication/2025-YGG-PerspectivesInPlay.pdf

References

Zhou, Y., Ye, J., and Xue, H. (2022). Web3: A survey on decentralized applications and blockchain-based internet. *Computer Science Review*, *44*, 100468. https://doi.org/10.1016/j.cosrev.2022.100468

Zwitter A and Hazenberg J (2020) Decentralized Network Governance: Blockchain Technology and the Future of Regulation. *Front. Blockchain* 3:12. https://doi.org/10.3389/fbloc.2020.00012

Chapter 3
Digital Assets and Tokenization

Abstract Chapter 3: "Digital Assets and Tokenization" unpacks the concept of tokenization and how in-game items, currencies, and identities are being represented as tradeable, ownable digital tokens. Readers will explore how NFTs and blockchain-based assets enable the exchange of real-world value, creating new monetization models for both developers and players. The chapter explores the rise of secondary markets where virtual items are bought, sold, and traded across platforms, introducing the concept of interoperability and ownership beyond a single game. It also examines the regulatory complexities emerging around digital asset markets, including legal frameworks, financial oversight, and consumer protection. As the lines blur between virtual and real-world economies, this chapter provides a critical foundation for understanding how tokenized ecosystems are reshaping identity, commerce, and the future of play.

Keywords Digital assets · Tokenization · Non-fungible tokens (NFTs) · Blockchain gaming · GameFi · In-game economies · Interoperability · Decentralized finance (DeFi) · Smart contracts · Secondary markets · Regulatory frameworks · Digital property rights · Player ownership · Esports tokenization · Virtual asset governance

Introduction

Digital assets are units of value that exist in digital form and can be owned or transferred electronically (Tapscott and Tapscott 2016). Tokenization of digital assets in games is creating economic opportunities and fostering a player-driven economy. The market for tokenized assets could reach $10 trillion by 2030. (Boston Consulting Group and ADDX 2022). Tokenizing real-world assets like real estate unlocks global access to investment opportunities (OECD 2020). This chapter examines tokenization, in-game items, currencies, and identities as tradeable, ownable digital tokens. Readers will explore how NFTs and blockchain-based assets enable the exchange of real-world value, creating new monetization models for developers and players. The chapter examines the emergence of secondary markets where virtual items are bought, sold, and traded across platforms, with interoperability and ownership extending beyond a single game. The chapter addresses some of the technical challenges, including interoperability and metadata standards. It explores the regulatory complexities emerging around digital asset markets, including legal frameworks, financial oversight, and consumer protection. Finally, this chapter provides a critical foundation for understanding how tokenized ecosystems reshape identity, commerce, and the future of play.

Tokenization

Tokenization is the process of turning real or digital assets like in-game items into digital tokens that can be stored, transferred, or traded on a blockchain. It enables the possibility of creating a digital version of something valuable (such as a concert ticket or a piece of land), which can then be sold or shared. It also creates provability of ownership.

NFTs have been described in Chap. 2. NFTs represent individual assets with unique properties. When these NFTs are tokenized on-chain, they are owned by the player, not the publisher. They can be bought, sold, or lent across marketplaces. This introduces a secondary market where value is determined by demand, rarity, and utility, rather than developer pricing.

Tokenization can offer multiple benefits, including improved access to investment, increased efficiency, and reduced reliance on intermediaries (World Economic Forum 2020). Tokenization enables faster transactions and settlements, with quicker transactions facilitated through automation and smart contracts. It also improves traceability and transparency, as an immutable shared ledger keeps track of all actions on a given asset, providing visibility to all parties. Tokenized assets enable quicker transactions with less paperwork. Many manual operations can be automated and streamlined using smart contracts, while clearing and settlement processes may be simplified and built more efficiently.

Token Standards

Token standards are a set of rules that enable the creation and management of digital assets (Krishnan 2020). These rules are outlined in technical documents that define the methods researchers, developers, and innovators must follow when creating new tokens. The Ethereum community has developed multiple token standards (Buterin 2014), which are detailed in the Technical Compendium. In summary, ERC-20 is the standard for fungible tokens — all tokens are equal (e.g., 1 USDC = 1 USDC). With ERC-721, each token has a unique ID and is widely used in art and gaming

NFTs. ERC-1155 is a hybrid and can represent both fungible (e.g., gold) and non-fungible (e.g., sword) tokens in one contract. Finally, ERC-6551 extends NFTs into token-bound accounts, where an NFT can act like a smart contract wallet holding assets and other NFTs. More detail can be found in the technical companion.

Tokenization and In-Game Economies

Previously, in digital gaming, players could spend hours unlocking skins, acquiring weapons, or building characters; however, these activities could not be monetized. Tokenization is changing this paradigm. Tokenization enables the conversion of in-game items, currencies, or achievements into cryptographic tokens on a blockchain. Value in games becomes portable, programmable, and owned by the player. This will challenge the economic philosophy of gaming, as it challenges the traditional model of extractive monetization, where value flows one way. Instead, tokenization will facilitate an open, player-driven economy, where gamers can own, trade, and co-create digital assets that retain value beyond any single game. Tokenization enables ownership or rights attached to an asset to be split into small units or tokens, which can be traded, held, bought, sold, and exchanged. The ability to exchange that value is the building block for the future of gaming.

One of the most potent aspects of tokenization is programmability. Game assets can evolve or be enhanced based on usage, achievements, or the passage of time. A sword can change form because the token metadata can be updated securely on-chain. This turns digital items from static inventory into living assets, each with a verifiable history and narrative.

Tokenization builds player sovereignty because players can transfer their assets to another wallet, lend them in a guild economy, stake them for in-game rewards, or use them as collateral in DeFi protocols. In this way, virtual items become a financial instrument, a collectable, a reputation badge, or a gateway to exclusive experiences, giving players control over their digital assets.

Tokenization transforms these assets into fungible tokens (like ERC-20 s), whose supply can be transparently managed, traded on exchanges, and even integrated with DeFi systems. For example, a player earns game tokens through quests or tournaments. These tokens can be traded for other cryptocurrencies or fiat. Players can stake them for governance, rewards, or yield. This play-to-earn loop gives time spent in games a tangible economic dimension, especially relevant in emerging markets where gaming offers real income potential. Tokenized gaming assets are also composable, meaning they can be combined or repurposed across ecosystems. Developers can build on existing assets and reward the original creators.

The convergence of tokenized assets and DeFi is the basis of GameFi. GameFi enables players to farm tokens through gameplay, stake NFTs for in-game bonuses or governance, borrow or lend gaming assets through NFT lending platforms, and fractionalize high-value NFTs for collective ownership. In this environment, games have become not only platforms for fun but also income-generating ecosystems, investment vehicles, and creative economies.

Designing sustainable in-game economies requires an approach that puts player experience, economic stability, and long-term value at the core. By prioritizing utility, managing inflation, and ensuring that games remain engaging beyond financial incentives, tokenization can create vibrant player-driven markets and governance systems. However, the early experience of play-to-earn models was unsustainable due to inflationary tokenomics, and their token-staking economies weakened once token prices stagnated and player numbers dropped (AINvest. 2025).

There are several key elements that are necessary for sustainable token economic systems within games (Kim et al. 2023; Ranandeh and Mirza-Babaei 2023; Thomas 2024). These are:

(i) *Utility-first tokens*—with clear in-game uses (e.g., crafting, upgrades, governance).
(ii) *Balanced supply and sinks*—mechanisms to regulate token inflation and player behavior.
(iii) *Engaging core gameplay*—games must be fun first, or economies will collapse when rewards shrink.
(iv) *Liquidity strategies*—ensuring that in-game assets have pathways to be traded without destabilizing the market.
(v) *Progressive decentralization*—gradually shifting governance from developer-controlled to community-led.

Tokenization and eSports

In eSports, tokenization is also used to allow brands, influencers, and creators to monetize experiences and services. Tokenization is reshaping the economic and engagement models of Esports by introducing digital assets that represent ownership, identity, and participation rights. Fan tokens are a prime example of how tokenization enables fans to participate more directly in the Esports experience.

Community gaming, an Esports tournament platform, uses blockchain to manage automated tournament payouts and participation tokens. These tokens serve as proof of entry and enable real-time, gas-efficient payment distribution through smart contracts. This model reduces overhead, increases transparency, and enables micro-tournaments with token rewards, making it ideal for grassroots Esports and amateur players seeking monetization opportunities.

ZED RUN, although not a traditional Esports title, offers a model for Esports-related NFT integration. Virtually Human Studio has begun integrating tournament formats where participants race tokenized digital horses. Applying this to mainstream Esports, platforms are now exploring ways to mint limited-edition NFTs of in-game highlights, skins, or event passes, mirroring the success of NBA Top Shot.

This provides fans with digital memorabilia that they can trade or showcase, thereby enhancing both emotional and economic connections to their teams and players.

Though best known for its play-to-earn focus, Yield Guild Games (YGG) has also ventured into competitive gaming structures. YGG tokenizes membership and ownership in gaming assets, which are then lent to players often in developing markets to compete in tournaments and earn a share of winnings. This model is spreading into Esports, particularly in mobile-first games, enabling players with limited capital to participate in revenue-generating competitive play. (Case Study Chap. 4).

MetaGame offers a glimpse into decentralized Esports leagues. In these systems, decisions regarding tournament rules, prize distribution, and sponsorship allocation are made by token holders through a voting process. Projects like Illuvium DAO and Aurory are also experimenting with integrating tokenized governance for future Esports leagues built on Web3 principles. Tokenization enables ownership, rewarding participation, and decentralizing decision-making. In an industry traditionally driven by sponsorships, streaming revenues, and tournament prize pools, tokenization creates new models for monetization, fan engagement, and community governance.

These emerging models demonstrate that tokenization is transforming Esports economics and community dynamics. As the sector matures, tokenization could democratize Esports funding, increase transparency in revenue sharing, and offer new forms of identity, recognition, and reward for both players and fans. From amateur tournaments to global franchises, the integration of blockchain-based tokens is creating an infrastructure where everyone involved in the Esports ecosystem can become a stakeholder.

Tokenization and Secondary Markets

Traditionally, game economies were closed ecosystems. Players had no legal ownership, no ability to resell, and often lost access entirely if the game shut down or they were banned from it. In cases where secondary markets emerged, such as the gray-market trading of CS: GO skins or World of Warcraft gold, they often violated terms of service, were plagued by scams, and lacked transparency and accountability. Tokenization can change this paradigm by turning virtual items into NFTs or fungible in-game tokens. This enables developers to formalize ownership and enable secure, transparent, and open trade on or off-platform. These assets exist on public blockchains and can be stored in wallets, traded on decentralized exchanges, lent out, or integrated into other digital environments.

For example, a rare skin in a battle royale tournament can become a verified, tradable digital asset. It can be sold on marketplaces like OpenSea or Magic Eden. It is possible to use it as a 3D avatar in a Metaverse platform like The Sandbox or stake it in a DeFi-style protocol to earn yield. This is the foundation of interoperable digital property, where in-game items hold tangible value and utility beyond their original platform.

One of the earliest large-scale examples of tokenized secondary markets in gaming was Axie Infinity (Case Study), where players could breed, trade, and battle NFT creatures called "Axies." The Axies, along with virtual land and other in-game assets, could be traded openly on the game's proprietary marketplace as well as on broader Ethereum-based platforms. At its peak, some Axies sold for thousands of dollars, and the ecosystem supported a thriving P2P economy, including third-party marketplaces, analytics tools, and leasing arrangements. Although Axie's economy later faced sustainability challenges, its model demonstrated the power and pitfalls of tokenized markets, specifically the need for economic balance, utility, and regulation.

Beyond simple buying and selling, tokenization introduces financialization to virtual assets. Platforms like Double Protocol, ReNFT, and IQ Protocol now allow players to rent out their NFTs, such as characters, weapons, or wearables, to other players for a fee, creating passive income streams. Similarly, games with native tokens (e.g., $SAND for The Sandbox or $ILV for Illuvium) offer staking mechanisms, where users lock tokens to earn yield or gain access to premium content.

This secondary economy mirrors financial markets, turning gamers into investors, lenders, and entrepreneurs. It also raises important questions about regulation, taxation, and consumer protection, particularly as real-world money becomes deeply integrated into digital play.

Tokenized secondary markets offer potential for player empowerment and innovation. They also introduce new risks: speculation can distort gameplay if asset prices outweigh utility; regulatory ambiguity exists around the classification of game tokens as securities or virtual property and interoperability limitations still depend heavily on cross-platform collaboration and standardization. These are discussed in more detail below. Despite these challenges, secondary markets powered by tokenization are reshaping the gaming landscape. Tokenization promises enhanced liquidity, but in practice, secondary markets for tokenized assets are often illiquid or underdeveloped. While tokenization is often associated with liquidity benefits, the lack of deep, regulated secondary markets significantly constrains real-world liquidity (European Securities and Markets Authority [ESMA] 2021).

The Regulatory Horizon

A central challenge in tokenized gaming is the lack of regulatory clarity. Depending on the jurisdiction, gaming tokens might be classified as securities, commodities, or unregulated digital goods. These classifications carry vastly different legal implications. For developers, the ambiguity complicates compliance, especially when issuing tokens, enabling player-to-player exchanges, or integrating in-game economies with external markets. Without clear guidance, developers risk noncompliance with securities laws, tax codes, or consumer protection statutes.

Gaming platforms now operate at the intersection of entertainment and finance. As such, they are increasingly subject to anti-money laundering (AML) and counter-terrorism financing (CFT) regulations. Platforms that allow token exchanges or facilitate real-money withdrawals must implement Know Your Customer (KYC) procedures, monitor transactions, and report suspicious activity. These requirements introduce new compliance costs and demand operational expertise traditionally reserved for fintech institutions.

The financialization of gameplay also introduces a new layer of consumer risk. As virtual assets gain real-world value, the potential for fraud, speculative bubbles, and market manipulation grows. Unsuspecting players may be enticed into risky or predatory schemes disguised as gaming features. In response, regulators are calling for higher disclosure standards, including mandatory whitepapers that detail technical and financial risks, ethical marketing guidelines, and transparent tokenomics. Protecting players from loss, manipulation, or unfair practices is fast becoming a cornerstone of tokenization governance.

Gaming is a global phenomenon, but regulation is typically local. A platform issuing tokens in one country and serving users in another must navigate a complex patchwork of laws. This fragmentation compounded by the absence of internationally harmonized digital asset standards creates legal uncertainty and exposes developers to enforcement risks. It also complicates scaling and integration, hindering efforts to build seamless, interoperable gaming ecosystems. The lack of harmonized regulatory frameworks across jurisdictions may result in legal uncertainty, increased compliance costs, and fragmented markets (OECD 2020).

Tokenization redefines ownership within virtual environments. Players may own unique digital items, resell them, or hold fractional stakes in game assets. However, these practices disrupt traditional intellectual property and licensing frameworks. Developers must address unresolved questions around royalties, resale rights, usage restrictions, and smart contract enforcement. As asset ownership moves from code to commerce, new legal definitions of digital property and user rights will be required.

The convergence of AI and blockchain introduces further complexity. AI is increasingly used for fraud detection, pricing models, content generation, and personalization within games. When combined with tokenized economies, these systems must be transparent, fair, and explainable. Regulators will need to coordinate across domains to address algorithmic bias, data privacy, and automated decision-making, especially when real money is at stake.

Technical and ethical hurdles persist. Blockchain scalability remains a barrier for fast-paced games requiring low-cost, high-frequency transactions. Security vulnerabilities, such as smart contract exploits, wallet hacks, and phishing, pose risks to both players and platforms. The volatility of token markets can destabilize gameplay and incentivize speculation over fun, while onboarding remains inaccessible to mainstream users unfamiliar with wallets, gas fees, and cryptographic jargon. Additionally, the blurred line between play and work raises ethical concerns, especially in play-to-earn ecosystems where gameplay may resemble gig labor more than entertainment.

Tokenization relies on blockchain technologies that may still lack scalability, security, and interoperability for institutional-grade adoption. Distributed ledger technologies are still maturing, and current implementations may not meet the performance and resilience standards required for systemic financial infrastructures (Bank for International Settlements 2019).

Virtual assets have transformed financial systems globally, offering transparency, efficiency, and broader access to digital financial services. However, these benefits are accompanied by substantial risks, particularly in relation to money laundering, terrorism financing, and proliferation financing. There remains regulatory uncertainty around how tokens are classified. Tokenized systems can be vulnerable to hacking, smart contract bugs, and key management failures. The immutability of smart contracts means that any bugs or vulnerabilities may be irreparable and subject to exploitation (Lyons and Nesenbergs 2020).

A Model Law for Responsible Innovation

Some regions are taking steps toward clarity. The Commonwealth Secretariat has developed a Model Law for Virtual Assets, offering a principle-based, technology-neutral framework for licensing, AML/CFT compliance, and investor protection. It excludes closed-loop tokens and stablecoins that are already under central bank jurisdiction, allowing for flexibility while supporting innovation. This law could serve as a global benchmark, particularly for gaming platforms that issue NFTs, run token sales, or integrate stablecoins for payments and rewards.

The Commonwealth Model Law for Virtual Assets notes that while virtual assets can facilitate remittances and financial inclusion, especially in emerging markets like India, Nigeria, and Pakistan, they are also susceptible to illicit financial activities due to their pseudonymous and borderless nature. Moreover, the rapid growth of ransomware attacks, where virtual assets are often used as payment, underscores the urgency of establishing effective anti-money laundering and countering the financing of terrorism (AML/CFT) frameworks. The Model Law responds by advocating for strong regulatory mechanisms, including licensing, registration, supervision, and enforcement provisions that align with the Financial Action Task Force (FATF) Recommendations, particularly the "Travel Rule," which mandates the identification of originators and beneficiaries in digital asset transfers. Without such regulatory safeguards, the use of virtual assets could threaten financial market integrity, consumer protection, and national security. Thus, the Model Law seeks to equip Commonwealth member states with a harmonized legal framework that balances innovation with financial stability, helping jurisdictions to mitigate risk while fostering a trustworthy environment for digital financial growth (Commonwealth Secretariat 2024).

A particularly challenging issue is compliance with the Financial Action Task Force's Travel Rule, which requires identifying both sender and recipient in digital asset transfers. For gaming companies facilitating peer-to-peer transactions, remittances, or cross-border trades, this rule presents significant challenges, especially as adoption remains fragmented across jurisdictions. A harmonized,

Commonwealth-wide registry of licensed VASPs could address this gap, enabling safer and more compliant value flows.

Conclusion

Tokenization holds immense promise for the future of gaming, but its success depends on the evolution of thoughtful, adaptive governance. Developers, regulators, and communities must collaborate to create systems that are secure, inclusive, and transparent. Smart compliance will be a competitive advantage, while player protection and legal clarity will be prerequisites for scale. In this next phase of gaming, the code must work, but so must the rules. Tokenization is not just a technical innovation; it is a structural shift in how value, rights, and relationships are managed in virtual worlds. As such, it demands a regulatory response as sophisticated as the technology itself.

The long-term vision of tokenization in gaming is to establish an infrastructure layer for player-centric economies. As the line between games, finance, identity, and social spaces continues to blur, tokenized assets will underpin the next generation of experiences. Tokenization can transform gaming from an entertainment medium to an economic participation platform. It puts the player at the center, not just of the game, but of the value it creates.

In the long run, tokenized in-game economies will blur the line between gaming, work, and creative entrepreneurship. Players will own their digital labor, co-create the value of game worlds, form DAOs to govern game economies, and earn income through participation, not just purchase. As digital and physical identities converge, in-game economies may even become the foundation for new forms of digital citizenship, employment, and community.

Cross-Chapter Insights

This chapter explores token economies and blockchain-enabled monetization. *Axie Infinity* catalyzed play-to-earn microeconomies, which are further institutionalized in *Yield Guild Games* (Chap. 4). The asset ownership mechanisms explored here are similar to those found in *The Sandbox* (Chap. 2) and *Roblox* (Chap. 10). Security, compliance, and infrastructure tools, such as Chainalysis and TRM Labs, covered in the Technical Compendium, highlight the backend systems that make tokenized economies viable. Emerging biometric assets in *Neurable* (Chap. 9) hint at a future where digital value may even include brain-based credentials.

Case Studies

Axie Infinity—Play-to-Earn and the Rise of Digital Microeconomies

Game/Platform Name: Axie Infinity
Developer/Publisher: Sky Mavis
Year Released: 2018
Genre: Blockchain-based creature battler/Play-to-Earn
Technology Stack: Ethereum blockchain, Ronin sidechain, ERC-721 NFTs, Smooth Love Potion (SLP) and AXS tokens

Axie Infinity redefined the relationship between players and digital ownership by allowing users to earn real income through gameplay. Players collect, breed, and battle creatures called Axies—NFTs that can be traded or sold. The game popularized the "play-to-earn" model and sparked a wave of blockchain games attempting to emulate its success

Innovation

Introduced NFT-based characters and assets tradable on blockchain
Smooth Love Potion (SLP) earned through gameplay and used for breeding
AXS governance token allows staking and DAO participation
Custom Ronin sidechain built to avoid Ethereum gas fees and enable mass adoption
Axie created a digital microeconomy blending NFT ownership, community finance, and gameplay.

Impact

2.5 million daily active users at its peak in mid-2021
Generated $1.3B+ in revenue in 2021
AXS token hit $10B market cap in November 2021
Filipino players earned above minimum wage during the COVID-19 lockdowns
Sparked the rise of Yield Guild Games (YGG), enabling crypto-financed player onboarding

Challenges and Controversies

SLP token oversupply led to inflation and price collapse
$625 M Ronin bridge hack exposed security flaws
Accusations of Ponzi-like reliance on new player inflows

Regulatory scrutiny around the classification of Axie-based income and activities

Axie's collapse revealed weaknesses in early blockchain game economics and security.

Lessons and Legacy

For developers: Sustainable tokenomics, burn mechanisms, and compelling gameplay are crucial.

For players: Earnings carry speculative risk, and ecosystem success is not guaranteed.

For policymakers: Axie raised urgent questions on digital labor, taxation, and consumer protection.

Future Outlook

Axie origins (free-to-play) lowers barriers for new users
  Expanded land gameplay introduces farming and Metaverse features
  Builder's Program funds third-party games using Axie IP
  Tokenomics reform aims to stabilize the ecosystem and reduce SLP inflation
  Axie remains a foundational case in how digital economies emerge—and collapse—in real time.

Steam and Epic Store—Competing Gateways to the Digital Gaming Marketplace

Platform Names: Steam and Epic Games Store
  Parent Companies: Valve Corporation (Steam), Epic Games
  Year Launched: Steam (2003),
  Genre: Digital distribution platforms for PC games and software
  Technology Stack: Proprietary storefront architecture, in-app purchase systems, multiplayer APIs, game engines (e.g., Unreal for Epic), DRM tools, community overlays

Steam and the Epic Games Store are two of the most influential PC game distribution platforms. While Steam set the standard for digital game sales and community features, Epic disrupted the market by offering developers better revenue splits and free games to attract users. Together, they define the commercial infrastructure of PC gaming

Innovation

Steam pioneered cloud saves, automatic updates, and robust mod integration via the Steam Workshop

Epic offered an 88/12 revenue share in favor of developers (compared to Steam's 70/30), putting pressure on incumbent models.

Both platforms offer cross-platform multiplayer integration and social features.

Epic's Free Games Program introduced weekly giveaways of AAA and indie titles to drive adoption.

These storefronts are not just sales hubs—they shape player discovery, indie success, and platform loyalty.

Impact

Steam had over 132 million monthly active users in 2023 and over 30,000 games in its library

Epic Games Store reached 270 million users and 68 million monthly active users in 2023

Over $2.7 billion was spent on the Epic Store in 2023, with $950 million on third-party games

Steam's review system and community features influence game visibility and user trust

Epic's exclusivity deals have sparked debates over platform fragmentation and user experience.

Challenges and Controversies

Steam's open publishing model allows for low-quality asset flips and issues with discoverability.

Epic faced backlash for securing exclusives and lacking basic community tools at launch.

Both platforms have struggled with the moderation of user content, review bombing, and algorithmic visibility.

Data privacy and refund policies have come under regulatory scrutiny in various countries.

Distribution platforms are no longer neutral—they are active participants in the ecosystem's economics and culture.

Lessons and Legacy

For developers: Storefront terms, visibility tools, and community ecosystems matter as much as game quality.

Case Studies   51

For players: Platform choice impacts access, pricing, and social features.For policymakers: Storefront operators function like digital utilities and require oversight for fair access and transparency.

Future Outlook

Expansion of subscription models (e.g., Steam Family Sharing, Epic's potential Game Pass-like service)
   Growth of regional pricing and alternative payment systems
   Integration with Web3 and blockchain-based asset ownership via third-party integrations
   Greater emphasis on modding, user-generated content, and creator monetization tools
   The battle between Steam and Epic is shaping the digital shelves of gaming's future—and redefining who holds power in a decentralized industry.

Yield Guild Games (YGG)—Turning Play-to-Earn into a Global Talent Guild

Platform/DAO Name: Yield Guild Games (**YGG**)
   Founders: Gabby Dizon, Beryl Li, "Owl of Moistness"
   Year Launched: 2020
   Core Products: YGGDAO, regional SubDAOs (e.g., **YGG** Pilipinas, IndiGG), Guild Advancement Program (GAP), Scholar Sponsorships
   Tokens: YGG(ERC-20 governance/rewards)
   YGG is a decentralized network of gaming guilds that buys NFT game assets and lends them to players, called scholars, who share a portion of their in-game earnings with the guild. YGG rose to prominence during the Axie Infinity boom and now supports 80+ games and infrastructure projects.

Innovation

NFT assets are leased to players who earn and share rewards.
   Regional/gaming guilds (e.g., YGG SEA) operate semi-independently while contributing to the main DAO.
   Guild Advancement Program: Tracks skills with soul-bound NFTs, forming "Metaverse résumés."
   Web3 Metaversity: Free courses in Web3 skills; rewards include tokens and NFTs

Impact

Raised $12.5 M in 31 s during the 2021 token sale
   Backed 80+ Web3 games and projects
   Nearly 30,000 active scholars (Mar 2022)
   YGG Pilipinas community surpassed 95,000 by 2024
   Token price around $0.17 (June 2025)
   YGG provided life-changing income during the peak of the play-to-earn era and transitioned toward talent development, training moderators, marketers, and Esports professionals.

Challenges and Controversies

P2E Collapse: Token devaluation in 2022 led to a shift to the "play-and-own" model.
   Speculative Users: Incentives attracted short-term participants; YGG now uses proof-of-play and education gates.
   Volatility: Treasury assets tied to market conditions.
   Legal Ambiguity: Scholar earnings raise questions of employment and taxation.

Lessons and Legacy

For developers: Guilds boost user bases but require sustainable game economies.
   For players: Web3 guilds provide pathways to long-term digital work.
   For policymakers: YGG underscores the need for frameworks for digital labor and reward sharing.

Future Outlook

Soul-Bound Reputation Layers: Restrict privileges to proven contributors.
   Esports and Media Brands: New revenue streams through teams and content.
   Guild Partnerships: Onboarding traditional clans via infrastructure.
   Expanded Metaversity: Adds AI-assisted coursework and credentials.
   YGG is evolving into a decentralized talent engine—exporting infrastructure and play-to-earn expertise to a broader Web3 economy.

References

AINvest. (2025, April 10). *Play-to-earn model collapses as Web3 gaming funding drops*. AInvest.com. Retrieved from https://www.ainvest.com/news/play-earn-model-collapses-web3-gaming-funding-drops-10-april-2025-2507/

References

Bank for International Settlements (BIS). (2019). Distributed ledger technology in payment, clearing and settlement: An analytical framework

Boston Consulting Group and ADDX. (2022). *Relevance of on-chain asset tokenization in 'crypto winter'*. https://www.bcg.com/publications/2022/relevance-of-asset-tokenization-in-crypto-winter

Buterin, V. (2014). Ethereum white paper. https://ethereum.org/en/whitepaper/

Commonwealth Secretariat. (2024). *Model Law on Virtual Assets: A regulatory framework for Commonwealth member countries*. Commonwealth Secretariat. https://thecommonwealth.org/publications/model-law-virtual-assets

ESMA. (2021). Report on trends, risks and vulnerabilities. https://www.esma.europa.eu/sites/default/files/library/esma50-165-2042_trv_report_no1_2021.pdf

Kim, H., Kim, H.-S., and Park, Y.-S. (2023). Evaluating and managing tokenomics for non-fungible tokens in game-based blockchain networks. *arXiv*. https://doi.org/10.48550/arXiv.2306.13672

Krishnan, R. (2020). *Tokenization standards on Ethereum: ERC explained*. [White paper]. https://medium.com

Lyons, T., and Nesenbergs, K. (2020). Risks of blockchain and smart contracts in financial services. Journal of Digital Banking, 4(2), 121–132.

OECD. (2020). *The tokenisation of assets and potential implications for financial markets*. https://www.oecd.org/finance/The-Tokenisation-of-Assets-and-Potential-Implications-for-Financial-Markets.pdf

Ranandeh, V., and Mirza-Babaei, P. (2023, October). Beyond equilibrium: Utilizing AI agents in video game economy balancing. *CHI PLAY Companion '23*. https://doi.org/10.1145/3573382.3616092

Tapscott, D., and Tapscott, A. (2016). *Blockchain revolution: How the technology behind bitcoin is changing money, business, and the world*. Penguin.

Thomas, D. (2024, August 30). *The evolution of tokenomics: From utility tokens to security tokens …* Medium. https://medium.com/@daisygarciathomas/the-evolution-of-tokenomics-from-utility-tokens-to-security-tokens-and-beyond-8f124ef8bf36

World Economic Forum. (2020). *Digital assets, distributed ledger technology and the future of capital markets*. https://www.weforum.org/reports/digital-assets-distributed-ledger-technology-and-the-future-of-capital-markets/

Chapter 4
Building the New Gaming Economy

Abstract "Building the New Gaming Economy" explores how gaming is spawning new forms of digital labor, from full-time streamers and Esports athletes to virtual asset designers and game modders. With platforms like Twitch and YouTube Gaming enabling monetization and community engagement, and Web3 technologies powering ownership and income via gaming guilds, the line between work and play is being redrawn. A particular focus is given to emerging markets where gaming offers accessible income opportunities and a gateway to the digital economy. Readers will uncover how virtual economies, decentralized platforms, and token-based incentives are democratizing wealth and transforming livelihoods. As gaming continues to scale, it is a powerful engine for inclusive economic growth.

Keywords Web3 gaming · Play-to-earn · GameFi · Tokenization · Decentralized finance (DeFi) · Non-fungible tokens (NFTs) · Gaming guilds · Esports economy · Creator economy · Virtual real estate · Metaverse platforms · Digital labor · DAOs · Digital identity · Inclusive digital economies

Introduction

Gaming is rapidly evolving into a thriving economic ecosystem where players are consumers, creators, entrepreneurs, and investors. This chapter explores how gaming catalyzes new forms of digital labor, from full-time streamers and Esports athletes to virtual asset designers and game modders (who modify video games, usually by adding content, features, or functionality). With new online spaces like Twitch and YouTube Gaming, where individuals can live-stream video game gameplay and interact with viewers, content creators can build an audience and share their passion for gaming. These spaces act as social networks centered around video game content, where viewers can discover new games, watch skilled players, and engage with a community. Twitch and YouTube Gaming enable monetization and community engagement.

Behind this, Web3 technologies power ownership and income via gaming guilds, and the line between work and play is redrawn. This is particularly important for emerging markets, where gaming offers accessible income opportunities and serves as a gateway to the digital economy. As outlined in Chap. 3, Web3 technologies bring ownership, interoperability, and decentralization to gaming. Token economies also challenge traditional corporate revenue models. Instead of centralized profits, value circulates through players, creators, and communities. Readers will discover how virtual economies, decentralized platforms, and token-based incentives democratize wealth and transform individuals' livelihoods. As gaming continues to scale, it is no longer just entertainment; it's a powerful engine for inclusive economic growth. This shift from play to productivity is redefining labor, value creation, and ownership in gaming, and blurs lines between user and producer, fun and work.

Gaming has evolved from a leisure pursuit into a vibrant digital economy, where gaming now intersects with finance, labor, and even education. From streaming and Esports to virtual economies and blockchain-based ownership, the gaming industry is rapidly becoming a foundational component of the digital economy. This chapter examines this shift and its creation of new forms of value and opportunity, particularly in underserved and emerging markets.

The scale of in-game economies is growing, and players spend millions annually on virtual items, skins, upgrades, and digital real estate. Yet the innovation goes far deeper than spending. With the blockchain and tokenization, these in-game items are becoming assets with real-world liquidity. Virtual economies now support full ecosystems of trade, speculation, investment, and entrepreneurship. For example, in Massively Multiplayer Online Role-Playing Games (MMORPGs), players can farm resources and sell them for fiat, in blockchain games, and in Metaverse platforms, players can mint NFTs and list them on decentralized marketplaces, and digital landowners lease property to creators, event organizers, and brands. What began as play has matured into a self-sustaining, multi-layered economic system that drives revenue, employment, and financial flows across borders.

New Economic Models

GameFi: The Fusion of Gaming and Decentralized Finance

In the evolution of digital economies, GameFi is merging the worlds of DeFi with the interactive, immersive nature of gaming. DeFi principles of open, permissionless, and peer-to-peer financial infrastructure are now increasingly being applied to the gaming sector. This integration has catalyzed new economic models where players are not just consumers but active participants in the value chain.

The core of GameFi lies in tokenized gaming economies. Players can earn, own, trade, and stake in-game assets such as tokens, NFTs, or virtual currencies that hold real-world value. As with DeFi, GameFi is underpinned by smart contracts that enable seamless, trustless transactions between parties without centralized oversight. This decentralization empowers players, giving them more control over their digital property and how they choose to monetize their gameplay experiences.

The Play-and-Own model emphasizes ownership rather than continuous monetary reward. Another layer of GameFi is the Create-to-Earn model, where players and content creators contribute to game development and they receive royalties or rewards in tokens. Platforms like the Sandbox and Roblox, though differing in their degree of decentralization, exemplify how user-generated content becomes a valuable asset class, with creators monetizing their creativity.

GameFi also blurs the boundaries between gaming and content consumption. In Watch-to-Earn or Engage-to-Earn ecosystems, players and fans receive token rewards for interacting with content, be it livestreams, voting on governance proposals, or participating in community forums.

The tokenization of in-game economies has added liquidity, speculation, and real-world implications to what were once purely virtual activities. Just as DeFi created composable financial layers, GameFi creates composable economic layers for entertainment. Games like EVE online, with its in-game currency ISK, show how virtual economies can rival the GDP of small nations. The ability to exchange in-game wealth for fiat currency on external markets further enhances the legitimacy of GameFi as a financial ecosystem.

Governance also plays a pivotal role. Many GameFi platforms are evolving into decentralized autonomous organizations (DAOs), where token holders have the right to vote on game updates, economic rules, or community grants. This introduces a new form of player-driven governance, blending gameplay with civic participation. The DAO model transforms passive players into co-creators and stewards of the gaming universe, democratizing development in unprecedented ways.

GameFi exemplifies how the principles of DeFi including composability, decentralization, and financial sovereignty are finding fertile ground in the gaming world. It has ushered in a new paradigm where gameplay, creativity, and community engagement are monetized and tokenized. For regulators, developers, and players alike, GameFi presents both a tremendous opportunity and a new frontier of challenges.

Play-to-Earn Games

Play-to-Earn (P2E) games marked a transformation of the gaming economy, where players could monetize their time and skill, earning real-world value through gameplay. P2E created a new model of economic participation in digital worlds. However, after an initial surge in 2021–2022, the P2E ecosystem faced significant volatility, forcing a wave of reinvention.

Early pioneers like Axie Infinitie, (Case Study), The Sandbox (Case Study), and Decentraland introduced the opportunity of digital ownership and rewards. During COVID, entire communities, particularly in Southeast Asia, generated livelihoods from gameplay. However, the token economies were largely inflationary, driven by user growth rather than intrinsic game value. When token prices crashed and daily active users declined, designers realized that games must be fun first, sustainable second, and profitable third. New models have emerged which emphasize digital asset ownership without promising unsustainable income streams, including Play and Earn, Play, and Create (Naavik 2024).

Traditional gaming guilds were communities centered around mutual support and shared gaming experiences. In contrast, crypto gaming guilds have transformed into profit-driven organizations, focusing on monetizing player activities. These guilds often recruit players from developing nations, offering them opportunities to earn income through P2E games without upfront investments.

"The Dark Side of Crypto Gaming Guilds" (Jirásek 2022) critically examines the ethical and socioeconomic implications of crypto gaming guilds within the play-to-earn (P2E) ecosystem. The model led to exploitative practices, as players may receive only a fraction of the earnings, with guilds and investors taking significant cuts. This shift opens the door to the potential exploitation of players, who may be viewed more as labor resources than community members, who undertake minor repetitive tasks. The P2E model's reliance on continuous influxes of new players and investments also raises questions about its economic structure, which resembles pyramid schemes, where early participants benefit at the expense of newer ones. On the other hand, crypto gaming guilds have provided some players with income opportunities and skill development. Instances of community support, such as fundraising for disaster relief, demonstrate the potential for positive social impact when ethical considerations are prioritized. While crypto gaming guilds present innovative avenues for income generation in the digital age, they also pose significant ethical and socioeconomic challenges. Yield Guild Games in the Philippines offer an interesting case study.

Play-and-Own (PandO)

Play-and-Own (PandO): Emphasizes ownership of in-game assets (NFTs, skins, characters) rather than just earning. In Illuvium, players capture and own NFT-based creatures (Illuvials) and gear, which are usable in battles and tradable on marketplaces. The emphasis is not on daily earnings but on true ownership of digital assets with long-term value and rarity.

Create-to-Earn

Create-to-Earn: Players and creators earn by contributing content, mods, or virtual experiences. In the Sandbox players and artists, use VoxEdit and Game Maker to design 3D assets, games, or entire experiences. These can be sold as **NFTs** on the

Sandbox marketplace, allowing creators to monetize their work. Virtual landowners can also rent space or host paid events.

Watch-to-Earn/Engage-to-Earn

Watch-to-Earn / Engage-to-Earn: Players are rewarded for streaming, voting, commenting, or engaging in communities. Galxe rewards users with tokens and NFTs for engaging with Web3 projects, completing quests, watching tutorials, or participating in community campaigns.

Economic Opportunity in Esports

Gaming is expanding beyond entertainment into several adjacent and overlapping sectors. Competitive gaming is a spectator and professional sport, with revenue from media rights, sponsorship, and betting.

The rise of Esports as a global entertainment phenomenon has redefined not only how games are played but how digital economies are built. At the heart of this transformation lies a powerful tool: non-fungible tokens (NFTs). More than just digital collectables, NFTs are increasingly serving as the economic scaffolding upon which new value systems are being constructed in competitive gaming.

In Esports, NFTs offer new ways for players, teams, fans, and developers to generate income, participate in ownership models, and build decentralized ecosystems. Where traditional Esports monetization relied heavily on advertising, sponsorships, and centralized prize pools, NFTs introduce a participatory economy where digital assets can be minted, traded, and monetized directly by the community.

Tokenized Team Assets: Esports organizations are beginning to tokenize parts of their brand; team logos, limited-edition merchandise, digital trophies, and player cards; allowing fans to purchase, trade, or even stake them. These NFTs can grant holders voting rights on team decisions, early access to merchandise, or exclusive content. In this way, fans become stakeholders, not just spectators. The model mirrors sports franchises, but with greater liquidity, traceability, and community engagement.

NFTs as Tournament Tickets and Rewards: Tournament access passes can now be issued as NFTs, providing verifiable and transferable digital credentials. Unlike static digital tickets, NFT passes may evolve with time; accruing metadata like attendance, victories, or interactions; adding scarcity and narrative value. For example, winning a championship might "upgrade" the NFT, enabling resale at a premium or unlocking future rewards.

Reward systems are also transforming. Instead of centralized prize pools, players may earn tokenized in-game assets, which can be traded on secondary markets. This has opened the door to sustainable play-to-earn models within Esports tournaments, where performance directly correlates to tangible economic benefit.

Creator Economies in Competitive Gaming: NFTs are blurring the line between professional gamers and creators. Streamers and Esports players can mint highlight moments, customized avatars, or exclusive training content as NFTs. These digital assets are sold or traded with fans, creating passive income through royalties each time the NFT changes hands. Smart contracts ensure that creators receive compensation on every secondary sale, institutionalizing long-term income from one-time moments.

Fractional Ownership and Sponsorship: NFTs enable new forms of micro-investment. Esports teams or rising stars can tokenize a share of their future earnings or tournament winnings, allowing fans to hold "fractional stakes" in a player's career. It democratizes sponsorship and brings crowdfunded support to Esports. Fans become backers, with skin in the game and aligned incentives. This also reimagines scouting; supporters can identify talent early, buy in, and profit from their rise.

Interoperable Digital Goods Across Games and Metaverses: As the Esports and Metaverse sectors converge, NFTs can act as interoperable assets; cosmetic skins, digital banners, or emotes usable across multiple games or platforms. This increases the utility and value of Esports assets while also offering seamless fan engagement in tournaments, streaming platforms, and virtual events. NFT interoperability introduces a fluid economic system that is not bound by a single developer's platform.

However, alongside opportunity comes risk. The very features that empower economic participation; scarcity, resale, and anonymity can be exploited for wash trading, rug pulls, or speculative bubbles. Esports is no exception. Without thoughtful regulation and platform accountability, there is a risk of over-financializing the competitive experience, turning community-driven ecosystems into profit-driven ones. The true promise of NFTs in Esports lies not in hype but in utility-first design, where each token enriches gameplay, deepens engagement, or offers genuine participation in the Esports economy. Esports is demonstrating that the digital arena is not just a battleground for glory but also for wealth creation, creative expression, and economic inclusion.

Metaverse and New Economic Opportunities

In addition to the Play-to-Earn, Play-and-Own, and Move-to-Earn models, the Metaverse is opening new frontiers for economic activity, blending creativity, commerce, and community ownership.

Tokenized Economies and Virtual Labor: At the heart of the Metaverse's economy are tokenized environments where virtual currencies and assets hold real-world value. Games like *EVE Online*, with its in-game currency ISK, have shown that digital economies can rival the GDPs of small nations. These currencies are not confined to gameplay but can be traded in external markets. In-game labor; mining, crafting, trading; translates to meaningful economic activity, especially in contexts where access to traditional income is limited.

Social Tokens and Community Economies: Social tokens are redefining relationships between creators and their audiences. Musicians, artists, and influencers can issue tokens to fans, unlocking access to exclusive content, experiences, or decision-making rights. These tokens foster loyalty and enable fans to become stakeholders in the success of the communities they support.

DAOs and Community Governance: Decentralized Autonomous Organizations (DAOs) have introduced a new model of digital democracy. In platforms like *Decentraland*, holders of tokens such as LAND or MANA can vote on development priorities, allocate grants, or shape platform rules. This bottom-up governance ensures that ecosystems evolve in line with the community's values and aspirations, not just corporate interests.

Meta-Commerce and Phygital Trade: Metaverse is also transforming commerce. Brands can now create immersive virtual storefronts where users purchase **NFTs** representing both digital and physical goods. Protocols like *Boson* and platforms like *Highstreet* facilitate these "phygital" exchanges, allowing **NFTs** to function as smart receipts redeemable in the real world. This hybrid retail model merges experiential shopping with blockchain-enabled logistics and ownership.

Metaverse-as-a-Service (MaaS): Metaverse-as-a-Service platforms are reducing barriers for creators and businesses to enter the virtual world. By providing infrastructure and templates for shops, galleries, classrooms, or clinics, MaaS platforms democratize access to the Metaverse and accelerate adoption across sectors like education, tourism, and healthcare.

Digital Identity and Livelihoods: For younger generations, particularly Gen Z and Gen Alpha, digital identity is intrinsically linked to economic opportunity. Selling avatar fashion, designing experiences, hosting virtual concerts, or participating in global DAO projects are not just hobbies; they're career pathways. In many emerging markets, the Metaverse is seen as a viable route to economic mobility and digital entrepreneurship.

Health, Education, and Wellness Tokens: Beyond gaming and commerce, the Metaverse is creating new models in service sectors. *Move-to-Earn* platforms promote wellness, *Learn-to-Earn* models incentivize micro-credentialing and upskilling, and tokenized health applications reward users for participating in healthy behavior or community support. These innovations are particularly promising for vulnerable populations, offering access, flexibility, and engagement in new ways.

The Metaverse is reshaping global economic paradigms, introducing inclusive, decentralized, and user-led models of value creation. By rewarding participation, creativity, and community governance, these ecosystems challenge traditional notions of labor and ownership. As these economic models continue to evolve, they will be vital tools for empowerment, innovation, and inclusion in a digitally interconnected world.

Virtual Real Estate in Gaming

Gaming has emerged as a powerful parallel economy; one in which virtual real estate, secured through blockchain-based tokens, is becoming an asset class of its own. From purchasable parcels in Metaverse platforms to rentable in-game venues, tokenized virtual land is redefining both the structure and scope of property ownership in digital realms.

In traditional real estate, tokenization facilitates fractional ownership, reduces entry barriers, and increases liquidity. These same principles now power the booming virtual real estate market within gaming environments like *The Sandbox*, *Decentraland*, and *Voxels*. Here, land is represented as NFTs, which are traded on open markets and often sold in limited quantities. Each parcel carries unique attributes; location, proximity to popular venues, or developmental potential; and functions as a programmable, monetizable unit of value.

The economic opportunity lies in the fusion of gameplay and investment. Virtual landowners can develop their properties into monetized spaces: Esports arenas, NFT galleries, branded experiences, or exclusive social hubs. These in-game properties generate income through ticketed events, advertising partnerships, leasing agreements, and gamified experiences. Much like physical real estate, virtual plots accrue value through development, network effects, and scarcity.

For investors, this new frontier offers lower friction and global accessibility. The liquidity of tokenized virtual land tradable 24/7 on NFT marketplaces makes it distinct from its real-world counterpart, which often suffers from bureaucratic delays and illiquidity.

Gaming tokenization also enables entirely new economic roles. Game developers can issue land parcels during pre-launch phases to raise capital and distribute ownership democratically. DAOs often form around these Metaverses, governing land use, event hosting rights, or collaborative urban design. Communities, rather than centralized studios, now shape the economic geography of virtual worlds. Fractional ownership is lowering the barrier to entry. Through smart contracts, land parcels can be divided into fungible tokens, enabling investors to own a share of a high-value district or Esports stadium. This not only democratizes access but also introduces real estate investment dynamics into player economies. Players become landlords, traders, and developers, roles once unimaginable in traditional gaming ecosystems.

However, risks remain. As with physical real estate, speculative bubbles can form. Regulatory uncertainty over digital property rights in many jurisdictions. Looking forward, tokenized virtual real estate will be a core asset class within gaming economies. Its economic logic mirrors that of physical property such as location, ownership, development, and yield but it also expands what is possible. Properties can evolve, self-govern, and plug into multiple interoperable worlds. In this sense, the tokenization of gaming real estate is not simply a digital replica of traditional markets; it is the architecture of a new, programmable economic paradigm.

Digital Fashion and Collectables

As gaming becomes more immersive, social, and interoperable, players increasingly seek to express their identities through avatars, wearables, and custom assets. Digital fashion and collectables are rapidly emerging as core economic drivers within gaming ecosystems. Fueled by NFTs, this new digital consumer economy is reshaping how value is created, exchanged, and perceived in virtual worlds.

In the traditional fashion industry, scarcity, exclusivity, and brand identity are central to value creation. NFTs bring these same attributes into digital environments. In gaming, fashion is no longer just cosmetic; it's capital. Wearables and skins are now tokenized, verifiable, and tradeable assets with built-in scarcity and provenance. With NFTs, these assets are no longer locked to a single platform. Players can buy, sell, and display them across interoperable Metaverses, transforming digital clothing into a form of self-expression, social capital, and investment.

Major fashion brands are moving fast to capture this market. Gucci, Nike, and Adidas have all launched NFT fashion items that either exist solely in the Metaverse or bridge physical and digital ownership. Nike's acquisition of RTFKT (a digital fashion studio) and its development of NFT-based sneaker drops illustrate how gaming-native assets are becoming status symbols. These NFTsneakers are not only worn by avatars but also unlock access to exclusive in-game content or real-world merchandise. For fashion houses, this opens new revenue streams and allows them to engage Gen Z audiences on the platforms where they spend most of their time, inside games.

Avatars have evolved from default characters into extensions of the self. Players now curate their digital appearance with the same attention as their physical presence, creating demand for high-quality, limited-edition fashion assets. NFTs make this economy possible. Every NFT-based wearable is provably owned, limited in supply, and often upgradeable, making them both expressive and economically valuable.

Creators and designers can now sell directly to players without intermediaries, generating revenue through primary sales and secondary royalties. Platforms like *The Sandbox* and *Decentraland* have embraced this model, allowing players to create, mint, and sell wearable NFTs. Beyond wearables, digital collectables are transforming fandom and gaming culture. Players are collecting rare in-game items, art pieces, or sports memorabilia not only for gameplay utility but also for status and speculative gain. The mechanics are familiar; scarcity, limited editions, and verified provenance; but now operate in a decentralized and player-driven market.

Gaming NFTs often grant exclusive access to tournaments, guilds, or creator content, turning collectables into membership keys or prestige markers. Trading platforms and secondary markets enable liquidity, making it possible for players to build portfolios of digital goods with real-world value. As seen with projects like Bored Ape Yacht Club and NBA Top Shot, cultural cachet and social belonging often amplify the financial value of collectables, creating vibrant communities where owning a token becomes a badge of identity and influence.

Legal and Commercial Complexities

While the opportunities are immense, digital fashion and collectables are also testing the boundaries of intellectual property and brand control. Legal battles, such as Nike vs. StockX over unauthorized NFTsneakers highlight the friction between decentralized creation and trademark enforcement. These precedents will shape the legal contours of fashion in gaming and determine how brands protect their digital assets.

Despite this, the convergence of gaming, fashion, and NFTs is laying the foundation for new hybrid economies, part entertainment, part speculation, and part self-expression. For developers, it offers a lucrative model of microtransactions reimagined as digital ownership. For players, it enables identity, creativity, and earning potential in equal measure.

Health and Education

Gamification techniques are increasingly being used in health and education. It is likely that many will be approved for medical use. In education, the influence of games will extend ever more deeply into all forms of education and skill training. For a more extensive exploration of gaming in health and education, see Chap. 6.

Gaming in e-Commerce

Recent research highlights the transformative role of gamification in livestreaming e-commerce, emphasizing how thoughtfully integrated game-like features, such as intimacy points, fan levels, virtual gifts, quests, and fan clubs, can significantly increase user engagement and purchase intentions. These gamified artifacts are not merely superficial entertainment tools; they are strategically designed to fulfill consumers' psychological needs and enhance their interactive experience. One particularly powerful gamification tool, achievement visualization affordance, enables users to visibly track their progress and contributions, thereby eliciting feelings of accomplishment, self-worth, and social recognition (Nobre and Ferreira 2017). This gratification feeds into consumers' desires for entertainment, social bonding, self-improvement, and public acknowledgment. The study offers concrete recommendations for stakeholders in the livestreaming e-commerce ecosystem. For platforms and streamers, the integration of achievement-based and reward-based mechanics, such as pop-up achievement announcements and frequent incentives; can significantly enhance social engagement. These mechanics foster a sense of belonging, and personal recognition, which strengthens the user's emotional connection with the platform and their community.

In addition, interaction affordances, such as real-time gifting, and direct audio connections with streamers meet cognitive and social needs by facilitating deeper communication, promoting emotional exchange, and enhancing consumer-brand identification. Similarly, competition affordances like leaderboards and fan club challenges fuel users' motivation by encouraging knowledge acquisition, personal goal setting, and loyalty-building through both individual and group competition. The study also found continued watching is primarily driven by the satisfaction of cognitive, affective, and social needs, whereas purchasing behavior is more closely tied to the fulfillment of cognitive, social, and social integrative needs. To optimize both outcomes, livestreaming platforms must create emotionally engaging, socially interactive environments and ensure that clear, abundant product information is readily available to viewers.

Human Work in the Gaming Economy

The nature of work is being fundamentally reshaped by AI, blockchain, and immersive technologies. As gaming evolves into a foundational layer of the Metaverse, it is simultaneously becoming a platform for employment, entrepreneurship, education, and economic inclusion. No longer limited to entertainment, gaming now offers a gateway to livelihoods in a decentralized digital economy. This is discussed extensively in Chap. 10.

Global Access and Economic Inclusion

Perhaps most significantly, gamified education offers a lifeline to underserved communities. With only a smartphone and an internet connection, learners in developing regions can access world-class instruction, earn blockchain-verified credentials, and participate in global job markets. AI tutors break language and literacy barriers, while AR modules eliminate the need for expensive physical infrastructure. This form of borderless education offers not just skills, but income-generating opportunities, turning digital play into a path to prosperity.

The Metaverse also doubles as a career simulator. Through interactive role-playing, users can explore professions such as architect, doctor, game designer, or entrepreneur. AI avatars can guide them through practice pitches, public speaking drills, and negotiation strategies. These gamified journeys build both technical competencies and soft skills, preparing learners for real-world and virtual jobs alike. Participation is further rewarded with access to virtual internships, project collaborations, and exposure to decentralized hiring ecosystems.

As these technologies scale, the infrastructure, content, governance models, and outreach must grow with them. From high-quality simulations to decentralized AI tutors and cloud-based learning environments, the investment in digital education ecosystems is becoming both urgent and inevitable. Education, once viewed as preparation for work, is now the work. Students learn by doing, earn while learning, and contribute to the very systems they're engaging in. In this new paradigm, gaming is the classroom, the career center, and the global job board; all in one.

Cultural and Economic Implications

Gaming today has evolved far more than a source of entertainment; it now functions as a cultural operating system for the digital age. Within virtual worlds, players don't just compete or complete quests; they govern communities, enforce rules, and even engage in forms of virtual nation-building. This form of digital citizenship reflects a broader societal shift, where identity, responsibility, and participation extend beyond physical borders and into immersive, programmable environments.

At the heart of this transformation is a commitment to inclusive design; the creation of safe, diverse, and accessible gaming experiences that reflect the broad spectrum of players across gender, ability, geography, and culture. Developers are increasingly prioritizing environments where all users feel welcome, represented, and empowered to contribute. These design principles are not only ethical imperatives but also economic drivers, broadening market reach and deepening user engagement.

Gaming has also emerged as a launchpad for youth employment and entrepreneurship, particularly through Esports, digital asset creation, and decentralized governance. Players can build careers not only as competitors or content creators but as DAO leaders, virtual architects, and Metaverse educators. In this way, gaming acts as a career simulator and economic training ground, offering practical skills in digital finance, teamwork, and creative production.

Perhaps most transformative is the flow of value from virtual to real-world economies. Income generated through gameplay, whether via play-to-earn models, streaming, or digital asset sales, is increasingly being used to fund education, support families, and invest in real-world opportunities. Gaming has become a viable economic pathway, particularly for younger generations and those in regions underserved by traditional employment systems.

This potential is most visible in emerging markets, where gaming is bridging the digital divide. In Southeast Asia, Latin America, and Sub-Saharan Africa, mobile gaming is widespread due to affordable smartphones and internet access. Games like *Axie Infinity* became lifelines during the pandemic, providing thousands in the Philippines with income when other work vanished. In these regions, gaming is often the first introduction to digital wallets, cryptocurrency, and decentralized markets; tools increasingly necessary for participation in the global economy.

Web3 gaming is especially powerful in this context. By enabling true ownership of digital assets, wallet-based access, and cross-platform digital identities, these ecosystems remove traditional gatekeepers like banks or centralized platforms.

Players can build reputations, earn rewards, and govern platforms through DAOs, giving them not just a stake in the game but a stake in the platform itself.

In regions where formal employment is limited, gaming is becoming an on-ramp to the digital economy. It fosters financial inclusion, digital literacy, entrepreneurship, and community leadership. Moreover, it introduces sustainability considerations through energy-efficient blockchains, ethical AI design, and attention-aware platform mechanics. These innovations ensure that the growth of the gaming economy can align with broader goals of environmental stewardship and social equity. In sum, gaming is no longer a separate digital domain; it is the foundation of a new cultural and economic logic. It is how a generation is working, learning, organizing, and building futures; one digital interaction at a time.

AI and Blockchain Convergence: The Intelligent Infrastructure of the Future of Gaming

A silent revolution is underway in the gaming industry; one driven by the convergence of artificial intelligence (AI) and blockchain technology. Once viewed as parallel innovations, these technologies are now fusing into a powerful, intelligent infrastructure that is reshaping how games are developed, experienced, governed, and monetized. Together, AI and blockchain are laying the foundation for a new gaming economy; one that is decentralized, adaptive, immersive, and economically inclusive.

AI is becoming the operating system behind it. Whether powering life-like NPCs, streamlining in-game marketing, or detecting fraud in real time, AI has become the invisible engine driving adaptability, scalability, and hyper-personalization.

In game development, AI is now a co-creator. It can design procedurally generated worlds, write dynamic story arcs, fine-tune difficulty settings, localize content across languages, and even balance digital economies. The creative pipeline, once limited by time, budget, and headcount, is now elastic and intelligent. Game studios increasingly rely on AI not just for efficiency, but for creativity itself.

At the gameplay level, AI-powered NPCs are ushering in a new era of dynamic storytelling. Gone are the days of scripted, one-dimensional characters. Today's AI-driven entities evolve with the player, respond in real-time to decisions, and co-author emotionally rich, emergent narratives. Games become less linear and more participatory, giving rise to unique, player-driven experiences with every session.

Blockchain: Ownership, Identity, and Interoperability

Where AI brings intelligence and adaptability, blockchain provides the trust infrastructure needed to support decentralized and persistent gaming ecosystems. Through smart contracts, NFTs, and on-chain credentials, blockchain enables players to own their assets, verify their identities, and participate in community governance.

In places like the Philippines, blockchain-based digital identities are already being trialed for social programs and gaming platforms. These secure, interoperable IDs, linked to biometric and behavioral data, can support age verification, platform access, and reputation management. As gaming becomes more intertwined with finance, education, and work, such systems are vital to ensuring safety, trust, and compliance.

Blockchain also underpins player autonomy and platform accountability. Players are no longer just users; they are stakeholders. They can vote on game updates, co-create economies, and earn revenue from user-generated content, ushering in a participatory, co-governed future of gaming.

Decentralized AI Agents: Autonomy in a Tokenized World

One of the most powerful examples of this convergence is decentralized AI agents, autonomous digital actors operating within Web3 ecosystems. These agents can buy and sell NFTs, manage token portfolios, execute contracts, and even make gameplay decisions on a player's behalf. Decentralized AI redefines what it means to "play." Players interact with AI companions that learn from their style, optimize strategy, and negotiate digital value autonomously. Games become intelligent economies where human and machine collaboration drive growth, creativity, and value exchange.

This convergence also simplifies complexity. AI is now simplifying wallet management through to DAO governance through no-code interfaces and intelligent UX design, blockchain fades into the background. The result is a far better player experience: engaging, intuitive, and powered by invisible infrastructure.

Gaming as the New School

The impact of AI and blockchain extends beyond gameplay; it's transforming how people learn and build careers. In Web3-native gaming guilds like Yield Guild Games, players are no longer just gamers; they are scholars, content creators, community leaders, and asset managers. With AI-driven curricula, personalized feedback, and gamified learning modules, players can improve in areas like game moderation, DeFi strategy, storytelling, and XR development.

Verifiable credentials are issued on-chain, enabling players to build lifelong portfolios of knowledge, reputation, and work experience. The result is an education system that is decentralized, portable, and deeply embedded in the economic logic of gaming. Gamified AI education is creating a pathway for global talent to participate in the digital economy, regardless of geography, background, or institutional access.

Post-Quantum Horizons: The Coming Security Challenge

As AI scales, so too do the risks. The looming spectre of quantum computing threatens to undermine the cryptographic foundations of today's blockchain protocols. At AIBC, security experts warned that standards like ECDSA, currently used by Ethereum and Bitcoin, could be considered obsolete. The race is now on for post-quantum cryptography; a vital challenge if gaming ecosystems are to maintain security across assets, identities, and smart contracts. For the future gaming economy, quantum readiness must be built into the foundation.

In summary, the convergence of AI and blockchain enhances gaming in the following ways:

- *Game Design*: AI for procedural world-building, adaptive storytelling, and blockchain for tokenized asset creation and royalties.
- *Player Experience*: AI for NPC personalization, difficulty adjustment, and blockchain ownership of in-game items and achievements.
- *Economic Systems*: AI for dynamic pricing, fraud detection, and AI-driven agents, blockchain for transparent, immutable token economies.
- *Governance*: AI for sentiment analysis, decision support tools, and blockchain for DAO-based voting and smart contract execution.
- *Education and Training*: AI provides tutors, personalized curricula, and blockchain for on-chain credentials and decentralized learning.
- *Identity and Reputation*: AI for behavioral modeling, and player profiling, and blockchain for biometric-secured digital identities.
- *Marketplaces*: AI for autonomous trading bots, trend forecasting and blockchain for peer-to-peer NFT and asset exchanges.
- *Security and Compliance*: AI for risk modeling, bot detection, and blockchain for immutable transaction history and cryptographic trust.

Conclusion

The convergence of AI and blockchain is powering a new kind of infrastructure, one where players are creators, work is play, learning is lifelong, and every interaction is intelligent, traceable, and meaningful. The convergence of AI and blockchain ensures that the systems beneath our virtual worlds are as intelligent, decentralized, and human centric as the worlds themselves.

The new gaming economy blurs traditional boundaries: between play and productivity, user and creator, labor and leisure. With the rise of tokenization, decentralized governance, and AI-powered systems, games are becoming sovereign micro-economies where players can own land, earn income, build reputations, and co-govern digital worlds. From Twitch streamers and Esports athletes to digital landowners, avatar designers, and AI-native co-creators, the roles enabled by gaming ecosystems are reshaping the global future of work.

These ecosystems are not hypothetical; they are here and growing. As case studies like *EVE Online* demonstrate, virtual economies can rival the complexity and value of real-world markets. In regions with limited formal employment, gaming has become a pathway to digital literacy, economic inclusion, and financial independence. In the Metaverse, a player's outfit is no longer just cosmetic; it's capital. Their attention is a currency. Their gameplay is a livelihood.

But this transformation comes with responsibility. The expansion of token economies, the introduction of AI agents, and the gamification of labor introduce new ethical, regulatory, and social complexities. Platform designers, policymakers, and communities must ensure that the gaming economy remains inclusive, transparent, and sustainable. Digital labor must be respected, and economic systems must avoid the pitfalls of over-financialization or exploitative design.

The rise of AI and blockchain further amplifies gaming's economic potential, unlocking intelligent, decentralized systems that can scale creativity, personalize education, and build trust in digital environments. The convergence of these technologies is not simply enhancing games; it is redefining what it means to work, earn, learn, and belong in the twenty-first century.

Ultimately, gaming is not a subset of the economy; it is becoming the infrastructure of the next economy. It is where communities gather, value is created, and futures are imagined. As digital and physical worlds converge, gaming will not just reflect cultural shifts; it will drive them. It is time to stop thinking of games as playthings and start recognizing them as platforms for prosperity.

In the new economic order, the controller is a tool of agency, the avatar is a worker, and the virtual world is the workplace. Gaming is no longer where the future is forecast; it is where the future is forged.

Cross-Chapter Insights

This chapter's focus on guilds, streaming, and new creator platforms is deeply connected to play-to-earn models from *Axie Infinity* (Chap. 3) and the creator monetization tools in *Roblox* and *Fortnite Creative* (Chap. 10). The decentralized talent systems of *YGG* are paralleled by *Alethea AI*'s "train-to-earn" paradigm and *AI Dungeon* (Chap. 8), where users co-create narratives with AI. Platforms like *Discord* and *Reddit* (Chap. 10) further extend community coordination and content co-creation—key pillars of this evolving economic ecosystem.

Case Studies

EVE Online—ISK and the Emergence of Spacefaring Mega-Economies

Game/Platform Name: *EVE Online*
   Developer / Publisher: CCP Games (Reykjavík, Iceland)
   Year Released: 2003 (continually updated)
   Genre: Single-shard sci-fi MMORPG / Sandbox economy
   Technology Stack: Proprietary "Tranquillity" server cluster, Python-based Carbon engine, real-time market APIs, community-run data dashboards (e.g., EVE-Marketdata)

EVE Online is a persistent, single-shard universe where more than 8000 solar systems host a live player economy. Its currency, Interstellar Kredit (ISK), is fully player-generated and via the PLEX token can be legally bridged to real-world money. Annual ISK turnover has repeatedly surpassed US$ $5 billion, briefly eclipsing the GDP of Pacific micro-states such as Tuvalu or Palau.

Innovation

EVE pioneered the idea of a self-regulating player economy, single-shard design ensures every market order, and battle affects the entire universe.

   PLEX token bridge links ISK to fiat through CCP-approved trading, establishing a regulated gray-market exit.

   Open APIs and player analytics let community economists track money supply, mineral prices, and inflation in real time.

   Everything is player-made; ships, space stations, and citadels are all crafted from player-harvested resources, making industrial gameplay as deep as combat.

Impact

At its peak in 2022, the in-game economy of EVE Online reached staggering heights, with daily trade volumes in its virtual currency, ISK, outpacing the NASDAQ's share count of newly listed SPACs. This remarkable benchmark highlighted how virtual liquidity, driven purely by player behavior and digital assets, could rival real-world financial markets in complexity and scale.

   By 2024, EVE Online hosted around 340,000 monthly active pilots, most of whom were between 25 and 44 years old, with a strong representation from STEM professions. This demographic helped shape a sophisticated economic environment where gameplay extended far beyond combat or exploration.

   At the height of its activity, EVE's daily trade volume reached 1.3 trillion ISK, with an estimated annual turnover in 2022 equivalent to US$ $6 billion. These numbers rivaled the GDPs of small nations, cementing EVE's reputation as the most economically complex game in the world.

The game's cultural significance was equally pronounced. The infamous "Bloodbath of B-R5RB" in 2014, an all-out war between player factions resulted in the destruction of digital assets valued at over US$330,000, earning coverage in The Economist and becoming a case study in the cost of virtual conflict.

EVE Online's geographic reach spans global clusters in North America, Europe, and Russia, with a rapidly expanding presence in China following the relaunch of the Serenity server. These player bases have created regional hubs of influence and commerce, blending language, time zone coordination, and geopolitical dynamics into digital strategy.

Perhaps most striking is how corporations (player-run guilds) in EVE mimic real-world enterprises. These groups manage everything from HR and logistics to financial strategy, and many operate with the same discipline and structure as start-ups or trading firms. EVE's economy has attracted the interest of academic economists, who use the game's open data to model complex labor markets. Meanwhile, some players have leveraged their in-game trading acumen to launch careers in finance, proving that skills developed in a virtual economy can translate into real-world opportunities.

Challenges and Controversies

RMT and Black Markets: Despite PLEX, illicit ISK sales persist, driving bans and price volatility.

Economic Shocks: Balance patches or massive wars can trigger hyperinflation and resource scarcity.

Warfare-as-Grief: Blockades and extortion schemes test the line between emergent gameplay and harassment.

Scams Are Legal: EVE's laissez-faire ruleset permits Ponzi schemes and corporate espionage, sparking ethical debate.

Lessons Learned

Developers: A single-shard sandbox scales only with robust data tooling and active macroeconomic stewardship.

Players: Market literacy, logistics, and diplomacy are as valuable as PvP skill, transferable soft skills for careers.

Policymakers / Investors: Virtual economies can rival small-nation GDPs; taxation, AML, and consumer-protection questions are no longer hypothetical.

Case Studies 73

The Future Outlook

EVE's third decade focuses on:

Interoperability: CCP's upcoming *EVE Vanguard* FPS will share economics with the main shard.

AI-driven market monitoring: Machine learning anti-fraud tools to curb black-market ISK.

Player Governance 2.0: The Council of Stellar Management (CSM) is trialing on-chain voting to increase transparency.

If these initiatives succeed, *EVE Online* will remain the benchmark for large-scale virtual economies; and a living laboratory for digital asset regulation.

Twitch—Streaming as a Platform Economy

Game/Platform Name: Twitch

Developer/Publisher: Originally Justin.tv, acquired and rebranded by Amazon (2014)

Year Released: 2011 (Twitch rebrand), acquired by Amazon in 2014

Genre: Streaming Platform (live game streaming, social platform, creator economy)

Technology Stack: Cloud Infrastructure (AWS), real-time video streaming, AI/ML for moderation and recommendations, APIs for third-party integrations

Twitch is a live streaming platform that revolutionized how gaming content is consumed and monetized. It enables gamers to broadcast live content, build communities, and earn income through donations, subscriptions, ads, and sponsorships.

Innovation

Twitch pioneered the "creator economy" in gaming, turning gameplay into a spectator sport and monetizable career. Its innovation lies in blending live entertainment with real-time interaction, fostering community-led content economies. Unlike traditional broadcasting, Twitch allows viewers to directly engage, donate, and subscribe, creating new participatory experiences.

It established a platform-based gig economy where gamers, entertainers, and niche creators could earn income, independent of traditional Esports teams or publishers. The platform's API also fostered a vast ecosystem of extensions, stream overlays, and donation tools.

AI/ML tools manage content moderation, stream discovery, and user recommendations, which are essential for platform scalability.

Impact

Twitch viewers watch over 1.3 billion hours of content each month; more than Netflix in some demographic segments. While Twitch dominates in Western markets, regional platforms like Bilibili (China), Nimo TV (SEA), and AfreecaTV (Korea) offer culturally and linguistically tailored competition.

User Adoption and Demographics: By 2023, Twitch had over 2.5 million concurrent viewers and 140 million monthly active users, skewing toward Gen Z and Millennial males but with growing female and non-binary representation.

Economic Value Generated: Top streamers earn seven-figure incomes annually. Twitch has enabled hundreds of thousands of micro-entrepreneurs, especially in the US, Europe, and parts of Asia. It has become a critical revenue stream for professional gamers and indie creators alike.

Cultural/Social Influence: Twitch popularized game streaming, influencing YouTube, Facebook, and TikTok to enter space. It's "Just Chatting" category expanded content beyond gaming into commentary, music, activism, and education, signifying a cultural shift in digital interaction and entertainment.

Geographic Reach: While most popular in North America and Western Europe, Twitch's influence has grown in LATAM, Japan, and Korea. However, it faces regulatory and infrastructure limitations in China and parts of the Middle East.

Challenges and Controversies

Content Moderation and Harassment: Twitch has struggled with "hate raids," gender-based abuse, and moderation inconsistencies, especially affecting women, LGBTQ+, and BIPOC creators.

Revenue Share Tensions: Changes to subscription revenue splits (dropping to 50% from 70% for many streamers) triggered backlash, driving some creators to platforms like YouTube Gaming.

Platform Burnout: The "always-on" culture and pressure to stream long hours have caused mental health issues among creators.

Regulatory Issues: Concerns about gambling streams, age-inappropriate content, and lack of unionization or employment protections for creators have drawn scrutiny.

Lessons Learned

For Developers: Prioritize scalable moderation tools and robust community guidelines early on.

Transparency in monetization policies builds long-term loyalty.

For Players/Streamers: Streaming is labor-intensive and uncertain; successful creators treat it as a full-time business with audience management, branding, and scheduling.

Case Studies 75

Diversifying revenue beyond Twitch (Patreon, merch, YouTube) is crucial.

For Policymakers and Investors: Twitch reveals gaps in creator protections, digital labor rights, and platform accountability.

Live streaming platforms can be influential tools for soft power, education, and social mobilization but require proactive governance.

The Future Outlook

Twitch is likely to remain dominant in Western markets but will face increasing competition from decentralized and niche streaming platforms, especially those integrating blockchain-based creator rewards.

AI agents could eventually co-host streams or moderate content dynamically. Interoperability with Metaverse environments and VR integration (e.g., Twitch streaming from within games like VRChat) is a likely frontier.

As digital identity and creator monetization become more decentralized, Twitch's centralized model may need to adapt or risk disruption from Web3-native platforms.

Alethea AI—Train-to-Earn and the Dawn of Intelligent NFTs

Platform Name: Alethea AI
   Developer/Publisher: Alethea AI Labs
   Year Released: 2021
   Platform Type: Decentralized protocol for iNFTs (intelligent NFTs)
   Technology Stack: Ethereum, Polygon, CharacterGPT, ALI token, AI SDKs, AWS, DAO structure

Alethea AI is a decentralized protocol that introduces intelligent NFTs (iNFTs) interactive digital avatars powered by generative AI. Users train their iNFTs to engage in conversations and earn ALI tokens by contributing data to Alethea's shared intelligence engine. This "train-to-earn" model blends Web3 economics, conversational AI, and identity.

Innovation

CharacterGPT and No-Code Tools: Users can create avatars using natural language prompts to define personalities, memories, and skills.
   ALI Token Utility: Serves as incentive, access currency, and governance tool.
   Polygon Integration: Reduced gas fees allow broader participation.
   AI-Powered iNFTs: Digital agents capable of conversation, training, and interaction across dApps.

Impact

Over 180,000 daily iNFT interactions by 2025
    Partnerships with AWS, OpenSea, Polygon, Solana Mobile
    9+ billion ALI tokens in circulation (10B max supply)
    iNFTs used as tutors, brand avatars, and digital twins
    Global engagement with train-to-earn AI data economy

Challenges and Controversies

Data Quality Concerns: Spam or poor input risks degrading AI models.
    Token Volatility: ALI is prone to market speculation.
    Partial Centralization: AI operations are not yet fully decentralized.
    Ethical AI Debates: Use of conversational agents raises bias and authenticity issues.

Lessons and Legacy

For Developers: Design incentive systems with moderation and data integrity in mind.
    For Players: Participation offers ownership, but economic returns vary by use case.For Policymakers: Train-to-earn signals a shift in digital labor and AI commodification requiring new regulatory thinking.

Future Outlook

Multimodal AI: will bring facial/emotional expression to avatars.
    AI SDKs: Enable cross-platform deployment of iNFTs
    DAO Governance: Gradual decentralization of control and treasury by 2026.
    Alethea is building infrastructure for AI-native economic agents, where anyone can train, own, and deploy digital intelligence.

YouTube Gaming—The Rise of Game Streaming and Creator Economies

Platform Names: YouTube Gaming
    Parent Companies: Google (YouTube Gaming)
    Year Launched: YouTube Gaming (2015)

Case Studies

Genre: Game streaming, Esports broadcasting, influencer-driven live content-
Technology Stack: High-performance video streaming infrastructure, AI-powered recommendation algorithms, integrated monetization tools, APIs for third-party extensions

YouTube Gaming revolutionized the way audiences engage with games—transforming passive consumption into interactive entertainment. These platforms turned gamers into creators, and creators into full-time professionals, spawning a new category of digital labor and reshaping the media landscape around gaming.

Innovation

Live game streaming with community interaction through chat and emotes
Monetization via subscriptions, ads, donations (YouTube Super Chats), and sponsorships
Creation of affiliate and partner programs offering scalable income for streamers
Platform APIs enabling overlays, bots, and custom extensions
Streaming platforms unlocked parasocial interaction and turned gameplay into performative, revenue-generating content.

Impact

YouTube Gaming reached over 250 million logged-in viewers watching gaming content each month
Top streamers (e.g., Ninja, Pokimane, Valkyrae) became global celebrities with multi-million-dollar brand deals
Streaming supported the rise of games like Fortnite, Among Us, and Fall Guys by rapidly scaling exposure
Created full-time careers and micro-businesses for hundreds of thousands of content creators

Challenges and Controversies

Creator Burnout: Pressure to stream consistently led to mental health concerns
Content Moderation: Harassment, toxicity, and copyright violations plagued both platforms
Monetization Inequity: Smaller streamers struggle with visibility and income sustainability
Platform Power: Algorithmic control and policy shifts affect creator livelihoods unpredictably
Twitch and YouTube reflect broader tensions in the gig economy—between opportunity, precarity, and platform governance.

Lessons and Legacy

For Developers: Streamability and community engagement now influence game design and marketing.

For Players: Game streaming enables connection, learning, and even careers—but also carries risks of parasocial dependency.

For Policymakers: The creator economy demands clearer rules around digital labor, income tax, copyright, and online safety.

Future Outlook

Rise of AI streamers and virtual influences, reducing entry barriers while raising ethical questions

Integration of real-time commerce (live shopping) into gaming streams

Decentralized alternatives (e.g., Theta.tv) pushing for creator-owned infrastructure

Expansion into education, fitness, and corporate training through gamified streaming formats

Streaming isn't just a medium, it's an economy, a community, and a cornerstone of gaming culture.

References

Jirásek, M (2022), The dark side of crypto gaming guilds, Front. Blockchain, 01 September 2022. Volume 5 - 2022 | https://doi.org/10.3389/fbloc.2022.965604

Naavik. (2024). The evolution of Web3 gaming: From play-to-earn to play-and-own. https://naavik.co/digest/web3-gaming-2024-year-in-review/

Nobre, H., & Ferreira, A. (2017). Gamification as a platform for brand co-creation experiences. *Journal of Brand Management, 24*(3), 349–361. https://doi.org/10.1057/s41262-017-0055-3

Chapter 5
Bridging the Digital Divide Through Play

Abstract "Bridging the Digital Divide Through Play" shows that in many parts of the world, gaming is becoming a catalyst for digital inclusion. This chapter explores how mobile-first gaming is opening the door to connectivity, digital literacy, and economic participation in underserved regions. With smartphones as the primary access point, gaming is reaching remote and low-income communities, offering entertainment, education, and even income-generating opportunities. Readers will discover how telcos, governments, and Web3 startups are partnering to extend infrastructure and create new digital ecosystems across Southeast Asia, Africa, and Latin America. From grassroots Esports tournaments to mobile games with embedded financial tools, gaming is becoming a bridge to the digital economy. By highlighting scalable public–private models and real-world case studies, this chapter illustrates how play can empower the next billion users, transforming gamers into digital citizens and entrepreneurs.

Keywords Digital inclusion · Mobile-first gaming · Emerging markets · Financial inclusion · Blockchain gaming · Digital literacy · Play-to-earn · Telecom partnerships · Decentralized economies · Web3 infrastructure · Mobile money · Youth empowerment · Gaming guilds · Tokenized assets · Digital equity

Emerging Markets: The Future Growth Engine of Gaming

Gaming is becoming a catalyst for digital inclusion. This chapter examines how mobile-first gaming facilitates connectivity, digital literacy, and economic participation in underserved regions. With smartphones as the primary access point, gaming reaches remote and low-income communities, offering entertainment, education, and even income-generating opportunities. Readers will discover how telcos, governments, and Web3 startups partner to extend infrastructure and create new digital ecosystems across Southeast Asia, Africa, and Latin America. From grassroots Esports tournaments to mobile games with embedded financial tools, gaming is becoming a bridge to the digital economy. By showcasing scalable public–private models and real-world case studies, this chapter illustrates how play can empower the following billion users, transforming gamers into digital citizens and entrepreneurs.

Emerging economies are increasingly positioned as innovation frontiers in the digital age, driven by favorable demographics, mobile penetration, and infrastructural gaps that enable technological leapfrogging. With nearly 90% of the global youth population and billions of mobile connections, regions such as Africa, Southeast Asia, and Latin America offer fertile ground for mobile-first and blockchain-enabled gaming ecosystems.

In contrast to industrialized economies burdened by legacy systems, emerging markets often display greater institutional flexibility and openness to experimentation. The lack of traditional infrastructure has facilitated the rapid uptake of mobile money (e.g., M-Pesa), decentralized identity systems (e.g., Aadhaar), and crypto-enabled platforms (e.g., BloomX and Electroneum), enabling inclusive access to digital services and economic participation (OECD 2022; Electroneum 2025).

Gaming is emerging as a vehicle for financial inclusion and digital empowerment in these regions. Models such as play-to-earn, NFT-based microtransactions, and decentralized freelance platforms allow users to generate income, participate in governance, and access services without reliance on traditional banking or employment structures.

This chapter examines how emerging markets are not merely adopting global gaming trends but actively shaping them. By integrating scalable, decentralized, and mobile-native solutions, they are redefining both the purpose and potential of gaming within the global digital economy.

At the same time, many of these countries face low trust in traditional institutions because of historical instability, corruption, or inefficiency. In the absence of legacy systems, emerging markets are often more willing to embrace new digital infrastructure, whether for banking, education, or identity verification, exemplifying a remarkable openness to technology. Emerging markets are proving that a lack of traditional infrastructure can be an advantage. With minimal legacy systems to disrupt, these countries adopt modern solutions more fluidly. Examples include mobile money in Africa, India's Aadhaar biometric identity system for financial access, and Electroneum's app, which enables crypto-based airtime purchases across 140 countries.

The urgency of structural challenges, such as financial exclusion, lack of formal identity systems, or inadequate logistics, further fuels innovation. Over two billion people globally remain unbanked, yet many are connected through mobile devices. Blockchain provides a means to circumvent traditional financial structures. Services like M-Pesa and crypto-based remittance platforms, such as BloomX in the Philippines, showcase how financial inclusion is becoming a reality, empowering micro-entrepreneurs and gamers in rural areas to transact, earn, and play. Emerging markets demand leapfrogging solutions that can radically transform access and affordability.

This environment is often further enabled by regulatory flexibility. In many cases, governments are experimenting with sandbox frameworks, progressive digital policies, or public–private partnerships that encourage innovation. Without the weight of rigid legacy regulation, startups and technologists are more able to iterate and scale quickly.

Crucially, the private sector has emerged as a key catalyst for change. From mobile health apps in Kenya to blockchain-powered agricultural supply chains in India, and EdTech platforms in Latin America, companies are stepping in to solve problems that public systems alone cannot address. They are redefining what development looks like, less reliant on aid, more driven by entrepreneurship and digital infrastructure.

Mobile phone penetration is widespread: Africa has 1.08 billion mobile connections, and Asia-Pacific has over 4.3 billion. These populations are primed for digital-first solutions, including gaming, built around affordability, accessibility, and mobile integration. In this context, emerging economies are pioneering models of inclusive, tech-driven development. Traditionally consumers of Western-developed technologies, they are now shaping the future of digital transformation through leapfrogging outdated infrastructure and rapidly adopting mobile-first and blockchain-enabled solutions. Countries like India, Kenya, the Philippines, and Nigeria exemplify this shift, driving innovation in finance, digital identity, and mobile services.

Gaming is poised to become a gateway to digital and economic inclusion. As seen in the Philippines and Kenya, mobile-first design, combined with localized content and blockchain-backed microtransactions, offers both entertainment and income-generating opportunities. Platforms like AnyTask allow users to earn and spend in crypto, and game-based economies are creating new income models for underbanked populations.

Emerging markets are not just adopting gaming; they're defining its future. They bring mobile-first design principles tailored to network constraints, localized game economies embedded with cultural relevance, crypto-native populations are familiar with digital value exchange and regulatory openness to new forms of ownership, identity, and reward.

Emerging markets are home to nearly 90% of the global population under the age of 30, representing an enormous, digitally native demographic. These youth populations are highly receptive to mobile-first, digital-first services, including gaming. With over 4.3 billion mobile connections in Asia-Pacific and 1.08 billion in Africa, mobile phones have become the gateway to entertainment, education, and financial participation. This demographic alignment—characterized by youth, tech-savviness, and a mobile-first approach—positions emerging markets at the forefront of the next global wave of gaming.

Historically, over 2 billion people and 200 million small businesses in emerging markets lacked access to formal financial systems. Mobile money solutions, such as M-Pesa in Kenya, have transformed financial inclusion, enabling users to transact in national currencies via their phones. M-Pesa now processes over half of Kenya's GNP, demonstrating how leapfrogging traditional banking systems with mobile innovation can unlock economic participation. These same mobile rails are now powering game-based ecosystems, enabling players to pay, earn, and trade in virtual environments.

Emerging markets are among the fastest adopters of cryptocurrency, with the Philippines, Brazil, South Africa, Thailand, and Nigeria leading the globe in crypto ownership. This readiness is born from familiarity with mobile money and the need for low-cost, borderless financial tools. As blockchain gaming grows, these regions are expected to lead in the real-world applications of tokenized economies, play-to-earn models, and wallet-based gaming identities. The ability to bypass traditional infrastructure makes blockchain gaming particularly appealing for underbanked communities seeking new income streams.

Companies like BloomX in the Philippines have pioneered the use of cryptocurrency to reduce remittance costs, a critical need in a country where overseas remittances account for over 9% of GDP. During the pandemic, cash pickup locations closed, but mobile wallet signups surged, and crypto became a local store of value. Entrepreneurs began using crypto to buy digital goods and resell them in rural areas, turning gaming-adjacent behavior into micro-enterprises. BloomX is a Philippine-licensed cryptocurrency remittance and exchange platform, operating since 2015 under regulation from the Bangko Sentral ng Pilipinas (BitPinas 2022; Bloom Solutions 2024). Incorporated in Singapore with entities in the Philippines and Australia, it serves as a remittance aggregator, FX broker, and blockchain tech provider for money transfer services (Southeast Asia Globe 2023). BloomRemit offers APIs that enable money transfer operators to reduce settlement costs through real-time, smart trading with minimal volatility exposure (Forbes 2024). Since inception, they have processed hundreds of millions of USD via remittances, enabling instant P2P transfers without changes in customer behavior (Southeast Asia Globe 2023). They partner with local networks such as Palawan Pawnshop and banks to provide seamless P2P sending and pickup across the Philippines (BitPinas 2022).

BloomX pioneered smarter remittance routes, enabling smaller money transfer operators to engage in crypto payments without pre-funding foreign corridors. Their approach—seamlessly integrating cryptocurrency behind the scenes—reduces transaction costs significantly while maintaining familiar user experience (Southeast Asia Globe 2023; Forbes 2024). However, while the model is innovative, its long-term sustainability and scalability face critical challenges. These include dependency on volatile crypto markets, varying degrees of regulatory clarity across jurisdictions, and the infrastructural limitations of rural and low-bandwidth environments. For instance, sudden changes in crypto policy—as seen in India and Nigeria—can disrupt remittance pathways (OECD 2022). Moreover, despite its promise, adoption at scale will depend on user trust, agent network expansion, and interoperability with legacy financial systems. To ensure sustainability, platforms like BloomX must continuously adapt to evolving legal frameworks, maintain user protection mechanisms, and foster cross-sector collaboration with regulators, telecoms, and financial institutions.

Similarly, Electroneum, a mobile-based cryptocurrency, enables users in 140 countries to purchase airtime and data directly from their crypto wallets, converting virtual currency into a medium of exchange with real-world utility (Electroneum 2025). Electroneum has also expanded into electricity top-ups in several African nations, including Nigeria, Senegal, Mali, and The Gambia (Changelly 2025; BitScreener 2025). Current services support a wide network of telecom and utility integrations worldwide, and ETN is accepted by nearly 2000 merchants (Electroneum 2025; Forbes 2024).

AnyTask uses crypto payments with Electroneum, and sellers receive payment in ETN, purchasable or spendable directly through the integrated Electroneum ecosystem, supporting airtime, data, utilities, gift cards, and more (AnyTask 2025). The platform allows participation from freelancers in 140+ countries without requiring traditional bank accounts, providing zero seller fees and ETN wallet integration (AnyTask 2025). Freelancers can earn ETN and immediately use it for essentials—airtime, data, utilities—without needing a bank account (AnyTask 2025). By turning online freelancing into accessible income, AnyTask embodies how blockchain platforms are creating new jobs and financial pathways in markets with limited banking infrastructure.

Users can earn crypto and spend it directly on digital services. This mirrors the rise of game-based economies, where players in emerging markets earn tokens, sell digital assets, or participate in governance through decentralized autonomous organizations (DAOs), blurring the lines between play, work, and entrepreneurship.

Telecom companies in regions like Africa and Southeast Asia are now at the heart of gaming ecosystems. With vast prepaid user bases and strong distribution networks, they are positioned to deliver gamified services, offering airtime rewards, data bundles, and payment rails for gaming apps. These collaborations create low-friction entry points into gaming for millions who lack credit cards but have access to mobile money.

The combination of high mobile penetration, youthful populations, financial exclusion, and tech receptiveness means that emerging markets are poised to leapfrog traditional models—not just in payments, but in identity, asset ownership, and play-to-earn gaming. The success of M-Pesa is just the beginning. Full-scale blockchain adoption—embedded in gaming, freelance platforms, and virtual economies—could offer transformational opportunities to lift millions out of poverty and into a digital-first global economy.

With mobile-first access, a hunger for opportunity, and rapidly expanding crypto ecosystems, they are becoming innovation hubs where gaming, fintech, and blockchain converge. In this landscape, gaming becomes not just a tool for entertainment but a platform for empowerment, education, and economic participation.

Emerging economies are increasingly dominating the global gaming landscape, driven by rapid mobile adoption, youthful demographics, and expanding internet access. India, with an estimated 450 million gamers, is among the largest markets by user base, and its gaming industry is projected to grow from USD 4.3 billion in 2024 to USD 15.2 billion by 2033, at a compound annual growth rate (CAGR) of 15.2%. In the Philippines, gaming gross revenue reached PHP 410 billion (approximately USD 7.16 billion) in 2024, reflecting a 24–25% year-on-year increase and underscoring its strong mobile-first culture. Southeast Asia as a whole hosts around

277 million gamers, a figure expected to rise to 332 million by 2028, with mobile gaming as the dominant platform. In Latin America, the gaming population is estimated at 316 million, with revenue projected to reach USD 16.12 billion by 2030, while Sub-Saharan Africa is home to around 186 million gamers, predominantly on mobile devices. These markets illustrate the shift of gaming growth from traditionally dominant Western economies toward mobile-first, high-engagement regions in the Global South.

Gaming as a Gateway to Digital Inclusion

The concept of the digital divide provides a useful theoretical lens through which to understand gaming's role in digital inclusion. The digital divide has evolved to encompass disparities in usage skills, quality of access, and meaningful participation (van Dijk 2005). In emerging markets, these divides are often shaped by socioeconomic status, geographic location, gender, and infrastructure gaps. Gaming, particularly mobile-first and low-barrier platforms, has the potential to bridge this divide by functioning as an informal and intuitive entry point into the digital ecosystem. As van Dijk and Hacker (2003) argue, overcoming digital inequality requires not just access but also the ability to convert access into beneficial outcomes—a process gaming facilitates by offering economic, educational, and social opportunities through play. By embedding digital literacy and economic engagement into engaging and culturally resonant platforms, gaming moves beyond entertainment to serve as a vector for empowerment within digitally marginalized communities.

This chapter examines how mobile-first gaming provides a low-barrier entry point to connectivity, digital literacy, and economic participation, particularly in underserved communities across Southeast Asia, Africa, and Latin America. Through partnerships between telcos, startups, and governments, gaming is helping to transform smartphones into gateways to the digital economy.

Gaming is rapidly becoming a gateway to digital fluency, community engagement, and economic participation. In regions with limited access to traditional education or digital tools, gaming provides an intuitive and low-barrier entry point into the digital world. As more young people grow up interacting with mobile games, Esports platforms, and gaming have evolved into an infrastructure for inclusion. The appeal of play helps reduce resistance to digital adoption, enabling millions to learn digital skills informally through participation and collaboration.

In emerging economies, the mobile phone is the de facto gaming console. Unlike Western markets that evolved from PCs and consoles, mobile-first populations in Southeast Asia, Africa, and Latin America are skipping legacy platforms entirely. Telco-backed gaming bundles, prepaid data incentives, and Android-optimized games are redefining what accessibility means. This shift is turning smartphones into universal portals—not only for play, but for financial services, education, and social connection—blurring the line between leisure and infrastructure.

Games are increasingly used as tools for digital inclusion. In rural and underserved areas, gaming communities are often the first digital spaces where people create profiles, join networks, and engage in digital transactions. Localized content, culturally relevant narratives, and vernacular languages help bridge literacy and tech gaps. For women, youth, and marginalized populations, gaming creates safer, more familiar environments for online engagement, building confidence and digital literacy organically through shared experiences.

Telcos and public agencies are beginning to recognize gaming's role in digital transformation. By integrating gamified platforms into public education campaigns or social service access points, governments can expand reach and user engagement. Some initiatives link telco data incentives to educational game milestones, while others deploy game-based learning apps as part of national digital literacy programs. Public–private collaborations around mobile gaming are proving effective in bridging access and skill divides, especially where formal systems fall short.

In countries like the Philippines, gaming guilds have evolved into digital upskilling hubs, training players to become streamers, moderators, content creators, and Web3 community managers. With over 3.5 billion players globally, play is not just a pastime—it's a proving ground for digital talent. Micro-earnings from in-game assets, community contributions, and even competitive Esports are helping players turn their screen time into livelihoods, especially where traditional jobs are scarce or unstable.

Web3 technologies are enabling players to own their digital assets and participate in decentralized economies. In mobile-first and crypto-savvy regions, blockchain gaming allows users to earn, trade, and govern within localized digital ecosystems. From peso-backed stablecoins to regionally relevant NFTs, these innovations are creating new models for digital ownership that are rooted in local culture. The next frontier lies in the creation of portable digital identities and decentralized learning platforms, turning players into citizens of virtual economies with real-world value.

Gaming has emerged as a powerful tool for promoting social inclusion by introducing users to digital interfaces, communication tools, and financial systems in an accessible and engaging format. Through gameplay, individuals naturally acquire digital fluency, learn to navigate menus, manage virtual assets, and participate in online communities without requiring formal education. Gamified platforms are increasingly being used to support essential learning, from language acquisition to civic participation and health education. In East Africa, for instance, mobile games teach rural farmers about climate-resilient agriculture practices, while fintech apps in Southeast Asia use gaming mechanics to onboard users into savings and digital payment systems. Story-driven games targeted at young girls have been used to teach basic coding, fostering early interest in tech fields. These serious games foster cognitive engagement, build practical skills, and offer a gateway to more meaningful participation in the digital economy. By making learning fun and interactive, gaming helps to bridge the digital divide and empower marginalized communities.

Telco and Private Sector Partnerships

In many emerging economies across Southeast Asia, Africa, and Latin America, mobile phones have become the primary computing device for the majority of the population. This mobile-first reality has turned smartphones into the de facto gaming consoles of Global South. The rapid rise of mobile gaming in these regions is fueled by the affordability of Android-based devices, the availability of prepaid data plans, and the popularity of casual, low-bandwidth games that are easy to download and play. In places where broadband infrastructure is limited or unreliable, mobile gaming fills a vital gap in digital entertainment. In countries like Nigeria and Brazil, mobile games account for more than 80% of total gaming activity, while in Southeast Asia, markets such as the Philippines and Indonesia have seen explosive growth in mobile gaming communities. This surge is further amplified by the integration of gaming with social media platforms, allowing players to connect, compete, and share experiences in real time. As smartphone penetration continues to grow, mobile gaming is set to become not only the dominant form of play in the Global South but also a key driver of digital inclusion and economic opportunity.

Telecommunications providers play a pivotal role in scaling mobile gaming and reducing the digital divide. In some countries, telcos partner with game publishers to offer zero-rated access, allowing users to play without using their data. Others bundle game subscriptions with prepaid mobile plans.

Governments are also recognizing the potential of gaming. National innovation programs in countries like Kenya, Vietnam, and Colombia have begun funding game development hubs and supporting grassroots Esports initiatives. Public–private partnerships are emerging to build digital infrastructure, create content, and deliver inclusive digital services through gaming platforms.

Telecommunications operators in the Global South are fast becoming architects of entire gaming ecosystems. Across Africa and Southeast Asia, regions where most consumers are prepaid, unbanked, and mobile-first, telcos use their dominant billing rails to stitch together airtime rewards, data bundles, and friction-free payment options that let millions play (and sometimes earn) without ever entering a credit-card number.

Airtel Africa offered an early blueprint. In 2013, it partnered with India's Nazara Technologies to launch Airtel Games Club, a flat-fee subscription that unlocked more than 1000 mobile titles across Kenya, Tanzania, Nigeria, Ghana, Uganda, and Zambia. Players paid in local airtime—often just a few naira or shillings—turning leftover credit into instant entertainment (Steenkamp 2013). The model not only boosted data usage but also cemented Airtel's brand among young consumers on the continent, frequently dubbed the world's "mobile-only generation."

Today, telcos are scaling that logic into cloud gaming. In November 2024, MTN South Africa and sport-tech firm Telecoming unveiled MTN Cloudplay, a R79/month service that streams a 340-game library, straight to mid-range phones. Billing runs through MTN airtime or MoMo mobile money wallets, so hardware costs and payment frictions vanish (APO Group 2024). With 290 million MTN subscribers across Africa, even modest uptake can translate into millions of new gamers.

Gamified loyalty campaigns extend the trend. Nigeria's Globacom joined forces with startup Korrect Games in 2025 for a daily football-prediction platform that showers winners with instant airtime or cash. The promotion drew thousands of Glo subscribers, and 19 players walked away with awards of up to one million during the "Glo-Korrect Millionaire" finale (Daniel 2025). By mapping rewards directly to prepaid balances, Glo turns habitual sports fandom into a sticky gaming loop that feeds both engagement and ARPU.

Parallel developments are unfolding in Southeast Asia. In the Philippines, Smart Communications renewed its long-running partnership with MOONTON Games to power the 2024 Mobile Legends Professional League. Beyond streaming every match on Smart's Facebook page, the telco bundles "Unli 5G" offers that grant unlimited data during tournament windows—effectively subsidizing Esports participation while driving 5G adoption.

These cases share some common features:

- *Leverage prepaid billing rails.* By charging tiny daily or weekly fees to existing airtime or mobile money balances, telcos remove the credit-card hurdle that blocks many first-time gamers.
- *Bundle data as currency.* Game passes or tournament promos come packaged with discounted data, aligning operator revenue goals with player needs.
- *Gamify loyalty.* Prediction contests and reward programs recycle airtime or cash prizes back into telco ecosystems, increasing stickiness.
- *Act as distribution hubs.* With physical SIM networks and ubiquitous agent outlets, telcos bridge the gap between global publishers and last-mile consumers.

The opportunity is vast. Mobile gaming revenue in Africa alone is projected to grow at a 13 percent CAGR to 2025—an order of magnitude faster than core telco revenue (Digital Virgo 2022). In short, the fusion of telco billing infrastructure with gaming content is redefining how people play across emerging markets. The next billion gamers will not sign up with credit cards; they will subscribe, stream, and compete using a prepaid balance and a 4G or 5G signal.

As outlined in Chap. 4, gaming is increasingly emerging as a viable source of income, particularly in low-income and mobile-first settings. Through play-to-earn platforms, ad-based rewards, mobile tournaments, and embedded fintech features like digital wallets and micropayments, players are turning time spent gaming into tangible value. In places like the Philippines and Kenya, games have served as supplemental income sources during times of economic strain. Beyond playing, gaming ecosystems are also generating jobs in moderation, content creation, community management, and game testing. These new digital livelihoods offer accessible pathways for economic participation, especially for young people with limited formal employment opportunities.

While telecom companies have played a pivotal role in expanding digital access in emerging markets, their growing influence over digital ecosystems also presents significant risks. In regions with limited competition and regulatory oversight, telecom operators can become de facto gatekeepers to digital services, including gaming platforms, app marketplaces, and financial tools. This consolidation of infrastructure and access can lead to anti-competitive behavior, price manipulation, and the exclusion of smaller players from the market (World Bank 2021). Moreover, vertically integrated telecom firms may exert disproportionate control over data flows, monetization pathways, and platform prioritization, raising concerns about net neutrality and user privacy (GSMA 2023). In some cases, the bundling of services—such as zero-rated access to selected apps—may distort the digital marketplace, reinforcing platform monopolies and curating users' online experiences in ways that limit choice and diversity (UNCTAD 2022). These dynamics risk creating monopolistic digital enclaves where innovation is stifled and user autonomy is curtailed, particularly in countries where independent regulatory capacity is weak or compromised.

Scalable Models for the Next Billion

The scalability of Web3 gaming in emerging markets is shaped by a blend of infrastructure constraints, innovative deployment models, and grassroots community adoption. Africa, Southeast Asia, Latin America, and parts of Eastern Europe have become critical testbeds for scalable, mobile-first, and inclusive Web3 gaming ecosystems. Several key factors underpin their success:

1. Low-Cost, High Throughput Blockchain Infrastructure

    Emerging markets face constraints in transaction fees and network speed. Scalable Web3 gaming requires blockchains that combine high throughput, low fees, and energy efficiency. Blockchains like Solana and Polygon are preferred in these regions for their affordability and mobile friendliness (Choudhury 2022). For example, YGG Pilipinas in the Philippines adopted Polygon to enable low-fee play-to-earn models for Axie Infinity and similar games (Tan 2022). Celo, a mobile-first blockchain optimized for lightweight smartphones, is increasingly deployed in sub-Saharan Africa for gaming and financial applications (Celo Foundation 2023).

2. Layer 2 Rollups for Scalable Access

    To extend Ethereum's reach in bandwidth-constrained regions, Layer 2 solutions provide rollup-based scalability with drastically reduced fees. These are critical for enabling microtransactions in Web3 games without pricing out low-income users. Africa's Nestcoin utilizes Layer 2 s to build Metaverse Magna, a platform that offers affordable access to games and in-game assets across Nigeria, Ghana, and Kenya (Metaverse Magna 2023).

3. Mobile Optimization and Cross-Platform Engines

    In emerging markets, mobile devices are the dominant form of digital access. Game engines like Unity and Godot support lightweight builds and efficient rendering, enabling cross-platform functionality across low-end Android devices

(Geig 2022). Cocos2d-x, used in Vietnam and India, allows developers to build memory-efficient games with low-bandwidth consumption, an essential feature for mobile-first players in these regions (Nguyen 2023).
4. No-Code Tools and Local Developer Ecosystems

   No-code and low-code development platforms such as Buildbox and FlutterFlow empower local creators without extensive coding backgrounds to develop and monetize their games. These tools are critical for enabling talent in underserved tech ecosystems to contribute to the Web3 gaming economy. Kenyan startup Usiku Games builds Swahili-language games targeting rural youth, using Unity and low-code toolchains to reduce development overhead (Usiku Games 2023).
5. Community-Driven Models and Guild Infrastructure

   Web3 gaming communities in emerging markets thrive on social finance models like gaming guilds. Guilds such as Yield Guild Games (Case Study) and SnackClub provide scholarships, game onboarding, and asset lending that lower barriers to entry for gamers in low-income regions (Martinez 2023). YGG's sub-DAOs in the Philippines and Indonesia facilitate revenue-sharing schemes where players earn tokens through gameplay while guilds manage assets and infrastructure (Tan 2022). This model is now expanding into Brazil and Nigeria.
6. Regulatory and Compliance Adaptation

   Emerging markets often lack comprehensive digital asset frameworks. Services like TRM Labs and Chainalysis provide compliance infrastructure to gaming startups, helping them navigate cross-border regulation and avoid risks related to anti-money laundering (AML) and user fraud (Technical Companion).

   For instance, South Africa's National Treasury is piloting blockchain compliance sandboxes to foster safe experimentation in crypto-based gaming and fintech sectors (South African Reserve Bank 2023).
7. Token Standards and Economic Flexibility

   Games operating in volatile economic contexts, where fiat inflation and remittance costs are high, benefit from multi-token standards. ERC-1155 and ERC-6551 allow for hybrid asset models, where players hold bundles of fungible and non-fungible tokens in a single smart contract (El Messiry et al. 2023).

   In Argentina, the Sandbox partnered with local creators to issue tokenized land plots on Polygon and ERC-1155, enabling cost-effective asset ownership in local currency equivalents.
8. Edge Computing and Data Compression

   Given connectivity constraints in rural regions, edge computing and compression technologies ensure smoother gameplay. Platforms such as Unity Relay, Photon Fusion, and AWS Edge reduce latency by bringing processing closer to users. This is especially beneficial in African and Southeast Asian regions where mobile data is costly, and infrastructure is patchy. MTN's Esports Africa initiative is trailing edge network delivery with Unity to reduce lag in multiplayer tournaments across West Africa.

Scalability in emerging markets depends not only on technical elements but also on inclusive infrastructure, accessible tools, and community-based models. With mobile-first adoption, social incentives, and creative localization, these regions are pioneering sustainable models that offer valuable lessons for the global Web3 gaming economy. It is increasingly clear that well-designed, inclusive models are not only possible, they are already working at scale. The most scalable models share a few common traits: low entry barriers, inclusive monetization, public–private partnerships, and designs that reflect local realities.

Gaming ecosystems in emerging markets often blend commercial innovation with social value. Telcos, NGOs, cooperatives, and startups are playing complementary roles in building digital pathways that serve the unbanked, the underemployed, and the offline. Public–private partnerships are especially effective in reducing friction for new gamers, while NGO-led Esports leagues, educational gaming hubs, and youth tech incubators provide on-ramps to digital skills and micro-entrepreneurship. *Africacomicade* in Nigeria provides grassroots training and exposure for aspiring game developers through workshops, community events, and mentorship, supported by civil society partners (Africacomicade 2024). These initiatives illustrate how gaming can serve as a powerful tool not only for inclusion and economic participation but also for peacebuilding and community empowerment.

India's Jio offers a blueprint for scale. By embedding gaming directly into its mobile and broadband ecosystem, Jio removes common barriers like downloads, app stores, and payment set-up. Games are simply bundled into tiered data plans and billed as part of existing subscriptions, enabling frictionless access across income brackets and devices. This kind of infrastructure-level integration is what makes gaming both accessible and sustainable in price-sensitive markets.

In Southeast Asia, MyRepublic's "MyGamer" broadband offerings in Indonesia and Singapore show how performance-optimized packages, featuring static IPs and low-latency routing, can rapidly gain traction in regions with active gaming communities (Media OutReach Newswire (2025)). On the monetization side, the rise of direct carrier billing platforms like Xsolla enables gamers to purchase titles and in-game items using mobile balance rather than credit cards. This payment model has proven critical in emerging markets where formal banking access remains limited. With telcos acting as payment facilitators, the entire gaming value chain becomes more accessible, from first play to premium upgrades.

This success is grounded in a few key enablers:

- *Mobile-first access:* Smartphones and data plans are the primary digital entry point for most users.
- *Device-agnostic design*: Game bundles and platforms must support everything from low-end Android devices to high-performance smartphones.
- *Frictionless payments*: Carrier billing and mobile wallet integration are essential for onboarding users without bank accounts.
- *Optimized networks*: Real-time and cloud gaming demand low-latency infrastructure—something telcos are uniquely positioned to deliver.

To accelerate digital inclusion through gaming, governments and international development organizations can play a pivotal role. Policy interventions might include subsidizing data for educational games, funding community-based Esports initiatives, offering tax incentives for local game studios, and promoting digital literacy through school curricula. Governments should also include gaming in broader national digital transformation strategies, recognizing its potential to drive financial inclusion, youth engagement, and tech sector growth.

Risks and Challenges

While gaming offers opportunities for economic participation and digital inclusion, it also brings significant risks, particularly for players in emerging economies where regulatory safeguards and digital literacy are still catching up. Mobile addiction and screen dependency, encouraged by reward loops and constant mobile access, excessive playtime can displace essential activities. In many countries, the absence of public health guidelines or formal screen time education has left young people particularly vulnerable to compulsive gaming behaviors.

There is also the risk of over-monetization and financial exploitation. Popular free-to-play models often rely on "pay-to-win" mechanics, loot boxes, and microtransactions, designed not for player well-being but for-profit maximization. In settings where financial literacy is low and mobile money is widely used, players—especially children—can unwittingly overspend on in-game purchases or drain their prepaid balances without fully understanding the consequences.

The digital landscape also exposes users to a flood of scams, misinformation, and predatory content. Without oversight, these risks are compounded in multiplayer environments, where players may face cyberbullying, grooming, or manipulation.

There is a critical gap remaining in digital safety and content moderation frameworks. Many emerging markets lack adequate legal protections, ratings systems, or enforcement mechanisms to ensure safe and age-appropriate gaming environments. While global platforms may offer safeguards in wealthier regions, these are not always adapted or enforced in lower-income contexts.

Finally, there is a profound lack of parental and institutional guidance. Parents, teachers, and caregivers often have limited awareness or tools to guide safe and balanced digital play. National education systems have yet to catch up with the reality that mobile gaming is now a central part of childhood and adolescence. The path forward requires a multi-stakeholder response. Game developers must adopt responsible monetization practices, embed age-appropriate design, and implement localized financial safeguards. Governments should enact and enforce regulatory standards, launch digital literacy initiatives, and prioritize youth protection in national policy. At the community level, families and educators need culturally relevant resources to help children navigate the benefits and pitfalls of the gaming world safely.

As Web3 gaming expands into emerging markets, ethical design principles become increasingly critical to avoid exploitation, ensure digital inclusion, and protect vulnerable populations. In regions where income-generating gameplay may appeal to economically disadvantaged users, developers must guard against "play-to-survive" dynamics that risk digital labor exploitation and uneven power relations between players and asset holders. Ethical design involves transparency in tokenomics, culturally sensitive content, data privacy protections, and meaningful consent—particularly where literacy, digital infrastructure, or regulatory frameworks may be limited. It is essential that game mechanics promote autonomy, fair value exchange, and community governance, rather than extractive monetization. As discussed more comprehensively in Chap. 9, ethical frameworks should be embedded from design to deployment, with participatory input from local communities and attention to the unintended consequences of gamified financialization in emerging economies.

Conclusion

Gaming will be reframed as a developmental tool with the power to shape the digital futures of entire generations. In emerging markets, gaming is often the first point of contact with technology for millions. It is where young people begin to build digital literacy, where micro-entrepreneurs learn to transact, and where communities form across geographies and languages. Public and private actors must work together to create ecosystems that are not only commercially viable but socially transformative, designed with access, equity, and empowerment in mind.

The gamer of tomorrow is not just a consumer of digital content, but a creator, a collaborator, and a citizen of a globally connected world. Three key takeaways emerge: (1) Mobile-first, inclusive design is critical to onboarding the next billion users; (2) public–private-community partnerships must be prioritized; and (3) risk mitigation strategies are essential to ensure gaming empowers rather than exploits. Gaming in emerging markets provides a scalable infrastructure for economic opportunity, creative expression, and digital participation. The path forward lies in embracing this potential with intentional, inclusive, and context-aware design.

Cross-Chapter Insights

Mobile-first platforms like *Mobile Legends: Bang Bang* illustrate how gaming scales in bandwidth-limited or low-cost environments. These issues of access, infrastructure, and inclusion are reinforced by *Minecraft: Education Edition* (Chap. 6), which supports global education goals, and *Axie Infinity* (Chap. 3), which brought income to underbanked communities. If included case studies like *Carry1st* or *Facebook Connectivity in Africa* would further strengthen the regional analysis. Neurotechnologies like *NexMind* (Chap. 9) also offer promise for accessible, controller-free interaction—crucial for diverse abilities and environments.

Case Studies

Mobile Legends: Bang Bang—Mobile Esports (MLBB) at Scale

Game/Platform Name: Mobile Legends: Bang Bang
   Developer/Publisher: Montone, a subsidiary of ByteDance
   Year Released: 2016
   Genre: Multiplayer online battle arena (MOBA)
   Technology Stack: Unity, C++, JavaScript, Java (Android), Objective-C/Swift (iOS)

Mobile Legends: Bang Bang (MLBB) is a fast-paced 5v5 MOBA game designed for mobile platforms. It offers streamlined gameplay and accessibility for players on low-end devices. With short match durations and smart reconnection tools, MLBB became one of the most downloaded mobile games globally. Over time, it evolved into a comprehensive Esports ecosystem and introduced blockchain-enabled digital asset ownership.

Innovation

Ultra-fast session design: 10-min matches, <10-s matchmaking
   Smart offline reconnection with AI taking over disconnected players' avatars
   Continuous content updates: heroes, skins, maps, and seasonal events
   2024 launch of NFT hero skins and mystery boxes enabling digital asset ownership
   Adaptive matchmaking: player roles, ranks, and preferences inform balanced team assembly

Impact

User Adoption and Demographics
MLBB has reached lifetime app downloads of 695 million.

In June 2025, the title generated approximately 8.31 million app downloads, yet the all-time high was in April 2025, when the app generated 13.04 million app downloads.

In April 2025, Mobile Legends streams on the video platform Twitch collected a combined total of 2.2 million hours.

MLBB is mostly played by men (about 70%), although the game runs the MLBB Woman Invitational tournament. In 2022, Woman Invitational was one of the most viewed female Esports tournaments of the year, generating 2.1 million hours watched.

Economic Value Generated

The all-time in-app purchase revenue reached 1.7 billion U.S. dollars in 2025.

The game generated 111.83 million U.S. dollars in 2025 only.

In 2021, the app reached an all-time peak in the in-app purchase revenue of 230.73 million U.S. dollars.

Cultural/Social Influence

The game, designed for mobile phones, is widely accessible to be played on low-end devices, and therefore to players from different strata of society.

MLBB is tied to collaborations with celebrities, and even anime crossovers, like Attack on Titan or Star Wars; therefore, it has an influence on media creation, fashion, and art.

By popularizing Esports, MLBB has a strong influence on the economic development of East Asia countries. Teams like Blacklist International (Philippines) and RRQ (Indonesia) are known as cultural legends of the region.

Geographic Reach

The game is played worldwide, with special popularity in countries like the Philippines, Indonesia, Malaysia, and Myanmar.

Challenges and Controversies

Intellectual Property Controversies
In 2017, Riot Games filed a lawsuit against MLBB's original developer, Moonton, claiming that MLBB copied the elements of League of Legends.

Pay-to-Win Controversies
In the game, the players who have in-game assets like skins and armor get preferences.

Gaming Addiction and Academic Disruption
The popularity of MLBB is tied to poor academic performance among the youth.

Cultural Sensitivity Issues
The game includes numerous heroes from the historical and mythological backgrounds of Asian nations, and that creates the risk of offence when not handled properly.

References

Africacomicade. (2024). *Empowering African creatives through games and XR*. https://www.africacomicade.org

AnyTask. (2025). *Freelance marketplace overview*. https://www.anytask.com

APO Group. (2024, November 20). *Telecoming and MTN partner to launch cloud gaming in South Africa*. African Business. https://african.business

BitPinas. (2022). *Crypto regulation and remittance in the Philippines*. https://www.bitpinas.com

BitScreener. (2025). *Electroneum's global crypto services*. https://www.bitscreener.com

Bloom Solutions. (2024). *About us*. https://www.bloom.solutions

Celo Foundation. (2023). *Celo: Mobile-first blockchain for financial inclusion*. https://celo.org

Changelly. (2025). *Buy and sell crypto globally with Electroneum*. https://www.changelly.com

Choudhury, S. (2022). Gaming and blockchain in Southeast Asia: Adoption and friction. *Blockchain Use Cases Journal, 2*(3), 101–113.

Daniel, E. (2025, June 6). *19 rewarded in Glo-Korrect Millionaire Award*. The Guardian Nigeria. https://guardian.ng

Digital Virgo. (2022). *Africa mobile gaming trends and growth projections*. https://www.digitalvirgo.com/africa-mobile-gaming-trends/

El Messiry, M., Saliba, A., and Huang, L. (2023). ERC-6551: NFTs as Smart Contract Accounts. *Ethereum Improvement Proposals*.

Electroneum. (2025). *Electroneum global payment ecosystem*. https://www.electroneum.com

Forbes. (2024). *How Bloom Solutions is reshaping crypto remittance*. https://www.forbes.com

Geig, J. (2022). *Unity Game Development Cookbook*. O'Reilly Media.

GSMA. (2023). *The Mobile Economy 2023*. https://www.gsma.com/mobileeconomy

Martinez, J. (2023). Gaming guilds and digital labor in Brazil. *Journal of Play and Labor, 7*(1), 55–72.

Media OutReach Newswire. (2025, July 3). *MyRepublic launches exclusive GAMER broadband bundle with Magic: The Gathering's newest expansion—Edge of Eternities*. MyRepublic Press Release.

Metaverse Magna. (2023). *Building Africa's gaming superapp*. https://nestcoin.com

Nguyen, L. T. (2023). The rise of Cocos2d-x in Vietnamese mobile game development. *Asian Tech Trends Quarterly, 12*(2), 31–39. https://doi.org/10.1177/1461444818769694

OECD. (2022). *Crypto-assets and remittances in developing countries: Risks and policy responses*. Organisation for Economic Co-operation and Development. https://www.oecd.org

South African Reserve Bank. (2023). *Crypto innovation sandbox pilot report*. https://resbank.co.za

Southeast Asia Globe. (2023). *Crypto's role in financial inclusion in SEA*. https://www.southeastasiaglobe.com

Steenkamp, A. (2013, April 23). *Airtel, Nazara launch Games Club in Africa*. HumanIPO. https://www.humanipo.com/news/airtel-nazara-launch-games-club-in-africa/

Tan, K. (2022). Community-owned gaming in Southeast Asia: The YGG model. *Asian Blockchain Review, 5*(3), 18–26.

UNCTAD. (2022). *Digital Economy Report 2022: Cross-border data flows and development*. United Nations Conference on Trade and Development.

Usiku Games. (2023). *Localized African mobile games*. https://usikugames.com

van Dijk, J. A. G. M. (2005). *The deepening divide: Inequality in the information society*. SAGE Publications.

van Dijk, J., and Hacker, K. (2003). The digital divide as a complex and dynamic phenomenon. *The Information Society, 19*(4), 315–326. https://doi.org/10.1080/01972240309487

World Bank. (2021). *World Development Report 2021: Data for Better Lives*. Washington, DC: World Bank. https://doi.org/10.1596/978-1-4648-1600-0

Chapter 6
Gamifying Life, Learning, Health, and Consumer Behaviors

Abstract "Gamifying Life, Learning, Health, and Consumer Behaviors" shows how gamification—the use of game design elements in non-game contexts—is reshaping how people learn, heal, and engage with the world. This chapter explores how gamified systems are being integrated into healthcare, education, and consumer behavior to drive motivation, improve outcomes, and foster deeper participation. In healthcare, games are now tools for mental health therapy, physical rehabilitation, medication adherence, and even pharmaceutical education. In classrooms and virtual campuses, AI and the Metaverse are turning passive learning into immersive, skill-based journeys. For seniors, gamified platforms support mental agility, social connection, and well-being through accessible entertainment and community challenges. Readers will discover how these applications not only improve engagement but also offer measurable benefits to individuals and society. Whether it is through fitness trackers, interactive learning apps, or brain-training games, gamification is becoming a powerful force for behavior change and lifelong development.

Keywords Gamification · Digital Therapeutics · Serious Games · Metaverse Education · Immersive Technologies · Health Gamification · Learn-to-Earn · Move-to-Earn · Behavioral Design · Cognitive Training · Tokenized Wellness · AI Tutors · Biofeedback Gaming · Virtual Reality Therapy · Inclusive Game Design

Introduction

Gamification, the strategic use of game elements in non-game settings, has become a driver of engagement, learning, and behavior change (Deterding et al. 2011; Hamari et al. 2014). Today its impact spans education, healthcare, hospitality, mobility, and daily consumer life. At its core, gamification leverages well-established psychological principles such as rewards, feedback loops, and visible progression to foster intrinsic and extrinsic motivation (Sardi et al. 2017).

This chapter explores how gamified systems are integrated into healthcare, education, and consumer behavior to drive motivation, improve outcomes, and foster deeper participation. In healthcare, games are now tools for mental health therapy, physical rehabilitation, medication adherence, and even pharmaceutical education. AI and the Metaverse are turning passive learning into immersive, skill-based journeys in classrooms and virtual campuses. For seniors, gamified platforms support mental agility, social connection, and well-being through accessible entertainment and community challenges. Readers will discover how these applications improve engagement and offer measurable benefits to individuals and society. Whether through fitness trackers, interactive learning apps, or brain-training games, gamification is powerful for behavior change and lifelong development.

Gamification's effectiveness across domains such as education, health, and consumer engagement can be better understood through established behavioral psychology frameworks. Gamified systems optimize these models by enhancing user motivation through rewards and narratives, simplifying actions via intuitive interfaces, and providing timely prompts such as streak reminders or real-time feedback.

Gamification and Serious Games in Health Care

Serious games are fully developed games designed for a primary purpose other than pure entertainment, such as education, training, health interventions, or social impact (Michael and Chen 2006). These use game design elements (e.g., points, badges, leaderboards, challenges) in non-game contexts to increase user engagement, motivation, and behavior change (Deterding et al. 2011).

Unlike gamification, serious games are complete game experiences with defined rules, objectives, and immersive gameplay. Serious games and interactive narratives allow users to explore emotions and practice coping strategies in controlled, engaging contexts. For example, MindMaze and Akili Interactive's EndeavorRx incorporate evidence-based game mechanics to address conditions such as attention-deficit/hyperactivity disorder and depression, with clinical validation supporting their effectiveness (Patterson et al. 2019; Akili Interactive 2020).

Digital Therapeutics and Clinical Applications

Digital therapeutics are evidence-based, software-driven interventions designed to prevent, manage, or treat medical conditions. Often regulated or clinically validated, digital therapeutics may include gamified components but are developed under health standards and often prescribed by healthcare providers (Gerke et al. 2020). Digital therapeutics such as SuperBetter and the FDA-cleared EndeavorRx demonstrate the clinical promise of game mechanics for mental health support and ADHD treatment, respectively (Patterson et al. 2019; Akili Interactive 2020). Medication adherence apps like Mango Health use points and streaks to raise compliance rates (Kleinman et al. 2018), while wearables such as Fitbit harness social challenges to sustain engagement (Feng and Crowdhelia 2019).

Tokenizing Wellness: Health as a Digital Asset

Immersive technologies, blockchain incentives, and the expanding Metaverse are converging to gamify personal well-being, preventive care, and chronic disease management (World Economic Forum 2022). These gamified experiences engage users in positive health behaviors while embedding wellness into everyday life. This gamification model is now expanding into token economies, where healthy actions generate tangible rewards. Whether it's "move-to-earn" models that track steps with wearables or mental wellness games that reward mindfulness, users are compensated for behavior that improves their health. These games turn well-being into a participatory, rewarding experience.

One of the most promising applications of gamification in health is the "move-to-earn" model. "Move-to-earn" platforms, including Genopets, reward physical activity with tradable tokens, turning everyday steps into economic. These models gamify daily routines, making fitness both fun and financially incentivized.

Virtual fitness instructors, guided AR workouts, and smart avatars further enhance the user experience, offering motivation, personalized feedback, and progression systems akin to levels in a game. These systems tap into dopamine reward loops found in gaming, creating long-term behavioral engagement. This trend holds special promise for Gen Z and Gen Alpha—digital-native generations that respond better to interactive and gamified approaches than traditional health messaging. By speaking their digital language, gamified health tools can drive behavior change more effectively than lectures or leaflets.

At the core of this transformation lies the tokenization of health data. Powered by blockchain and NFTs, individuals can now securely store, manage, and even monetize their personal health records, biometric data, and wellness achievements. NFT-based health identifiers provide immutable proof of data ownership, enabling users to selectively share or license their de-identified information to research institutions, insurers, or wellness platforms. This marks a fundamental shift, from health data as a passive record to a personal economic resource. Individuals can now participate in data-driven health ecosystems as stakeholders, earning rewards while advancing precision medicine, diagnostics, and AI-powered healthcare solutions.

NFTs also facilitate seamless identity and access management in health and wellness services. A single NFT can verify a person's medical credentials, treatment history, or fitness program subscription, streamlining insurance claims, reducing administrative friction, and granting cross-platform access to virtual wellness offerings.

As telehealth, virtual yoga, and AI therapy scale across the Metaverse, such token-based identities will enable decentralized access to care. They also allow for better continuity and personalization of services, no matter which platform or provider the user chooses.

Gamified Mental Health and Emotional Wellness

Gamification is increasingly being applied as a therapeutic tool in mental health care, using immersive digital environments to support emotional well-being, resilience, and cognitive-behavioral change.

Virtual environments and avatars in the Metaverse also offer novel modalities for mental health support. These spaces facilitate peer interaction, mindfulness training, and therapeutic role-play, particularly benefiting individuals with anxiety, post-traumatic stress disorder, or autism spectrum conditions who may experience social barriers in traditional settings (Freeman et al. 2017). The capacity for users to remain anonymous or adopt expressive avatars has been shown to reduce stigma and promote openness in virtual therapy sessions (Cipresso et al. 2018).

Gamification represents a robust design paradigm to enhance user engagement, emotional regulation, and treatment adherence. The next frontier lies in adaptive games powered by biometric sensing—using data such as heart rate, facial tension, and voice modulation to dynamically adjust therapeutic content in real time. Such innovations could personalize interventions and offer just-in-time mental health support, bridging the gap between passive monitoring and active care (Riva et al. 2021).

The fusion of gaming and health is a present reality being rapidly shaped by technology and user demand. The Metaverse can be a force for wellness, empowerment, and global health equity, if built ethically and inclusively. Game developers, healthcare providers, public health experts, and patient communities must work together to design gamified health ecosystems that prioritize trust, joy, and efficacy. The goal is not just to make people play more, but to help them live better, longer, and more informed lives.

Video games are increasingly recognized as valuable tools in mental health care and therapeutic interventions. Once viewed predominantly through a lens of concern over negative psychological effects, games are now seen as promising digital therapeutics.

It is likely that a growing number of video games will be approved for medical use, potentially addressing conditions such as anxiety, depression, autism spectrum disorder, and cognitive decline. Games offer a compelling blend of engagement and repetitive practice that facilitates brain-training and behavioral reinforcement (Patterson et al. 2019). For example, digital games that incorporate cognitive tasks, such as working memory or emotional regulation exercises, can motivate patients through reward loops and progression mechanics. Regulatory pathways for digital therapeutics are expected to expand globally.

VR therapy is also gaining recognition, particularly for exposure-based interventions. VR enables patients to confront fears in controlled environments, simulating situations such as heights, flights, or social encounters. A 2022 meta-analysis found that VR-based cognitive behavioral therapy was as effective as traditional in-person treatment for severe anxiety and post-traumatic stress disorder, with no significant difference in clinical outcomes (Carl et al. 2022).

These applications are expected to become more widespread and accessible by 2030, with VR therapy potentially administered remotely or integrated into home-use adjunct tools. The emergence of biofeedback-integrated VR games will further allow patients to monitor and learn to control physiological responses like heart rate and breathing, gamifying stress management techniques (Findlay 2022).

Gaming is also showing promise for mood improvement and depression management. Casual and experimental games have been found to enhance mood and create a sense of accomplishment, with some designed to shift cognitive biases commonly associated with depression (Carras et al. 2018). As mental health needs rise, particularly among young people, therapists may integrate games into treatment plans. These could include cooperative games to foster social engagement or calming exploratory games for stress relief. In the future, mental health providers may maintain digital libraries of recommended game-based experiences tailored to individual patient needs.

Immersive Medicine and Metaverse Therapies

In Metaverse environments, avatars can represent patients and doctors alike. Clinical procedures, from diagnostics to surgery, are enhanced by digital twins and 3D visualization tools. Simulated medical education, powered by gamification and token incentives, enables students to earn credentials through experiential learning. VR sessions help treat anxiety, and phobias. Virtual group therapy, AI-guided mental health coaching, and wellness quests offer scalable, interactive care solutions. These interventions create a future where healing is immersive, data-driven, and always accessible.

Rehabilitation, Physical Fitness, and Pain Management

Games are also being used effectively in physical rehabilitation and fitness. "Exergaming" (exercise through gaming) and rehabilitation games encourage physical activity and engagement in therapeutic exercises. Stroke rehabilitation, in particular, has benefited from game-based interventions. A meta-analysis of 42 studies found that serious games significantly improved upper limb recovery post-stroke compared to conventional therapy alone (Laver et al. 2017).

Interactive VR environments that simulate tasks, such as balance training, obstacle navigation, or limb movement; motivate patients to practice with greater frequency and enthusiasm. These tools also provide real-time feedback, enhancing rehabilitation outcomes. With the expansion of telehealth, such systems are increasingly used at home, monitored remotely by therapists.

By 2035, game-based rehabilitation will likely be embedded into standard protocols for stroke, orthopedic recovery, and traumatic brain injury. These games will adapt to patient progress and deliver performance metrics to healthcare providers.

Fitness games, including VR boxing, dance, and movement-based adventures, are gaining popularity. These combine entertainment with physical exertion, promoting health in a format that is fun and habit-forming. As the distinction between games and workouts blurs, millions may meet exercise goals while adventuring in virtual spaces or participating in Esports-style fitness leagues (Hamari et al. 2014).

Games are also used for pain management. Immersive VR games have demonstrated analgesic effects by distracting patients during painful procedures or chronic pain episodes. VR analgesia is a technique that reduces the subjective experience of pain without pharmacological intervention (Hoffman et al. 2011).

Cognitive Training and Social Therapy

Cognitive games designed to improve memory, attention, and processing speed are being used for older adults and patients with cognitive impairments. While the efficacy of some commercial brain-training games remains under debate, emerging titles are increasingly evidence-based. By 2035, clinicians may prescribe cognitive gaming suites for early-stage dementia or post-injury cognitive rehabilitation (Lampit et al. 2014). Games also offer therapeutic social environments. Multiplayer games and virtual worlds enable individuals with autism, social anxiety, or PTSD to engage in safe, structured social interactions. This approach is expected to gain formal acceptance through clinical trials and programmatic integration.

Health Education and Workforce Training

Gamification is also enhancing medical education and health literacy. An example of a "learn-to-earn" model in healthcare is Virginia's Earn to Learn Nursing Education Acceleration Program, funded under the American Rescue Plan. In this program, pre-licensure Registered Nurse and Licensed Practical Nurse students engage in paid clinical apprenticeships as they complete their education, earning wages comparable to their current practice level while gaining hands-on experience and mentorship through partnerships between nursing schools and healthcare providers (Virginia Department of Health 2025). Studies indicate that such integrative, work-based models enhance workforce readiness and retention more effectively than traditional academic-only approaches (Virginia Department of Health 2024). A parallel initiative in California, CalGrows Learn-and-Earn, offers direct-care workers and family caregivers up to $30 per hour for completing approved training modules, along with a one-time $500 bonus for at least 15 hours of coursework (Futuro Health 2023). By coupling financial incentives with skill development, these programs support both immediate economic needs and the expansion of a competent, stable healthcare workforce. This model can be applied to peer-to-peer health education, where communities teach one another and earn rewards for their participation.

Future Outlook: Phygital Well-Being

As phygital technologies mature, health and gaming will no longer be separate spheres. They will be co-infrastructures designed for economic inclusion, personal agency, and collective well-being. The most valuable gameplay may well be the one that extends lives, connects communities, and sustains health.

Video games will increasingly be recognized as validated tools for mental health treatment, physical rehabilitation, cognitive enhancement, and social-emotional therapy. With mounting evidence supporting their efficacy, these technologies will transition from supplemental tools to core components of healthcare and wellness strategies. The fusion of gaming with therapeutic goals offers scalable, engaging, and personalized interventions, making healthcare not just more effective, but also more accessible and motivating.

MetaEducation: Global, Gamified, and Generative

The Metaverse education market is forecast to grow at a CAGR of 44.98% from 2023 to 2030, reaching USD 763.7 million (Fortune Business Insights 2023). Platforms such as Classcraft (role-play quests), Duolingo (streaks and leaderboards), Prodigy (math RPG), Roblox Education (user-generated coding worlds), Minecraft: Education Edition (immersive sandbox), and Kahoot! (quiz battles) illustrate how gamification is already transforming learning at scale (Classcraft Studios 2022; Duolingo 2023; Prodigy Education 2023; Roblox Corp. 2022).

There will be profound changes to how people learn, driven by technological advances, changing work dynamics, and the global digitization of knowledge. As jobs evolve and the half-life of skills continues to shrink, lifelong learning and rapid reskilling are becoming critical. The traditional education model, slow to update, geographically constrained, and often prohibitively expensive, is no longer fit for purpose.

The Metaverse will make education truly global and borderless. Where a person lives will no longer limit what they can learn or who they can learn from. This educational globalization will redefine opportunity. It will close geographical divides, empower marginalized communities, and offer a more equitable playing field for learners around the world. Education will become not only more accessible but also vastly cheaper, bypassing traditional gatekeepers and brick-and-mortar infrastructure.

To operate safely and efficiently across jurisdictions, self-sovereign identity systems will verify credentials, protect privacy, and ensure trust in borderless, virtual classrooms. Learners will own their academic records and reputations—portable and verifiable anywhere in the world.

Gamified education will blend learning with play to keep students engaged, motivated, and excited. Web3 mechanisms such as "Learn-to-Earn" will reward students with tokens for attending classes, completing assignments, and collaborating on peer projects. Students will no longer passively absorb information. They will embark on quests, complete missions, collect digital badges and NFTs, and level up through immersive educational experiences. Data analytics will personalize these journeys, adapting the learning curve based on the student's pace, preferences, and performance.

Precision learning will be enabled by powerful feedback loops, allowing real-time insights into strengths, weaknesses, and growth opportunities. This means that learning pathways can be highly customized, making education not just more engaging, but far more effective. Social Metaverse spaces will allow students to form study groups, co-create digital projects, and learn through social interaction and collaboration, making learning a shared, interactive adventure.

Artificial intelligence will become a collaborator in every learner's journey. Generative AI will create tailored content, act as tutors, simulate labs, and design adaptive curricula based on each learner's needs. AI-powered avatars will guide medical students through a virtual anatomy dissection or language practice.

Generative AI will also power automated assessments, real-time feedback, and dynamic curriculum creation. Teachers and institutions will be able to scale high-quality learning at a fraction of today's cost while focusing human effort where it matters most—empathy, mentorship, and creativity. Learners will move beyond rote memorization to develop higher-order cognitive functions of critical thinking, systems analysis, and ethical reasoning.

One of the Metaverse's greatest promises is inclusion. For people in remote regions, those with disabilities, or learners excluded from traditional schooling, MetaEducation could be life changing. A person confined to a wheelchair could participate in virtual sports education; a refugee child could access education from a conflict zone; a stay-at-home caregiver could earn a new credential.

With opportunity comes responsibility. As education shifts into immersive and gamified worlds, there is a need to address digital ethics, data privacy, algorithmic bias, and accessibility. Who owns student data? Can AI tutors perpetuate stereotypes? How to ensure fair rewards in learn-to-earn systems? How to prevent addiction or over-surveillance in gamified environments? Ethics-by-design must be a foundational principle in MetaEducation. Developers, educators, regulators, and learners must co-create an ecosystem that is inclusive, transparent, and accountable. (See Chap. 7).

Gamification and Serious Games in Education

Over the next decade, the influence of games will extend ever more deeply into education and skill training. The concept of gamification, applying game design elements (points, challenges, rewards) in non-game contexts, has proven effective in increasing engagement and motivation in learners. In the future, many school curricula around the world may routinely incorporate educational games and simulations. Games can make learning experiential; they provide immediate feedback, adapt to a learner's pace, and often teach collaboration and problem-solving implicitly. Many higher education and professional development programs will likely use game simulations for teaching complex concepts (for example, medical students using virtual surgery simulators, or business students managing a simulated company in a strategy game to learn management).

Gamification in a broader sense will also permeate daily life: apps for fitness, personal finance, or workplace productivity in 2025–2035 often include levels, badges, or friendly competitions to encourage user engagement (already apps like Duolingo or Fitbit do this, and the trend will continue). There will be more partnerships between game developers and educators to create content that is both pedagogically sound and genuinely fun. Additionally, assessment might be gamified: instead of or alongside traditional tests, students could be evaluated by their performance in educational games that measure skills more dynamically (like creativity, persistence, and strategic thinking).

What Will Learning Look Like in 2050?

By 2050, education may look radically different. Learners will enter virtual academies where they interact with peers across the world in multi-sensory learning environments.

Language learning will be powered by real-time immersive interactions with avatars and AI-powered "peers." Learning will be active, social, and creative, tailored to attention spans, cognitive diversity, and emotional needs. Credentials will be stored on blockchain, portable across jobs and countries, and recognized globally.

Gamification can support adult learning and workforce reskilling by transforming curriculum into bite-sized, trackable challenges. Virtual reality classrooms, powered by devices like Oculus or HoloLens, deliver high-fidelity simulations for engineering, medicine, and environmental sciences. Biofeedback tools are being integrated to adapt lesson intensity based on cognitive load and focus.

As the vision of MetaEducation takes shape, gamification is becoming a powerful force, reshaping how people learn. Education is moving beyond traditional classrooms into immersive, interactive environments where learning is not only effective but also engaging and enjoyable. A range of innovative platforms are already demonstrating how gamified learning experiences can capture attention, improve retention, and foster lifelong skills.

One of the early pioneers in this space is Classcraft, which transforms the classroom into a collaborative role-playing game. Students assume roles like warriors, healers, or mages and earn points by displaying positive behavior, completing tasks, and helping peers. Teachers become game masters, guiding students through narrative-based quests that align with academic goals. Classcraft has gained traction in over 75 countries, proving that gamification can build not just knowledge, but also empathy, cooperation, and social-emotional skills (Classcraft Studios 2022).

Language learning has also been revolutionized through gamification. Duolingo, one of the most popular apps in the world, uses a reward system of streaks, leaderboards, and virtual currency to motivate users. Learners engage in micro-lessons that offer instant feedback and allow steady progress over time. With over 500 million users globally, Duolingo has turned language acquisition into a habit-forming daily game (Duolingo 2023).

For younger learners, Prodigy brings math to life through a fantasy role-playing game. Aimed at students in grades 1 to 8, Prodigy blends curriculum-aligned math problems with epic quests and battles. Students answer questions to advance in the game, and the adaptive engine ensures each player gets content at the right difficulty level. Over 100 million children around the world have used Prodigy, transforming math from a source of anxiety into a captivating adventure (Prodigy Education 2023).

Gamified learning isn't limited to traditional academic subjects. Platforms like Roblox Education empower students to learn through creation. Within Roblox's expansive virtual world, students can design their own games, develop coding skills, and even monetize their creations using the in-game currency, Robux. Partnerships with organizations like Code.org and STEM.org have helped Roblox become a dynamic learning environment where creativity, technical literacy, and entrepreneurial thinking intersect.

Sandbox platforms like Minecraft: Education Edition are also supporting immersive education. This version of Minecraft allows students to collaborate in building projects that teach coding, science, history, and sustainability. Used in over 115 countries, Minecraft has shown that immersive, student-driven learning can be both fun and academically rigorous. Students are not only solving problems but also developing creativity, spatial reasoning, and collaboration skills that are essential in a digital future.

Gamified assessments have also been reimagined by platforms like Kahoot! which turn quizzes and tests into competitive games. With leaderboards, timers, and instant feedback, Kahoot! fosters engagement while allowing educators to track progress. With more than nine million educators using the platform worldwide, Kahoot! shows that even traditional assessment can benefit from game mechanics.

Together, these platforms illustrate that the future of education is already unfolding. As blockchain, AI, AR/VR, and decentralized identity systems mature, the next wave of educational platforms will include NFT diplomas, skill-based quests that replace standardized tests, and even DAO-run universities governed by students and educators. We'll see learners earning tokens for helping peers, creating content, or mastering micro-skills, all tracked in secure digital wallets.

Gamified education is about more than entertainment—it's a system that builds motivation, self-efficacy, and long-term engagement. It creates a model of learning where every interaction can be rewarding, every accomplishment is verifiable, and every learner has a personalized path to success. As MetaEducation takes hold, powered by the same dynamics that drive the gaming industry, the line between learning and playing will blur, ushering in a global, inclusive, and lifelong learning revolution.

Creating a truly global, gamified, and generative education system will not be easy. It will require collaboration across governments, tech companies, educators, and civil society. It will require infrastructure investment, policy innovation, and a deep commitment to equity and ethics.

The Silver Metaverse: Gaming and Later Life

The fastest-growing segment of the global games audience is now over sixty-five. Over the next decade, an unprecedented demographic wave, the arrival of 1.5 billion people aged 65 and older by 2050 (United Nations 2022), will collide with a maturing Metaverse. The result will be a new digital frontier coined the Silver Metaverse: a constellation of immersive game worlds, AI companions, and assistive robots designed to support longer, healthier, more connected lives. Age-friendly games and VR platforms, including BrainHQ, Lumosity, Fit Minds, and MyndVR, have shown benefits for cognitive resilience and social connection (Mahncke and Merzenich 2016; Czaja et al. 2019). Exergames and narrative problem-solving titles are clinically trialed for stroke, MCI, and mood disorders (Laver et al. 2020). Early VR presence studies suggest avatar-based group therapy can rival in-clinic outcomes (Freeman et al. 2017).

Retirement has always promised leisure, but until recently, "leisure" for many older adults meant a limited menu of television, radio, or the occasional bus trip. Physical ailments, fixed incomes, and mobility restrictions make it hard to maintain friendships or discover new hobbies. The Metaverse upends these constraints. Instead of typing on a flat social-media feed, seniors can slip on lightweight VR glasses and stroll through a photorealistic park to play chess with friends who may live thousands of kilometers away. Multiplayer titles like *Animal Crossing*, *Minecraft, and The Sims* will evolve into age-friendly virtual neighborhoods where grandparents decorate digital cottages, attend open-mic nights, or garden on floating islands.

By recreating the rituals of everyday life, eye contact, body language, and shared scenery, the Metaverse erases the alienation many seniors feel when navigating traditional online spaces. Crucially, these shared spaces do not have to be segregated by age. Mixed-generation guilds in massively multiplayer games already show how teens teaching grandmothers raid tactics, or older engineers mentoring young coders can reverse stereotypes and build genuine intergenerational understanding.

Loneliness rates soar in late life, especially after bereavement or hospitalization. Traditional online forums lack non-verbal nuance; in-person meet-ups require transport and stamina. In a Metaverse support circle, participants embody expressive avatars around a virtual hearth. Because voice proximity, gaze, and gesture are preserved, members build trust quickly, yet anonymity remains possible for those discussing grief, chronic pain, or diagnoses like Parkinson's. Trained facilitators can mute disruptive users, trigger calming environmental cues, or teleport the group to a serene shoreline for guided meditation. Early research into VR "presence" shows that such embodiment can reduce social anxiety and increase therapeutic rapport outcomes comparable to in-clinic group therapy.

Independence is a proven driver of psychological well-being in older adulthood. Here, gaming-adjacent technologies such as extended reality (XR) and AI create tools that feel liberating, not infantilizing. Imagine a virtual shopping district where a senior can walk into a digital shoe store, try on 3D slippers that conform to the exact scan of their feet, and pay with a secure tap of their pension-linked wallet, all without fearing online fraud. Because the products are rendered at life-size, buyers can judge color, texture, and fit before a drone delivers the physical item to the doorstep.

AI-equipped smart homes will monitor data like gait speed, fridge usage, and medication timing and turn these signals into gentle prompts or automatic orders. If the system detects an abnormal pattern, it can notify a caregiver avatar inside the same Metaverse space, preserving the resident's dignity while summoning help only when truly needed. Independence becomes a continuum, scaffolded by invisible technology rather than eroded by constant in-person oversight.

Robotic dogs that fetch slippers, humanoid assistants that carry groceries, and kitchen bots that dice vegetables are no longer science fiction. What makes them relevant to gaming is the *interface*: seniors often bond more easily with a cartoonish penguin on a screen than with a clinical dashboard. Social robots shaped like cats, seals, or friendly astronauts can speak through the same voice engine that powers game NPCs, telling jokes, reminding users to hydrate, or inviting them into a daily Tai-Chi quest line that counts reps and awards badges.

Because the robot's back-end is connected to the Metaverse, progress in physical therapy can unlock virtual travel tokens and complete exercise routines all week. By linking offline health behaviors to online rewards, designers tap intrinsic motivation rather than punitive alarms. Importantly, physical robots can also serve as bridge devices for seniors wary of full immersion. A tabletop companion that reads bedtime stories from grandchildren's avatars eases the adoption curve toward more advanced headsets.

New Economies of Purpose

Games have long rewarded mastery with virtual loot; older players often crave purpose over prestige. Platforms can channel this by transforming life experience into in-game currency. A retired teacher might mentor language learners in an educational sandbox, earning tokens redeemable for cultural tours. A former carpenter could host a virtual workshop on building birdhouses, then sell NFT blueprints that younger players print on real-world 3D printers. These micro-entrepreneurial pathways keep skills alive, supplement pensions, and foster dignity. Even legacy preservation can be gamified: seniors record life stories that AI curates into interactive quests for descendants. Grandchildren can "unlock" chapters of family history by completing tasks that reflect ancestral values, planting a tree, volunteering, or learning a traditional dish, thus weaving heritage into gameplay loops.

Silver Esports and Competitive Longevity

Competitive gaming need not fade with reaction times. Strategy titles, turn-based card games, and team management sims value pattern recognition and patience—traits that often sharpen with age. Senior-only leagues already exist for *League of Legends* and *Counterstrike*; by 2030, expect a dedicated Silver Esports circuit streamed on age-friendly platforms with larger HUDs and slower game clocks. Sponsorships by healthcare brands and retirement communities will create new revenue models, while intergenerational tournaments, grandparents versus grandchildren, could become holiday staples.

Lifelong learning extends brain health and social engagement. The Metaverse transforms MOOCs into experiential classrooms: art-history students fly through a reconstructed Florence, while a physics cohort manipulates planetary orbits in a shared solar lab. AI tutors adjust difficulty, and seniors can audit modules for free or earn micro-credentials that translate into part-time virtual jobs—museum guide, language coach, and citizen scientist annotating climate data. For residents of rural nursing facilities, such intellectual stimulation may combat cognitive decline more effectively than medication alone.

Realizing the Silver Metaverse will require coordinated action:

1. *Inclusive Standards*: Industry bodies should publish accessibility checklists specific to XR and seniors, analogous to the Web Content Accessibility Guidelines.
2. *Public-Private Subsidies*: Telecoms, insurers, and social-care agencies can bundle headsets and broadband with preventative-health programs, offsetting costs through reduced hospital admissions.
3. *Ethics Charters*: Loot-box limits, data-retention caps, and algorithmic-fairness audits should be codified into ESG reports and enforced by independent review boards that include gerontologists and senior advocates.

4. *Research and Evidence*: Longitudinal trials measuring VR's impact on depression, fall risk, and cognitive reserve will convert hype into reimbursable clinical pathways.
5. *Community Hubs*: Libraries and senior centers can host walk-in Metaverse pods, staffed by digital "concierges" who demystify equipment and foster peer-to-peer teaching.

The first generation to grow up with home consoles is now entering retirement. What they will demand next is not nostalgia but the chance to keep exploring, competing, laughing, and learning inside worlds limited only by imagination, not by arthritic knees or shrinking social circles. If developers, policymakers, and caregivers seize this moment, gaming will evolve from pastime to lifeline, from escapism to empowerment. The Silver Metaverse can become a vast, inclusive playground where age is not a barrier but a badge, evidence of stories earned, wisdom gained, and still-curious hearts ready for the next adventure.

To fulfil this vision, developers must confront specific barriers. Older adults vary widely in vision, hearing, dexterity, and cognition. Game UIs need scalable fonts, high-contrast modes, adjustable motion intensity, and voice-first navigation. Onboarding tutorials should assume zero prior controller experience, using slow-paced, gesture-based interactions.

Ethically, privacy is paramount. Biometric psychography, data streams of gait, gaze, and micro-facial expressions, can reveal mood disorders or medication side effects. Such insights are powerful for early intervention, but they also create lucrative advertising profiles. Clear consent dashboards, local on-device processing, and regulatory guardrails that prohibit targeted age-based manipulation are essential.

Gaming Meets Hospitality and Travel

Built on game engines, persistent social spaces and tokenized economies, this "play layer" turns travel from a linear transaction, search, book, go, into an ongoing, gamified relationship that begins months before departure and can linger long after return home. In effect, tourism is becoming a live-service game, and success will belong to brands that understand the design languages of guests, digital scarcity, and community progression.

Digital-twin replicas of cities, resort islands, or cruise ships give prospective guests something far richer than a glossy brochure. Drop an avatar into a faithful copy of Kyoto at cherry-blossom time, and the sensations—petal drift, temple bells, ambient chatter—hit the brain's presence circuits in ways a video never can. But the real power is interactivity: visitors can accept side quests, collect NFT souvenirs that unlock discounts on the physical trip, and leave verifiable reviews stamped on-chain so they cannot be faked or deleted.

For operators, this is live user-testing. A hotel can prototype room layouts or spa treatments in the twin and watch heat maps of avatar flow to refine real-world renovations. A theme-park script writer can A/B-test parade routes with thousands of virtual families' months before the gates open.

Tokenized Loyalty Becomes a Game Economy

Traditional points programs are opaque spreadsheets hidden behind logins; Metaverse loyalty behaves like a massively multiplayer online role-playing game economy. Airlines and hotel groups mint limited NFT badges for mileage milestones or seasonal events. Holders automatically receive airdropped upgrades or early-access slots to gastronomic pop-ups inside the virtual twin. More valuable still, these tokens grant governance votes on future amenities—pool redesigns, menu rotations, destination pop-ups—turning passive guests into engaged co-designers.

Because NFTs are self-custodied, travelers can trade or gift them on secondary markets, giving the loyalty graph real-world liquidity. Speculation alone is not the goal; rather, the ability to transfer value mirrors the way players sell cosmetic skins in *Fortnite* or rare swords in *Diablo*. The psychological effect is profound: travelers feel like stakeholders, not data points.

Travel's pain points such as, over-booking, ID checks, currency fees, map neatly onto game mechanics:

1. Over-booking becomes an inventory-management minigame. Each booking NFT carries a unique hash; once the supply for a given date is exhausted, no contract can mint more. Secondary trade is visible on-chain, allowing guests to resell or gift stays with zero risk of counterfeit vouchers.
2. Identity verification shifts to zero-knowledge proofs issued by "Known Traveller" wallets. Check-in kiosks read a cryptographic attestation, not a printed passport, shaving queues while preserving privacy, analogous to servers validating a gamer's license key without storing personal data.
3. Payments move through stable-coin rails that settle instantly and cost pennies. A Portuguese hostel owner receiving deposit tokens can swap them for local fiat or stake them in a community pool that funds area clean-ups, creating a virtuous feedback loop advertised in the lobby leaderboard.

The future of travel will be written in code, smart contracts, AI agents, and immersive simulations that turn every journey into a game. As the boundaries between digital and physical continue to blur, the travel experience is undergoing a fundamental transformation, one where the logic of gaming, progression, discovery, and rewards is becoming the new framework for hospitality and mobility.

With procedural heritage layers generated by AI, visitors can explore history as time-traveling role-players. These immersive reconstructions turn city breaks into living role-playing games, where each corner reveals quests, relics, and interactions with the past.

There will be a new kind of travel companion: the contextual NPC. These large language model-driven guides speak in the local dialect, recall returning visitors, and adapt their tone and challenge level based on user preferences. They can suggest hidden cafés, decode cultural rituals, or even lead scavenger hunts through digital twins of the city, always evolving, always personal.

Gamification also extends to real-world incentives. In the Metaverse, completing a sustainability quest, like navigating a digital carbon-neutral itinerary, could earn you a real-world benefit, such as an expedited visa or eco-travel voucher. "Skill-to-earn" mechanisms blend education with adventure, turning digital learning into tangible travel perks. Want to brush up on Italian? Complete the "language questline" and unlock a discount on your Rome-bound flight.

Even physical sensations are being integrated. Wearable haptics deliver subtle cues: a soft sleeve vibration lets you know your room-service order is on the way in VR, or a breeze emulator syncs to the live climate of your resort destination, deepening your connection between the virtual and the real. These sensory overlays bring the digital experience closer to the physical journey, enhancing immersion without replacing reality.

Ultimately, travel has always been about storytelling. The Metaverse doesn't change this; it magnifies it. Each traveler becomes a protagonist in a shared, persistent campaign. Hoteliers, airlines, backpackers, and baristas alike become co-creators, layering experiences, quests, tradable collectables, and loyalty tokens into the journey. These mechanics don't just serve to entertain, they foster community, deepen engagement, and respect the traveler's agency.

The real winners in this new frontier will be those who think like game designers: carefully balancing challenge and reward, crafting social connections, and offering meaningful choices. Done right, gaming mechanics won't replace the thrill of stepping onto foreign soil, they'll amplify it. They'll guide travelers from digital anticipation to physical immersion, and back again, level after level, journey after journey. In the gamified Metaverse of travel, every trip becomes a dynamic narrative, every touchpoint a potential quest, and every traveler a hero on an unforgettable path.

Gamification and the Future of Mobility

As the Metaverse begins to intertwine with real-world mobility, gamification is emerging as a key driver of transformation in the automotive and travel industries. What was once limited to entertainment or consumer engagement is now evolving into a full-fledged layer of immersive interaction that redefines how people experience transportation, from virtual test drives and in-car gaming to collaborative vehicle design and digital car ownership. This fusion of gaming, AI, XR, Web3, and automotive innovation is giving rise to a new frontier: Mobility-as-Experience.

Travel and automotive brands are importing live-service game design into loyalty, sales, and in-ride entertainment. Audi's Holoride synchronizes VR game motion with vehicle telemetry (Audi AG 2022). Skoda's Skodaverse and Acura's Decentraland showroom let guests test-drive or customize cars virtually (Škoda Auto 2023; Honda Motor Co. 2022). McKinsey projects in-car infotainment could yield USD 30–60 billion in annual value by 2030 (McKinsey and Company 2021). Digital-twin factories and design sandboxes—e.g., Ford x Gravity Sketch and BMW x Nvidia Omniverse—gamify engineering collaboration, cutting time-to-market by up to 50% (Ford Motor Co. 2021; Nvidia Corp. 2022).

The Gamified Showroom

Automotive brands are leveraging the immersive potential of gamification to reinvent customer engagement. Showrooms in the Metaverse offer more than just static displays—they are interactive environments where consumers can walk through digital twins of cars, customize features in real time, engage in virtual races, and use avatars as guides or virtual salespeople.

Acura and Skoda have pioneered this concept in Decentraland, allowing users to test-drive new models in game-like environments. Porsche and BMW are exploring the use of virtual brand ambassadors and gamified launch events to appeal to younger, digital-native audiences.

Gamification here serves multiple purposes: it educates, entertains, and informs potential buyers while generating brand loyalty and data insights. Just as gamers are drawn to achievements, unlockable content, and collectable assets, consumers now seek similar experiences in mobility. This is car buying reimagined as an immersive game, with NFTs, exclusive digital assets, and even virtual accessories linked to real-world purchases.

Driving Entertainment: The Car as a Game Console

In the future of mobility, the car itself becomes a gaming platform. Audi's Holoride project transforms in-car experiences into hyper-immersive adventures, synchronizing game motion with real-time vehicle movement. When the car accelerates, virtual objects rush toward the player; when it brakes, the game slows. This kind of sensory integration transforms mundane commutes into interactive entertainment, effectively turning every ride into a game.

Other automakers are experimenting with head-up displays and AR overlays. Mercedes-Benz, for instance, integrates traffic and navigation data with gaming-style dashboards. Holographic projections can show not only directions but also contextual information—like restaurant deals or nearby events—while offering interactive AR games for passengers. McKinsey estimates that in-car infotainment could generate $30–$60 billion in value by 2030.

These developments not only increase the appeal of travel but also unlock entirely new use cases. Autonomous vehicles can become moving classrooms, remote offices, or entertainment hubs. Children could engage with educational VR games during school commutes, while adults attend virtual meetings or play co-op games on immersive screens.

Gamification of Product Development

Gamification is not just for consumers—it's also transforming how cars are made. Companies like Ford and BMW use gamified design environments with digital twins and 3D collaborative modeling. Using tools like Gravity Sketch, developers, and designers explore new models, simulate road conditions, and test vehicle interiors in virtual sandboxes.

Designers now "play" with prototypes before physical models exist. They can simulate driving on a desert road or test acoustics in a virtual wind tunnel. Hyundai and Nvidia's DRIVE Sim platform even gamifies vehicle testing, allowing engineers to evaluate perception systems and decision-making under diverse virtual scenarios—from dense city traffic to unpredictable weather patterns.

These virtual environments reduce time-to-market by up to 50% and cut development costs dramatically. These are key benefits as automotive companies face increasing consumer demands for speed, sustainability, and personalization.

Repair and Maintenance with XR

Gamification is also redefining vehicle service and training. Daimler Trucks and BMW are piloting augmented reality (AR) programs to train technicians using virtual overlays, allowing them to learn step-by-step repairs without needing a physical vehicle. XR devices offer in-context guidance, speeding up learning curves and reducing error rates.

This approach extends to customers, too. If a vehicle encounters a minor issue, a technician avatar could walk the user through repairs at home using AR. For complex problems, the same system can direct the user to service centers. These tools increase transparency, reduce maintenance costs, and gamify diagnostics and user empowerment.

Community, Loyalty, and the Token Economy

Web3 mechanics are being integrated to gamify brand loyalty and ownership. Metaverse-enabled experiences are tied to NFTs and community tokens that offer access to gated content, like virtual car rallies, limited-edition accessories, and even decision-making power in vehicle development (via DAOs). The gamified community experience allows car brands to reward engagement, foster exclusivity, and monetize IP in entirely new ways. For instance, BMW's Metaverse launch of the iX1 in Milan allowed users to attend as avatars, interact with the model, collect exclusive NFTs, and engage in digital community activities. Mercedes collaborated with crypto-artists to create NFT tributes to their G-Class, blending car culture with digital collectables. In this emerging model, consumers aren't just buyers, they're players, creators, and stakeholders in branded ecosystems.

Gaming Meets Mobility in the Metaverse

Gaming is no longer confined to leisure, it is evolving into the interaction layer for everything from education to mobility. As the world transitions to autonomous vehicles, digital twins, and smart cities, gaming principles will be increasingly embedded into everyday experiences. The car becomes a game controller, allowing users to engage with their environment; a digital wallet, enabling seamless payment and data sharing via blockchain; a training tool, educating users and technicians through gamified simulations; and a social platform, where avatars connect in branded or user-created worlds. This convergence of gaming and mobility will define how Gen Z and Gen Alpha perceive car ownership, not as a possession, but as an experience. Loyalty, identity, and even social status will be gamified across both digital and physical realms.

The future of gaming is not just on a screen, it's on wheels. As mobility becomes immersive, interactive, and intelligent, gamification is the connective tissue tying together entertainment, commerce, design, and user experience. In this world, driving isn't just about getting from point A to point B, it's about unlocking levels, earning rewards, and participating in a broader digital universe.

Mobility, reimagined as play, has the potential to make transportation more enjoyable, accessible, and meaningful. For automakers, game developers, and digital architects alike, the opportunity is clear: build worlds where users don't just consume mobility—they live, learn, play, and grow through it.

A Playbook for Social Impact

Research indicates that gamification, when grounded in sound behavioral science and ethical design, can significantly improve engagement, knowledge retention, and health outcomes (Sardi et al. 2017). As AI, biofeedback, and extended-reality platforms mature, next-generation systems will offer increasingly personalized, adaptive, and equitable experiences, turning play into a potent force for lifelong development and social good.

Gamification is more than a trend; it is a foundational tool for human-centered design. Its strength lies in its ability to convert passive consumption into active engagement. As AI, biofeedback, and immersive platforms continue to evolve, the future of gamification will be increasingly adaptive, ethical, and personalized.

Cross-Cultural Applications of Gamification

Gamification is not a universally transferable solution; its design and efficacy are shaped significantly by cultural, economic, and social contexts. For instance, in South Korea, a highly digitized and competitive educational culture has fostered early adoption of gamified learning systems that emphasize mastery, competition, and status. Platforms like *Classting* and government-supported smart education initiatives integrate leaderboards, achievement badges, and AI tutors to boost student engagement and performance, often in high-pressure exam-oriented environments (Lee and Kim 2021). In contrast, Brazil has adopted gamification in education with a focus on inclusion, engagement, and addressing systemic learning gaps. Projects such as *Game Educação* use playful, low-cost mobile games to increase literacy and numeracy in underserved communities, often avoiding competitive elements in favor of cooperative and narrative-based learning.

In the health sector, cultural attitudes toward technology and wellness also shape gamification design. In South Korea, digital health is widely embraced, and gamified fitness and wellness apps—such as *WalkOn* or *S Health*—capitalize on social competition and real-time feedback, aligning with collectivist and technologically fluent demographics (Kwon et al. 2015). Conversely, Brazil's health gamification efforts often emphasize public health campaigns, community participation, and language accessibility. For example, gamified apps developed by *Fiocruz* target chronic disease prevention and sexual health education through collaborative storytelling and contextual cues, reflecting local health priorities and resource limitations (Rocha et al. 2019).

These contrasts underscore the importance of localization in gamification design. Elements such as reward systems, interface language, narrative framing, and social mechanics must be tailored to local preferences, norms, and digital infrastructures. Without cultural adaptation, gamified systems risk low engagement or unintended consequences. As gamification expands globally, developers and policymakers must engage in culturally responsive co-design to ensure both relevance and equity.

Limitations and Constraints

Despite the growing promise of health, education, and consumer behavior, several limitations must be acknowledged. Ethically, the use of behavioral nudges and reward loops raises concerns about manipulation, over-surveillance, and consent—particularly when applied to vulnerable populations such as children or the elderly (Zuboff 2019). Regulatory frameworks have yet to fully catch up with the decentralized, cross-border nature of gamified platforms, leading to fragmented standards around data privacy, digital identity, and the monetization of user engagement (Gillespie 2018). Cultural contexts also play a significant role in how gamification is received; mechanics that work in one region may clash with social norms or digital literacies elsewhere. Technically, barriers such as uneven internet access, limited device availability, and insufficient digital infrastructure can exacerbate existing inequalities, especially in low-resource settings (UNESCO 2022). Addressing these constraints requires not only adaptive design and inclusive regulation but also interdisciplinary collaboration to ensure gamification enhances, rather than undermines, social equity and user well-being.

Conclusion

As this chapter has demonstrated, gamification is no longer a peripheral strategy, it is a transformative force reshaping how individuals learn, heal, and engage with the world. From digital therapeutics and immersive education to tokenized wellness and age-inclusive Metaverse environments, the strategic application of game mechanics is enhancing motivation, personal agency, and measurable outcomes across life domains. However, the potential of gamification also comes with ethical imperatives: to design inclusively, protect privacy, avoid manipulation, and ensure equitable access across cultures and generations. As technologies like AI, XR, and blockchain converge, the next frontier of gamification will be adaptive, immersive, and deeply personalized. Ultimately, gamified systems—when grounded in sound behavioral science and guided by principles of ethics and inclusion, have the power to foster lifelong development, community resilience, and global well-being. The challenge ahead lies not in inventing new tools, but in deploying them responsibly to create systems of meaning, motivation, and care.

Cross-Chapter Insights

This chapter highlights gaming's impact on education and health through *Sea Hero Quest* and *Minecraft: Education Edition*. These themes resonate in *AI Dungeon* (Chap. 8), where generative storytelling promotes narrative learning, and in *Roblox* (Chap. 10), where young users develop game design and collaboration skills. Therapeutic potential also appears in *NexMind* (Chap. 9), which supports meditation and focus. These use cases affirm the emerging role of games in public health, cognitive training, and digital literacy—fields once far removed from entertainment.

Case Studies

Minecraft: Education Edition

Overview

Game/Platform Name: Minecraft: Education Edition
Developer/Publisher: Microsoft
Year Released: 2016
Genre: Sandbox gaming
Technology Stack: Bedrock Engine (C++), MakeCode (JS, Blockly), Python API (via WebSocket), Microsoft Azure, Classroom Mode (C#), World distribution via CDN

Minecraft was first released as an open-ended sandbox game. Over the years, it has evolved into a feature-rich platform, attracting immense communities and inspiring educational editions and spinoffs, such as Minecraft Dungeons and Minecraft Legends. Minecraft: Education Edition enables students worldwide to learn subjects such as math, science, history, and coding while exploring virtual worlds, conducting experiments, and solving problems in a creative environment.

Innovation

Minecraft: Education Edition is the first impactful and widely adopted game to tie gameplay to real-world curriculum standards.

The game enables teams of up to 30 students to collaborate on problem-solving in real time.

The game features ready-made worlds that cover topics in various subjects, from chemistry to history, allowing students to explore civilizations, ecosystems, or chemical reactions within a gaming environment.

Minecraft: Education Edition includes tools for coding, such as MakeCode and Tynker, which allow students to customize and automate tasks using JavaScript and Python.

The game gives teachers the power to regulate classroom activities by freezing students, setting spawn points, or rewarding them.

Impact

User Adoption and Demographics
Minecraft: Education Edition is used in more than 40 school systems across 115 countries worldwide.

The game has 15 million users globally.

In 2025, the platform added over 1.2 million students.

26 million hours of student playtime were logged in 2025 only.

Economic Value Generated
While the exact numbers of Minecraft: Education Edition's yearly earnings are not always separated from Minecraft's general statistics, it was reported that in 2018, the platform generated $175 million in revenue.

In 2025, the game was sold to 38 new institutions, resulting in the sale of 170,000 licenses.

Cultural/Social Influence
Minecraft: Education Edition influences education norms, pushing education toward game-based, student-centered learning.

The game empowers creativity in learning sciences and increases student motivation, engagement, and attendance, fostering a more enjoyable and accessible learning environment.

Additionally, the game promotes social cohesion by teaching students' collaboration habits.

Geographic Reach
Minecraft: Education Edition is popular worldwide, with the largest audiences in the United States, United Kingdom, and Canada, which collectively make up over 55% of Education Edition usage.

Challenges and Controversies

Simplified Science and Misconceptions
Some game features simplify complex scientific topics, which can lead to inadequate knowledge in students. Additionally, there are concerns that students, especially those of a younger age, will perceive elements as colored gaming blocks without a proper understanding of their atomic structure.

Commercialization of Education
As Microsoft Corporation develops the service, there is a risk that integrating Minecraft into study plans may present a risk of corporate influence in public education. Over-reliance on branded tools in the classroom can stimulate loyalty to the company producing them, working as a form of advertising.

Dependence on Gamified Environments
Students may become overly reliant on the gamified approach to learning, which provides immediate feedback and fast-paced tasks. This may negatively impact academic performance in subjects that are not well-suited for Minecraft or other games, which typically require traditional classroom settings. Additionally, dependence on gamified environments poses risks to learning abstract concepts that require complex problem-solving, which is difficult or impossible to translate into the gamified environment.

Sea Hero Quest—Gaming for Cognitive Science

Game/Platform Name: Sea Hero Quest
Developer/Publisher: Glitchers, in collaboration with Deutsche Telekom, University College London, and the University of East Anglia
Year Released: 2016
Genre: Mobile cognitive science game / Citizen science
Technology Stack: Unity, iOS/Android mobile platforms, cloud-based data collection and analytics

Sea Hero Quest is a mobile game designed to serve as both an entertainment platform and a large-scale neuroscience experiment. By guiding a boat through virtual waterways, players contribute anonymized data on spatial navigation—vital for understanding and diagnosing early signs of Alzheimer's disease. With over four million players globally, it has become one of the largest citizen science efforts in cognitive health.

Innovation

Gamified Data Collection: Gameplay is structured around navigation tasks that mirror lab-based cognitive tests
Massive Citizen Science: Enabled crowdsourced neuroscience data across diverse geographies, demographics, and age groups
Accelerated Research: What would take over 9000 years in lab conditions was collected in mere months
Diverse Cognitive Mapping: Provided a global dataset for understanding spatial ability variations tied to dementia risk

Impact

Over 4.3 million global players contributed to the study
Generated the equivalent of 15,000 years of lab data
Findings informed early Alzheimer's risk profiling based on spatial navigation
Contributed to refining diagnostic tools for early dementia detection
Strengthened cross-sector collaborations between telecoms, universities, and game developers

Challenges and Controversies

Data Privacy: Balancing anonymized user input with ethical standards in health research

Scientific Translation: Ensuring gameplay data correlates meaningfully with clinical findings

User Retention: Maintaining user engagement to ensure robust, long-session data

Lessons and Legacy

For Developers: Aligning game design with research aims enables impactful scientific contributions.

For Players: Citizen science through gaming can empower individuals to aid health research passively.

For Policymakers: *Sea Hero Quest* shows the value of regulatory clarity around digital health and data ethics in gameplay.

Future Outlook

Neurogaming Evolution: Future updates may integrate with wearables or VR for deeper analytics.

Diagnostic Tools: Builds precedent for mobile-first, data-rich medical assessments

Gamified Therapeutics: Opens new frontiers in behavioral diagnostics and therapeutic gaming

References

Akili Interactive. (2020). *EndeavorRx—The first FDA-approved treatment delivered through a video game* [White paper].

Audi AG. (2022). Holoride: Pioneering extended-reality in-car entertainment [Press release].

Carl, E., Stein, A. T., Levihn-Coon, A., Pogue, J. R., Rothbaum, B., Emmelkamp, P., & Powers, M. B. (2022). Virtual reality exposure therapy for anxiety and related disorders: A meta-analysis of randomized controlled trials. Journal of Anxiety Disorders, 84, 102453. https://doi.org/10.1016/j.janxdis.2021.102453

Carras, M. C., Kalbarczyk, A., Wells, K., Banks, J., Kowert, R., Gillespie, C., & Latkin, C. (2018). Connection, meaning, and distraction: The role of video game play in the lives of people with mental health challenges. JMIR Mental Health, 5(4), e16. https://doi.org/10.2196/mental.9530

Cipresso, P., Giglioli, I. A. C., Raya, M. A., and Riva, G. (2018). The past, present, and future of virtual and augmented reality research: A network and cluster analysis of the literature. *Frontiers in Psychology*, 9, 2086. https://doi.org/10.3389/fpsyg.2018.02086

Classcraft Studios. (2022). *Classcraft impact report: Gamifying classroom engagement.* https://www.classcraft.com

Czaja, S. J., Boot, W. R., Charness, N., Rogers, W. A., and Sharit, J. (2019). Improving social support for older adults through technology: Findings from the PRISM randomised controlled trial. *Gerontologist,* 59(1), 34–45.

Deterding, S., Dixon, D., Khaled, R., & Nacke, L. (2011). From game design elements to gamefulness: Defining "gamification." In Proceedings of the 15th International Academic MindTrek Conference (pp. 9–15). ACM.

Duolingo. (2023). *Duolingo press kit.* https://www.duolingo.com/press

Feng, Y., & Crowdhelia, E. (2019). The fitness benefits of competitive social challenges: An observational study of Fitbit data. Journal of Medical Internet Research, 21(3), e10954.

Findlay, G. (2022). Move-to-earn: A new model for health and gaming. Forbes Technology Council. https://www.forbes.com/sites/forbestechcouncil/2022/11/02/move-to-earn/

Ford Motor Company. (2021). *Designing the future: Ford and Gravity Sketch pilot immersive 3D design* [Media release].

Fortune Business Insights. (2023). *Metaverse in education market size, share and COVID-19 impact analysis.*

Freeman, D., Haselton, P., Freeman, J., Spanlang, B., Kishore, S., Albery, E., Denne, M., Brown, P., Slater, M., and Nickless, A. (2017). Automated psychological therapy using immersive virtual reality for treatment of fear of heights: A single-blind, parallel-group, randomised controlled trial. *The Lancet Psychiatry*, 5(8), 625–632. https://doi.org/10.1016/S2215-0366(18)30226-8

Futuro Health. (2023, November 1). *Futuro Health named as CalGrows Innovation Fund grantee* [Press release]. Futuro Health. aging.ca.gov+11futurohealth.org+11vdh.virginia.gov+11futurohealth.org+4futurohealth.org+4linkedin.com+4

Gerke, S., Stern, A. D., Minssen, T., & Cohen, I. G. (2020). Digital health and digital therapeutics: Ethical and regulatory challenges. The American Journal of Bioethics, 20(9), 10–23. https://doi.org/10.1080/15265161.2020.1793857

Gillespie, T. (2018). *Custodians of the Internet: Platforms, content moderation, and the hidden decisions that shape social media.* Yale University Press.

Hamari, J., Koivisto, J., & Sarsa, H. (2014). Does Gamification Work?—A Literature Review of Empirical Studies on Gamification. 2014 47th Hawaii International Conference on System Sciences, Waikoloa, HI, 6-9 January 2014, 3025–3034. https://doi.org/10.1109/HICSS.2014.377

Hoffman, H. G., Patterson, D. R., & Carrougher, G. J. (2011). Use of virtual reality for adjunctive treatment of adult burn pain during physical therapy: A controlled study. The Clinical Journal of Pain, 16(3), 244–250. https://doi.org/10.1097/00002508-200009000-00010

Honda Motor Company. (2022). Acura launches virtual showroom in Decentraland [Press release].

Kleinman, L., Shah, A., Shah, N., Phatak, H., Viswanathan, H., Fazel, S., Smith, J., Doll, H., & Shah, S. (2018). Improving medication adherence with a gamified mHealth app: Results from a pilot study. Patient Preference and Adherence, 12, 1767–1775.

Kwon, S., Kim, H., and Kim, J. (2015). The effects of a mobile health application on users' physical activity in South Korea. *Healthcare Informatics Research*, 21(2), 125–133. https://doi.org/10.4258/hir.2015.21.2.125

Lampit, A., Hallock, H., & Valenzuela, M. (2014). Computerized cognitive training in cognitively healthy older adults: A systematic review and meta-analysis of effect modifiers. PLOS Medicine, 11(11), e1001756. https://doi.org/10.1371/journal.pmed.1001756

Laver, K., George, S., Thomas, S., Deutsch, J. E., & Crotty, M. (2017). Virtual reality for stroke rehabilitation. Cochrane Database of Systematic Reviews, 2017(11), CD008349. https://doi.org/10.1002/14651858.CD008349.pub4

Laver, K., George, S., Thomas, S., Deutsch, J. E., and Crotty, M. (2020). Virtual reality for stroke rehabilitation. *Cochrane Database of Systematic Reviews, 2020*(11).

Lee, M. J., and Kim, M. (2021). Educational gamification and policy in South Korea: A case study of smart learning. *Educational Technology Research and Development*, 69, 293–312. https://doi.org/10.1007/s11423-021-09983-9

Mahncke, H., and Merzenich, M. (2016). BrainHQ: Evidence summary for cognitive training in older adults. *Posit Science White Paper*.

McKinsey & Company. (2021). Unlocking new value from in-car entertainment.

Michael, D., and Chen, S. (2006). *Serious games: Games that educate, train, and inform.* Thomson Course Technology.

Nvidia Corporation. (2022). *BMW Group and Nvidia bring Omniverse to life in digital-first factory of the future.* https://blogs.nvidia.com/blog/bmw-group-nvidia-omniverse/

Patterson, B., Marks, D., and Redrick, B. (2019). Gamification as a platform for mental health interventions: Review of the evidence. *JMIR Serious Games, 7*(2), e14720. https://doi.org/10.2196/14720

Prodigy Education. (2023). *Prodigy math game: Impact report.* https://www.prodigygame.com/main-en/blog/prodigy-math-game-impact-report/

Riva, G., Wiederhold, B. K., and Mantovani, F. (2021). Neuroscience of virtual reality: From virtual exposure to embodied medicine. *Cyberpsychology, Behavior, and Social Networking, 24*(1), 19–25. https://doi.org/10.1089/cyber.2020.29184.gri

Roblox Corporation. (2022). *Roblox education annual report.*

Rocha, T., Barreto, I. C., and Lima, D. L. (2019). Gamification and digital strategies for health promotion in Brazil: A systematic review. *Revista de Saúde Pública, 53*, 107. https://doi.org/10.11606/s1518-8787.2019053001282

Sardi, L., Idri, A., and Fernández-Alemán, J. L. (2017). A systematic review of gamification in e-health. *Journal of Biomedical Informatics, 71*, 31–48.

Škoda Auto. (2023). Škodaverse: Exploring automotive innovation in Web3 [Press release].

United Nations, Department of Economic and Social Affairs. (2022). *World population prospects 2022: Summary of results.*

Virginia Department of Health. (2024, September 20). *VDH awards more than $4.5 million to Earn to Learn program recipients.* vdh.virginia.gov+4vdh.virginia.gov+4schev.edu+4

Virginia Department of Health. (2025). *The Commonwealth's Earn to Learn Program.*

World Economic Forum. (2022). The future of health: Digital therapeutics and the Metaverse. https://www.weforum.org/agenda/2022/08/the-metaverse-and-healthcare-digital-therapeutics/

Zuboff, S. (2019). *The age of surveillance capitalism: The fight for a human future at the new frontier of power.* PublicAffairs.

Chapter 7
Gaming and Ethics: Safeguarding the Future of Digital Play

Abstract This chapter "Gaming and Ethics: Safeguarding the Future of Digital Play" explores the complex intersection of gaming, mental health, digital well-being, and ethical design. From the growing concern around internet gaming disorder to the positive use of games in therapy and emotional resilience, the mental health impact of gaming is multifaceted. Readers will examine how game mechanics, monetization strategies, and AI-driven systems can either support or exploit players. The chapter also addresses inclusivity, representation, and the social responsibilities of developers and platforms. As regulators begin to scrutinize the sector and parental concerns increase, ethical frameworks are becoming essential to ensure safe, equitable, and sustainable gaming ecosystems. With Environmental, Social, and Governance (ESG) principles entering the conversation, the industry stands at a crossroads—one that will define the future of responsible play. Gaming is increasingly social, with multiplayer experiences, Esports, and online communities playing a central role. While concerns about gaming addiction persist, research also highlights the positive effects of gaming, such as stress relief, cognitive development, and social connection. Solutions such as regulation and voluntary guidelines are explored. However, the success of such efforts will depend on the technical complexity of the systems as well as the ethical clarity of societies and regulators.

Keywords Artificial Intelligence · Adaptive gameplay · Procedural content generation · Intelligent NPCs · Generative AI · Reinforcement learning · Player personalization · Emotion-aware systems · AI narrative design · Ethical game design · Real-time game adaptation · AI agents · Voice synthesis · Co-creative storytelling · Metaverse infrastructure

Introduction

As gaming becomes a global cultural and economic force, it will confront a plethora of ethical challenges. This chapter explores the complex intersection of gaming, mental health, digital well-being, and ethical design. From mental health to algorithmic bias, loot boxes to inclusivity, gaming must now confront the social and moral implications of its design, distribution, and impact. As gaming cements its place as an influential medium that shapes identities, behaviors, and communities across the world, it is essential to engage in a conversation on ethics.

The same design techniques that make games captivating also introduce profound ethical dilemmas. Immersive worlds—whether on a phone, a console, or a head-mounted display—can automate exploitation at unprecedented speed and scale. Once a predatory mechanic or biased algorithm is hard coded into a game system, its effects can ripple out to billions of users in real time. In this chapter the question is: How to preserve gaming's benefits while preventing its hidden harms?

Modern game algorithms optimize relentlessly for attention, rewarding players with intermittent wins, loot boxes, or social validation loops that make "just one more round" hard to resist. For a small but significant minority, especially adolescents—this design can tip into addiction. The World Health Organization now recognizes internet gaming disorder; sufferers exhibit symptoms ranging from anxiety and depression to disrupted sleep and physical inactivity. The moral challenge is clear. When does persuasive design become predatory design?

Virtual-reality headsets promise richer learning and play, yet they also expose young users to unique cognitive and physical risks—eye strain, disorientation, even subtle shifts in neuroplasticity. Age verification tools lag far behind hardware sales, leaving children vulnerable to inappropriate content and predatory strangers. Policymakers face a balancing act: uphold a child's right to explore digital worlds while ensuring those spaces are age-appropriate, transparent, and safe.

Immersive platforms capture vast volumes of behavioral data, gaze patterns, pupil dilation, voice stress, even gait, and breathing rhythms. This can reveal intimate preferences and emotional states, yet meaningful consent is almost impossible when data capture is continuous and opaque. As connected devices multiply, each sensor becomes a potential breach point for identity theft, manipulation, or discrimination. The central ethical questions are stark: Who owns this data? How is it protected? And how can players exercise real agency over their digital selves?

As this chapter will show, ethics is needed to enable a rapidly accelerating industry to move forward safely. By embedding moral principles into code, policy, and culture, it is possible to ensure that gaming remains a force for creativity, community, and human flourishing and not a factory of addiction, exploitation, and surveillance.

Ethical Design

As parents and communities work to support children's mental health in the digital age, game developers and publishers must be held to account for the ethical design of their products. Too often, the mechanics of commercial games are engineered not for play or creativity, but for maximum engagement and monetization. This creates environments that exploit attention, encourage compulsive behavior, and make it difficult for vulnerable users, especially children, to disconnect.

Loot boxes (chance-based rewards similar to gambling), pay-to-win mechanics, where money buys competitive advantage, and dark patterns that trick users into more screen time or purchases are now widespread across free-to-play and even premium titles.

Such systems often blur the line between entertainment and exploitation. Children may not fully understand what they are consenting to, whether it's a microtransaction, a data collection pop-up, or a user agreement buried in fine print. This raises serious ethical questions about informed consent, manipulation, and digital autonomy.

Ethical gaming comprises: (i) transparency in game mechanics and monetization, (ii) age-appropriate design, including limits on in-game purchases and targeted ads, (iii) built-in well-being tools, such as screen time reminders or parental dashboards, (iv) data privacy by default, especially for minors, and (v) commitment to diversity and inclusion, both in character design and development teams.

Developers must move beyond "maximize engagement" toward an ethos of digital well-being. Game creators shape experiences that influence childhood development. With that influence comes responsibility. By adopting ethics-by-design, studios can innovate not only technologically but morally, creating games that are both successful and socially responsible.

Parents, regulators, and players all have a role to play in demanding this shift. Parenting in the digital age requires a mindset shift. Gaming is not an enemy to be eliminated, but a reality to be navigated. The goal isn't zero screen time, but meaningful screen time, where children are emotionally safe, socially connected, and mentally well. Digital games will be part of this generation's world. With guidance, structure, and empathy, gaming can be a powerful force for creativity, connection, and resilience. What matters most is not how often children play, but how consciously they engage.

Game Design Ethics: Mechanics, Monetization, and Manipulation

Modern game design often walks a fine line between engagement and exploitation. Monetization strategies such as loot boxes, gacha systems, and microtransactions have drawn comparisons to gambling, particularly where real money is exchanged for randomized rewards. These mechanisms tap into deep psychological triggers and can encourage compulsive spending, especially among children and vulnerable users.

Game mechanics also include so-called dark patterns: design elements that manipulate players into longer play sessions or unintended purchases. Reward schedules, fear-of-missing-out timers, and endless content loops are widely used in free-to-play games. Ethical design requires a conscious departure from these practices in favor of transparency, agency, and player well-being.

Online Toxicity, Harassment, and Moderation Challenges

The social side of gaming has amplified issues of harassment and toxicity. Online multiplayer environments often become breeding grounds for bullying, racism, misogyny, and homophobia. Despite efforts by platforms to implement moderation tools, many communities remain unsafe or unwelcoming for marginalized players. Game studios and publishers bear a growing responsibility to create respectful environments. Some are investing in AI moderation, player reputation systems, and community reporting tools. However, moderation remains a complex and resource-intensive challenge. Real progress requires combining technological solutions with cultural change, inclusive leadership, and community engagement.

Bias and Inclusion in AI and NPC Design

As AI is increasingly used to generate game content, from dialogue to behavior, concerns arise about bias and fairness. Non-playable characters (NPCs), if trained on biased datasets or designed without inclusive oversight, may reinforce stereotypes or exclude certain identities. This extends to gender roles, racial representation, and language patterns.

Ethical AI in gaming requires diverse development teams, inclusive training data, and continuous audit of generated content. Developers must take care not to encode discriminatory assumptions into seemingly neutral systems. Inclusivity should be a design principle, not an afterthought.

Equity, Access, and Inclusive Representation

Ethical gaming also involves who is represented and how. Historically, many games have excluded or misrepresented women, people of color, LGBTQ+ individuals, and people with disabilities. In response, a growing movement within the industry champions equity and inclusive design. This includes gender-diverse character options, accessibility features like subtitles and remappable controls, and storylines that reflect a range of human experiences. Equally important is diversity within game studios themselves. Inclusive development teams are better positioned to reflect the realities of diverse players.

ESG, Sustainability, and the Ethical Game Company

The ethical responsibilities of gaming companies are increasingly viewed through an ESG lens. Environmentally, industry must address energy consumption, especially from blockchain-based games and cloud computing. Socially, companies are being called to demonstrate inclusive hiring, safe community building, and cultural accountability. Governance involves transparency in data practices, fair labor conditions, and ethical monetization policies. Forward-looking studios are publishing ESG reports, engaging in sustainability initiatives, and embracing ethical leadership. As investors and consumers demand more responsibility, ESG frameworks offer a roadmap for the ethical evolution of gaming companies.

As the global gaming industry continues to scale—economically, technologically, and culturally—there is a growing need to align its evolution with principles of Environmental, Social, and Governance (ESG) responsibility. Ethical gaming goes beyond mechanics and monetization; it includes how games are produced, consumed, and regulated across the digital and physical worlds.

Environmental Responsibility in Gaming

While digital entertainment may seem like a low-impact, the industry's carbon footprint is significant, from energy-intensive data centers and always-on cloud gaming platforms to e-waste and physical product distribution. Sustainable gaming models are emerging, with strategies such as (i) shifting to all-digital releases and eliminating unnecessary packaging; (ii) optimizing cloud infrastructure for energy efficiency; (iii) sourcing eco-friendly merchandise and hardware components; and (iv) offering carbon offsetting for major events and Esports tournaments. Gaming companies increasingly recognize their role in supporting the broader sustainability agenda by reducing emissions, limiting waste, and investing in green innovation.

Social Impact and Inclusion

The social dimension of ESG in gaming is critical. Games have the power to shape narratives, build communities, and influence behavior, particularly among youth. Responsible gaming frameworks now prioritize: (i) mental health and screen time awareness; (ii) inclusive design for players of all ages, genders, and abilities; safe digital spaces, especially for children and vulnerable groups; and empowerment of underrepresented voices in development and leadership. Gaming is also being used as a tool for education, skills development, and economic opportunity, especially in emerging markets where mobile-first access can bridge digital divides.

Gaming, Mental Health, and Navigating a Digital Childhood

With over three billion gamers worldwide, digital play has become a central part of modern childhood. Games are no longer just fleeting pastimes or distractions—they are environments where young people learn, socialize, and shape their identities. But as gaming becomes increasingly immersive, accessible, and commercially engineered to drive engagement, parents face the challenge of balancing the benefits of gaming with its potential mental health risks? This section unpacks the relationship between gaming and mental health, highlights warning signs of problematic use, and offers parents evidence-based strategies to raise emotionally resilient, digitally literate children.

The Psychological Impact of Gaming

Contrary to outdated fears, gaming offers a range of psychological benefits. Studies show that moderate gaming can support cognitive development, boost problem-solving skills, and foster creativity. Cooperative multiplayer games strengthen teamwork, empathy, and social bonding, especially valuable in an increasingly virtual world. Games also provide emotional regulation by offering a sense of mastery, achievement, and escapism for children navigating stress, anxiety, or social challenges.

However, not all gaming is beneficial. Games designed with reward loops, variable reinforcement, and real-money microtransactions can foster compulsive behavior, especially in young, developing brains. The World Health Organization now recognizes Internet Gaming Disorder (IGD) as a mental health condition. Though only a minority of players are affected, those who can experience depression, anxiety, social withdrawal, and sleep disruption.

High-risk users often fall into patterns of avoidance: they game to escape real-world problems but become increasingly disconnected from real-life responsibilities and relationships. Left unchecked, this can create a cycle of low self-esteem, dependency, and deteriorating mental health.

Importantly, these signs must be understood in context. A child playing for several hours on weekends may be perfectly healthy, especially if they remain socially and academically engaged. What matters most is functionality—whether gaming interferes with other domains of a child's life.

Gaming is a cultural force that needs systemic support, not just family-level rules. Schools can incorporate digital literacy and wellness curricula, teaching students how to recognize manipulative game design, manage screen time, and use games for learning and creativity. Public health campaigns can normalize help-seeking and reduce the stigma around gaming disorders.

Governments and platforms also share responsibility. Stronger age verification systems, restrictions on exploitative monetization (like loot boxes), and transparent algorithms would reduce harm, particularly to children. Regulation should focus on ethical design, user safety, and consent-based data practices.

Governance, Regulation, and the Metaverse

Regulators around the world are beginning to scrutinize the gaming industry. Governments in countries such as the UK, Belgium, and South Korea have introduced legislation targeting loot boxes, screen time, and data protection. Governance in gaming means more than compliance; it's about embedding ethics at every level of design and decision-making. This includes transparency in algorithms and monetization models; fair play standards and anti-toxicity measures; informed consent for data collection and usage; and inclusion of ESG metrics in reporting and executive accountability. By integrating ESG values into strategy, companies can future-proof their platforms and contribute to a healthier, more equitable digital society.

Monetization Ethics and Fair Play

Ethical concerns surround monetization strategies beyond addiction. Players and regulators are concerned about fairness. For example, "pay-to-win" mechanics (where spending money gives gameplay advantages) are widely criticized. It is likely that regulatory bodies like consumer protection agencies will step in for false advertising or unfair trade practices if a game marketed as competitive hides de facto required purchases.

Another aspect is gambling in gaming includes real-money betting on Esports or casino-style mini-games within games. Regulators will need to ensure that gambling elements are kept away from minors and that games with such content are properly rated and partitioned. Some jurisdictions might require any game that simulates gambling (even with virtual currency) to carry adult age ratings.

Cheating and hacking also fall under an ethical umbrella, affecting fair play. Game companies are employing increasingly sophisticated anti-cheat systems to ensure a fair environment. However, privacy concerns arise here, too. There have already been lawsuits and even arrests for selling cheats in some countries. In the future, cheating in games might be a criminal offence in certain contexts (especially if tied to Esports betting fraud or large-scale hacking operations).

Consumer rights in the digital age also mean regulators might push for more transparency in terms of game odds (for random drops), clearer pricing (no hidden costs), and easier dispute resolution (like refunding accidental purchases made by children, as enforced in the Epic case). The industry is learning to proactively address these issues: for example, major platforms now often require password re-entry for purchases to prevent accidental buys by kids, and some have implemented spending caps or warnings for young users.

In conclusion, the next decade will see a solidification of the legal and ethical framework around gaming. There will likely be a set of best practices (some voluntary, some legally mandated) covering data privacy, community moderation, fair monetization, and health impacts. Gaming companies that adapt and lead in these areas (ensuring player well-being and trust) will build better reputations and long-term customer loyalty, whereas those that resist may face litigation, fines, or backlash from increasingly aware consumers. By 2035, a mature global gaming industry will be one where enjoyment and profit are balanced with ethical responsibility and compliance with worldwide norms and laws.

Regulatory Responses to Ethical and Legal Challenges in Gaming

As the gaming industry matures into a global digital ecosystem, regulatory frameworks are evolving to address a broad spectrum of ethical and legal challenges. These include data privacy, toxicity and moderation, gaming addiction, gambling mechanics, microtransactions, and consumer rights. A comparative overview of international responses reveals increasing alignment toward transparency, child protection, and fair design.

Data Privacy

The European Union's General Data Protection Regulation (GDPR), implemented in 2018, marked a significant shift toward stringent data governance in gaming. It mandates explicit user consent, limits on data use, and transparency in data handling practices. In the United States, the Federal Trade Commission (2022a) has similarly escalated enforcement actions. Notably, Epic Games was fined $520 million in 2022 for violating children's privacy protections under the Children's Online Privacy Protection Act (COPPA), including the use of "dark patterns" to manipulate purchases (NPR 2022). By 2030, a global convergence around robust privacy standards, mandatory age verification, and penalties for manipulative interface designs are anticipated.

Toxicity and Moderation

The issue of online toxicity—encompassing hate speech, bullying, and harassment—has prompted the deployment of AI-driven moderation technologies. Concurrently, Riot Games and Ubisoft launched the "Zero Harm in Comms" initiative to develop AI systems capable of detecting nuanced and contextual abuse (Hamilton 2022). Future regulation may enforce rapid content removal obligations under platform accountability laws, with an increasing focus on enhanced parental controls and community-based codes of conduct.

Gaming Addiction

Gaming addiction gained formal recognition as a clinical condition when the World Health Organization (WHO) included "Gaming Disorder" in its International Classification of Diseases (ICD-11) in 2019. Several nations have responded with restrictive policies. China, for instance, implemented a curfew in 2021 limiting minors to 3 h of online gaming per week (Pearson 2021a). South Korea's "shutdown law," effective from 2011 to 2021, prohibited minors under 16 from gaming between midnight and 6 a.m. (Engadget 2021). Looking ahead, countries are expected to adopt educational interventions, optional usage limits, and design standards that discourage compulsive play patterns.

Loot Boxes and Gambling

Loot boxes, a controversial monetization mechanic offering randomized rewards, have come under increased regulatory scrutiny. Belgium declared paid loot boxes a form of illegal gambling in 2018, leading to a de facto ban (Greo 2022). Other jurisdictions have introduced mandatory disclosure of odds or age-based access restrictions. The industry has responded by labeling games with "Includes Random Items" through self-regulatory bodies such as ESRB and PEGI. By 2035, regulatory landscapes will likely feature a combination of outright bans, adult-only ratings for gambling-like mechanics, and enhanced oversight for games involving real-money transactions.

Microtransactions and Downloadable Content (DLC)

Growing concern over exploitative monetization practices has prompted calls for greater transparency in microtransactions and downloadable content. Several countries are exploring laws requiring clear disclosure of item odds and pricing. Legal actions against misleading in-game advertising are on the rise, as consumer protection bodies respond to deceptive monetization schemes. In response, many developers are moving toward fairer models—eschewing "pay-to-win" dynamics—in favor of cosmetic-only or skill-neutral purchases.

Consumer Rights

The question of digital ownership has emerged as a central consumer rights issue. The European Union is exploring the legal right to resell digital games and enforce stronger refund protections. Some digital platforms, such as Steam, already offer no-questions-asked refunds for games played under 2 h. By 2030, a more harmonized global approach to consumer rights in gaming is expected, including clearer definitions of ownership, refundability, and the legal status of virtual goods.

Data Privacy and Consumer Protection

The exponential growth of the gaming industry has intensified scrutiny over data privacy and consumer protection practices. Contemporary video games increasingly collect extensive personal and behavioral data, including user interactions, purchasing behavior, and location tracking. As a result, global regulatory frameworks are evolving to enhance transparency and user control. The European Union's General Data Protection Regulation (GDPR), implemented in 2018, and the United States' Children's Online Privacy Protection Act (COPPA) (Federal Trade Commission (2025) exemplify legislative efforts to safeguard minors and enforce informed consent.

Notably, Epic Games faced a record $520 million settlement in 2022 for breaching COPPA and deploying manipulative interface designs (FTC 2022a; NPR 2022). This case signaled a growing intolerance for unethical data practices. Looking forward, legal regimes are expected to enforce robust age verification, opt-out mechanisms for targeted advertising, and clear consent pathways for biometric and behavioral data (FTC 2022b). In-game assets, increasingly perceived as investments, are prompting debates around digital ownership, resale rights, and consumer entitlement to refunds.

By 2035, privacy-by-design is anticipated to become a core requirement in game development, ensuring that security, data minimization, and transparency are embedded throughout the product lifecycle.

Moderation and Harassment

Toxic behavior in multiplayer gaming environments, including harassment, hate speech, and bullying, remains a persistent issue. Game developers are investing in AI-driven moderation systems to address this challenge.

Companies like Riot Games and Ubisoft have launched the "Zero Harm in Comms" initiative to research and implement AI moderation attuned to the complexities of gamer language (Hamilton 2022). However, concerns persist regarding the risks of false positives, algorithmic bias, and surveillance-related privacy intrusions. Legislative frameworks such as the EU's Digital Services Act (DSA) (2024) are increasingly mandating game platforms to ensure the swift removal of illegal content, mirroring expectations placed on social media platforms.

By 2035, industry norms may require transparent moderation systems, behavior reporting tools, and age-sensitive communication settings. Moderation quality may also influence content ratings, reinforcing its importance to platform accountability and user trust.

Gaming Addiction and Play Time Regulation

The addictive potential of video games has prompted regulatory responses worldwide. In 2019, the World Health Organization officially recognized "gaming disorder" as a behavioral health condition characterized by impaired control over gaming and prioritization of gaming over daily activities. This acknowledgment catalyzed policy interventions, particularly in Asia. In 2021, China imposed a three-hour weekly gaming limit for minors and mandated real-name verification systems (Pearson 2021). South Korea previously enforced a nightly "shutdown law" but later transitioned to flexible parental control systems (Engadget 2021).

To support healthier gaming habits, developers are incorporating wellness features such as screen time trackers, cooldown reminders, and parental dashboards. Ethical concerns also surround game mechanics that leverage psychological triggers, such as daily login rewards and fear-of-missing-out loops. These designs are increasingly under scrutiny for fostering compulsive use, particularly among vulnerable populations.

Loot boxes remain a particularly contentious issue. Often likened to gambling due to their randomized rewards, loot boxes have been banned or restricted in several jurisdictions. Belgium, for example, classified them as illegal gambling in 2018, though enforcement remains inconsistent (Greo 2022). By 2035, a global patchwork of policies is expected, ranging from outright bans to mandated disclosures of reward probabilities and age restrictions. In response, developers are shifting toward alternative monetization models perceived as more transparent and less exploitative.

How to Approach Ethics in Gaming

As the gaming ecosystem expands into the Metaverse, blockchain-based economies, and AI-driven storytelling, the need for ethical foresight becomes urgent. Developers, publishers, policymakers, and communities must work together to ensure that innovation serves the public good. A responsible gaming future is not only possible, but also essential.

Several principles can guide ethical game development: (i) Autonomy: respecting player agency and informed choice, (ii) fairness: ensuring equal access and opportunity, (iii) transparency: disclosing monetization models and data use, (iv) accountability: responding to harm and enabling redress.

Industry efforts include the creation of codes of conduct, third-party certifications, and cross-industry collaboration on ethical standards. A "Player Bill of Rights" could include protections against manipulation, abuse, and data misuse, along with rights to inclusive representation and fair treatment.

Solving these dilemmas demands a multi-layered response: (i) Industry design codes that favor inclusive mechanics over "pay-to-win" monetization. (ii) Regulatory frameworks that bring gaming, VR, and Metaverse platforms under child protection, privacy, and consumer-safety statutes. (iii) Transparency mandates algorithms that shape in-game economies, matchmaking, and content feeds, and (iv) digital literacy programs that equip parents, teachers, and young players to recognize manipulation and manage screen time responsibly.

Who Sets the Rules?

Traditional MMOs were sovereign kingdoms: if Blizzard banned a *World of Warcraft* account, appeal options were limited. In a federated Metaverse, multiple governance models will coexist corporate platforms, community DAOs, and national-level sandboxes (e.g., Seoul's municipal Metaverse). Ethical pluralism must therefore address:

- *Jurisdiction*—Does harassment in a US-run shard fall under Californian law if both avatars originate in Kenya?
- *Due-process rights* for bans, asset seizures or algorithmic demotion.
- *Stakeholder representation*—Token-weighted voting risks plutocracy; one-player-one-vote is Sybil-prone. Hybrid schemes may allocate council seats to developers, players, civil-society experts and child-advocacy NGOs.

Designers should bake constitutional layers—revocable smart contract modules that define rights, duties, and amendment pathways—directly into the protocol.

Leading studios and event organizers are beginning to fold Metaverse ethics into broader ESG dashboards, such as environmental, emissions intensity per play-hour; social, diversity metrics within dev teams, accessibility compliance, mental health resource uptake. Voluntary standards could certify virtual worlds that meet thresholds for inclusivity, data minimization, and carbon neutrality, allowing parents, investors, and advertisers to choose responsibly.

Ethics-By-Design Checklist for Developers

Stakeholder mapping: Includes children, marginalized groups, and disability advocates in pre-production workshops.

- *Threat modeling*: Imagine worst-case abuse and design countermeasures *before* launch.
- *Privacy impact assessment*: Document each data field, retention period, and sharing pathway; obtain a third-party audit.
- *Dynamic welfare metrics*: Track not only daily active users but also healthy-session ratios, reporting friction, and consent revocations.
- *Red-team simulations*: Hire ethical hackers and social engineers to stress-test moderation, smart contracts, and supply chains.

Just as medical researchers follow the Belmont Principles and software engineers, the ACM Code of Ethics, the gaming industry needs a *Metaverse Ethics Charter* grounded in five pillars:

- *Human dignity*: Avatars deserve respect; design must prevent dehumanization.
- *Autonomy and Consent*: Players control data, identity and time investment.
- *Fairness and Inclusion:* No exploitative monetization; accessible by design.
- *Transparency and Accountability*: Clear rules, explainable algorithms, appeal routes.
- *Planetary stewardship:* Commitment to climate-aligned operations.

The lesson from two decades of social media is clear: governance, safety, and equity cannot be retrofitted. They must be coded at genesis. Game makers, once artisans of fun, are now custodians of digital civilization. The controllers are in our hands; the outcome is still to be played.

Ethics in the Metaverse—The Next Frontier for Gaming

Games are expanding into a persistent, 3D internet, the Metaverse, built on game engines, social platforms, virtual-reality hardware, and blockchain economies. For the first time, the technical substrate of gaming will carry not only stories and quests, but also real identities, labor, property rights, and political speech. Decisions coded today—about data, monetization, moderation, or governance—can be replicated at machine speed to reach billions tomorrow. That shift turns questions that once belonged to philosophy seminars into pressing design requirements. Ethics is no longer a layer of public relations; it is infrastructural.

Identity, Avatars, and Moral Agency

In legacy multiplayer titles, an avatar was a throw-away skin; in the Metaverse, it is a portable, biometric signature of the self. Motion-capture rigs, head-mounted displays, and voice chat capture millions of data points—gait, gaze, respiration, micro-expressions—that can uniquely identify a player. That same dataset can reveal a person's age, mood, and even medical condition. Avatars, therefore, raise two overlapping ethical puzzles.

- *Authenticity and ownership*—Who controls the avatar's data profile? Web3 enthusiasts promise self-sovereign identity embedded in player-controlled wallets, yet most large platforms still gate avatars behind proprietary databases. If a player is locked out, does her digital "person" cease to exist?
- *Moral accountability*—When an avatar commits sexual harassment or incites hate inside a virtual lobby, who is liable: the account holder, the publisher, or the AI moderation stack that failed to intervene? Current jurisprudence treats such incidents as "user-generated content," but embodied VR makes the experience indistinguishable from a real-world assault for the victim.

Game studios must therefore treat identity as sensitive infrastructure: employ zero-knowledge proofs for age verification; store the minimum viable biometric footprint; offer revocable consent dashboards; and design escalation pathways that respect both due-process and survivor protection.

Data Ethics: Surveillance at Scale

Twenty minutes in a VR headset produces roughly two million telemetry records. Unlike cookies in Web 2.0, these data are continuous, involuntary and deeply intimate. They can be recombined into what legal scholar Brittan Heller calls *biometric psychography* (2020) a map of subconscious preference and vulnerability. Left unregulated, these streams invite abusive advertising, political manipulation and predatory pricing. Ethical stewardship therefore demands: (i) data minimalism, collect only what is mission-critical for gameplay; disallow "function creep" into targeted ads; (ii) differential privacy for aggregated analytics; right-to-be-forgotten hooks that let players delete or port their avatar histories across worlds; and real-time transparency dashboards that show, in plain language, how data fuel recommendations or dynamic pricing.

Monetization and Economic Justice

Web3 game economies promise "play-to-earn," interoperable NFTs and decentralized autonomous organizations (DAOs) that share revenue with players. But tokenization also introduces casino-like mechanics into children's sandboxes. Ethical red flags include: (i) loot boxes and gacha—chance-based purchases resembling gambling; (ii) pay-to-win upgrades that convert socio-economic inequality into in-game power; and (iii) speculative asset bubbles where influencers dump worthless tokens on naïve fans. Responsible design requires transparent odds disclosures, spending caps for minors, and ring-fenced tutorial zones where fiat or crypto purchases are disabled. DAOs should publish open ledgers of treasury flows and adopt conflict-of-interest rules mirroring traditional co-op governance. Where revenue sharing is touted, studios must also disclose downside risk: volatile token prices, gas fees, and smart contract exploits.

Mental Health and Well-being

The Metaverse inherits both the benefits and pathologies of gaming, but at higher fidelity. On the positive side, immersive play can teach collaboration, build resilience and provide safe rehearsal spaces for identity exploration. On the negative side, variable-reward loops, endless progression tracks, and competitive social comparison can drive compulsive use. WHO's recognition of internet gaming disorder underscores the need for preventative guardrails, including session-time nudges (e.g., color desaturation after 90 min); opt-in cooldowns that temporarily lock reward accrual; mindfulness modes that surface breathing exercises inside loading screens and integrated crisis-support links for players exhibiting at-risk behavior (detected, for instance, through prolonged late-night sessions combined with negative chat sentiment). Parental dashboards must translate these signals into plain language insights—sleep debt, expenditure, social network health—so families can co-create balanced media plans.

Child Safety and Content Moderation

Fully spatial, voice-driven worlds multiply existing moderation challenges: AI must parse nuance in dozens of languages, detect non-verbal harassment (e.g., an avatar cornering another), and respond in milliseconds. Suggested safeguards include: (i) Safe-circle bubbles—a tap enabling personal space force-fields; (ii) voice-to-text transcripts stored ephemerally for rapid review of abuse claims; (iii) human-in-the-loop escalation paths that empower trained moderators to override flawed automation; and (iv) granular age gates backed by privacy-respecting verification (e.g., cryptographic attestations from guardians rather than facial scans). Studios should publish quarterly enforcement transparency reports to build accountability.

The Metaverse will become the game board on which much human interaction unfolds. This raises the ethical stakes from personal hobby to societal infrastructure. Based on current trajectories, the next decade could yield inclusive worlds that enhance creativity, mental resilience, and global cooperation. However, there is an ever-present risk of building extractive digital worlds that monitor, manipulate, and monetize all aspects of human existence.

Conclusion

The rapid convergence of game engines, social networks, extended-reality hardware, blockchain economies, and AI are turning entertainment spaces into full-fledged social infrastructures. Immersive games, whether experienced on a mobile screen or in a head-mounted display, now mediate friendships, education, commerce, and even civic life. As this book has illustrated, an ethical approach to these environments cannot be an afterthought bolted onto a finished product; it must be embedded from the first line of code to final content moderation policy.

At a global level, leading technology and policy bodies already recognize that digital ethics is inseparable from Environmental, Social, and Governance (ESG) goals. Data-center energy use, labor conditions in game production, and the fairness of algorithmic matchmaking all sit on the same continuum of social responsibility. For gaming companies, ESG is not a reporting chore; it is the operational expression of values that keep virtual economies healthy and player communities safe.

Yet voluntary corporate pledges are not enough. Just as financial markets operate under a shared grammar of accounting rules, the interactive-media ecosystem now needs a Universal Code of Digital Ethics—a living charter that can be localized but never ignored.

Such a code would articulate baseline duties for every stakeholder in a game or Metaverse experience:

Developers commit to "ethics-by-design," publishing impact assessments on data privacy, loot-box mechanics, and carbon footprints before launch. Publishers and platform holders implement transparent due-process mechanisms so that bans, de-monetization, and content removals are appealable, auditable, and free from hidden bias. Regulators harmonize child safety, accessibility, and consumer protection standards across borders, recognizing that avatars do not respect jurisdictional boundaries. Investors include safety KPIs—such as healthy-session ratios, diversity scores, and carbon intensity—term sheets, and executive-compensation packages. Players and civil-society groups gain standing in governance councils, DAO treasuries, and standards bodies, ensuring that marginalized voices inform policy from the outset.

To operationalize this code, the industry should pursue an implementation toolkit that mirrors best practice in other critical domains. Think of ISO 20121 for sustainable events or the medical device industry's Good Clinical Practice guidelines—repurposed for virtual worlds. The toolkit would provide maturity models, red-team playbooks, audit rubrics, and disclosure templates that any studio, large or small, could adopt.

Finally, the community must nurture a translational ethos: converting academic insights about bias, addiction, and privacy into actionable checklists for designers and product managers. Interdisciplinary task forces that unite ethicists, engineers, lawyers, educators, and—crucially—young players themselves will be essential for testing assumptions against real-world use cases.

As the boundaries between physical and digital life continue to dissolve, the ethical dimensions of gaming are no longer theoretical, they are urgent, complex, and deeply human. The rise of the Metaverse has introduced new frontiers in moral reasoning, with avatars acting not only as digital extensions of self but also as agents within immersive social environments. With the ability to form relationships, express identity, and even commit acts of violence or harassment, avatars raise profound questions: Do they possess moral rights? Can they commit moral or legal wrongs? And where does accountability lie, on the code, the platform, or the person behind the screen?

In these virtual worlds, crimes once confined to imagination, harassment, defamation, sexual assault, and identity theft, are taking new forms. Moderating such behavior is no longer about deleting a comment; it's about policing fully embodied actions in persistent, shared realities. Questions arise of avatar impersonation, deepfake pornography, and algorithmic manipulation how to distinguish between an avatar and a human, and does that distinction matter?

These challenges cannot be addressed by regulators or platforms alone. Developers and designers are the architects of these worlds, and with that power comes ethical responsibility. It is no longer acceptable to treat harm as a glitch or edge case. Ethics must be embedded into the digital architecture itself. That means considering user safety, psychological impact, and consent at every stage of development. It means designing with foresight, not just functionality.

Could software developers be bound by professional ethical codes, much like doctors or engineers? Should communities demand transparency from platforms about how algorithms shape experiences and outcomes? As virtual economies and identities take root in daily life, these questions move from academic speculation to public necessity.

Ethical game development is not a constraint, it is a commitment to building virtual worlds that reflect our highest values, not our darkest impulses. It is a collective responsibility: developers, regulators, ethicists, parents, educators, and players themselves must collaborate to ensure that the online worlds are ones worth inhabiting. Because when three billion people log in, what happens in virtual spaces is not separate from society; it is society.

Cross-Chapter Insights

Ethical questions of data use, moderation, and well-being arise throughout the book. The mental health challenges seen on *Twitch and YouTube Gaming* (Chap. 4), the child safety concerns in *Roblox* (Chap. 10), and the neurodata privacy issues in *Neurable* and *NexMind* (Chap. 9) all intersect here. Games like *Sea Hero Quest* (Chap. 6) also raise ethical questions around health data in gameplay. This Chapter frames these case studies in a broader context of design responsibility, platform governance, and digital rights.

References

Brittan Heller, Watching Androids Dream of Electric Sheep: Immersive Technology, Biometric Psychography, and the Law, 23 *Vanderbilt Journal of Entertainment and Technology Law* 1 (2020) Available at: https://scholarship.law.vanderbilt.edu/jetlaw/vol23/iss1/1

Engadget. (2021). South Korea scraps gaming curfew law for young players. https://www.engadget.com/south-korea-scraps-gaming-curfew-080104837.html

EU (2024) Digital Services Act, https://commission.europa.eu/strategy-and-policy/priorities-2019-2024/europe-fit-digital-age/digital-services-act_en

Federal Trade Commission (2025) PART 312—CHILDREN'S ONLINE PRIVACY PROTECTION RULE (COPPA RULE), Authority:15 U.S.C. 6501 through 6506. Source:78 FR 4008, Jan. 17, 2013, as amended at 90 FR 16977, Apr. 22, 2025, unless otherwise noted.https://www.ftc.gov/legal-library/browse/rules/childrens-online-privacy-protection-rule-coppa

Federal Trade Commission [FTC]. (2022a). FTC finalizes record-breaking settlement with Epic Games over children's privacy violations. https://www.ftc.gov/news-events/news/press-releases/2022/12/ftc-finalizes-record-breaking-settlement-epic-games-over-childrens-privacy-violations

Federal Trade Commission [FTC]. (2022b). FTC action against Epic Games leads to $245 million refund for Fortnite consumers. https://www.ftc.gov/news-events/news/press-releases/2022/12/ftc-action-against-epic-games-leads-245-million-refund-fortnite-consumers

Greo. (2022). Loot boxes in Belgium: Persistence despite the law. *Gambling Research Exchange Ontario*. https://www.greo.ca/Modules/EvidenceCentre/Details/loot-boxes-in-belgium

Hamilton, K. (2022). Riot and Ubisoft team up for AI toxicity project. *The Verge*. https://www.theverge.com/2022/11/16/riot-ubisoft-ai-zero-harm-in-comms

NPR. (2022). Epic Games will pay $520 million for privacy violations and unwanted purchases. https://www.npr.org/2022/12/19/1143997273/epic-games-fortnite-ftc-fine

Pearson, J. (2021). China cuts gaming time for kids to one hour. *Reuters*. https://www.reuters.com/technology/china-tightens-gaming-curbs-minors-2021-08-30/

Chapter 8
AI and Adaptive Worlds

Abstract *"AI and Adaptive Worlds"* explores how AI will revolutionize game development and user experience through adaptive systems, procedural content generation, and intelligent non-player characters (NPCs). Readers will discover how AI-driven tools enable developers to create expansive, dynamic environments and storytelling that respond to each player's actions. From real-time personalization to emotion-aware characters and auto-generated quests, AI transforms static gameplay into living, evolving ecosystems. The chapter also examines using neural networks, reinforcement learning, and generative AI tools to streamline design, enhance player immersion, and reduce production costs. As AI continues to evolve, it promises to democratize game creation and unlock new forms of interactive entertainment that learn, adapt, and surprise.

Keywords Artificial intelligence in games · Adaptive gameplay · Procedural content generation · Intelligent NPCs · Reinforcement learning · Generative AI · Narrative design · Player personalization · Emotion-aware systems · AI ethics · Game economy automation · Decentralized gaming · AI-driven storytelling · Voice AI · Regulatory frameworks in gaming

Introduction

Artificial intelligence is no longer a background tool—it's the architect of new game worlds. This chapter explores how AI revolutionizes game development and user experience through adaptive systems, procedural content generation, and intelligent non-player characters (NPCs). Readers will discover how AI-driven tools enable developers to create expansive, dynamic environments and storytelling that respond to each player's actions. The chapter also examines the use of neural networks, reinforcement learning, and generative AI tools to streamline design, enhance player immersion, and reduce production costs. As AI continues to evolve, it promises to democratize game creation and unlock new forms of interactive entertainment that learn, adapt, and surprise. Handcrafted vs AI narratives are compared. The themes of adaptivity, automation, co-creation, and ethics are discussed. The relevance to the future of work and digital economies is covered in Chap. 10.

AI as the New Architect of Game Worlds

Artificial intelligence has shifted from a back-end tool to a front-line creative force in modern game design. AI now generates quests and builds dynamic worlds and personalized experiences in real time. It enables games to become responsive, fluid ecosystems where every player's journey can be unique. As AI capabilities expand—from machine learning to generative neural networks—developers are building intelligent systems that enhance immersion, reduce production costs, and redefine what a game can be.

Deep learning models are also transforming how games learn and evolve. In titles like Dota 2, OpenAI trained bots surpassed professional players using reinforcement learning. These bots observed, adapted, and refined strategies over millions of iterations.

Frameworks like Unity ML-Agents and TensorFlow allow developers to create game-specific agents that learn from players or simulate behaviors. AI opponents can now mimic player tendencies, making each session more personal and challenging. In future applications, these systems may serve as adaptive mentors, teaching players rather than defeating them.

As with all AI, bias and ethical design must be considered. AI-generated content may replicate stereotypes, exclude marginalized identities, or respond inappropriately if trained on flawed data. Deepfake voices can be misused for manipulation. Adaptive difficulty could unintentionally disadvantage certain players or invade their privacy.

Developers must ensure transparency, fairness, and accountability in AI systems. Consent, explainability, and inclusive datasets are foundational to ethical game AI. As games become more adaptive, they must also protect autonomy and player trust.

AI is pushing games toward a new frontier—one of living, evolving worlds that learn, adapt, and respond. From procedurally generated galaxies to emotionally aware characters and personalized quests, artificial intelligence is redefining interactivity.

This shift democratizes game creation, enabling smaller teams to build complex experiences. It also challenges designers to maintain human values in increasingly intelligent systems. As AI becomes the architect of the digital realm, it is up to creators to ensure these adaptive worlds remain imaginative, inclusive, and ethically sound.

Procedural Content Generation and World-Building

One of AI's most transformative contributions to gaming is procedural content generation. Using algorithms like Perlin and Simplex Noise or even more sophisticated generative adversarial networks, AI can create vast, intricate environments on the fly. Titles like No Man's Sky offer players galaxies of unique planets, each with distinct terrain, life forms, and ecosystems, all generated by code. These systems don't just save development time—they expand the playable universe beyond human imagination. Procedural tools like Houdini enable designers to define constraints while AI fills in the details. Yet the challenge remains balancing randomness with intentional design. The most successful examples combine procedural scale with handcrafted touchpoints.

AI is able to tailor experiences to individual players. Through real-time analytics, reinforcement learning, and player profiling, games can adjust difficulty, pace, and narrative based on personal play style. The "AI Director" in Left 4 Dead dynamically changes enemy spawns and item placements to maintain tension and flow. The Nemesis System in Shadow of Mordor creates rivalries that evolve based on player choices. These adaptive systems increase engagement by aligning the game with the player's emotional and cognitive state.

Intelligent NPCs and Emotional Adaptation

Non-player characters (NPCs) have long been constrained by static dialogue trees and predictable patterns. Now, AI is giving NPCs goals, emotions, and the ability to adapt. Techniques like goal-oriented action planning and behavior trees allow NPCs to make decisions based on their motivations, current context, and past interactions.

More advanced models integrate affective computing to read player emotion—via dialogue tone, biometric sensors, or gameplay patterns—and adjust NPC behavior accordingly. For example, a virtual ally might become more supportive when detecting frustration, or an opponent might taunt when sensing overconfidence. These systems deepen player immersion by transforming NPCs into responsive, emotionally intelligent agents.

Voice AI and Conversational Interactivity

AI-powered voice synthesis is enhancing immersion through dynamic, emotionally rich audio. Tools like Replica Studios and Resemble.ai allow for the creation of nuanced, real-time voice lines that react to gameplay. This means NPCs can speak lines they've never been explicitly recorded for yet still sound consistent and natural.

In narrative-heavy games, voice AI allows characters to comment on unexpected player actions or express empathy, fear, or joy without requiring hours of pre-recorded dialogue. These systems bring games closer to true conversational interactivity.

Human-AI Collaboration in Storytelling

Generative AI, especially large language models, is revolutionizing narrative design. Instead of hand-writing every line of dialogue or mission prompt, tools like Ubisoft's Ghostwriter and Inworld AI can generate variations, fill world lore, or even invent new quests in real time. For example, AI Dungeon by Latitude, which uses GPT to create endless player-driven stories. Players propose actions or dialogue, and the AI continues the narrative in a way that feels surprisingly coherent. This democratizes storytelling, allowing players to co-author their journeys. While still requiring curation and moderation, these systems vastly accelerate content creation.

Game development, once a labor-intensive and highly specialized process, is being radically reimagined through AI. AI agents can now generate level designs, create storylines, populate environments with adaptive NPCs, localize content into dozens of languages, and even test for bugs. In multiplayer online games and live service titles, AI can fine-tune player experiences, adapt economies on the fly, and moderate interactions in real time.

At the same time, for players, these technologies enable richer, more personalized journeys. NPCs that evolve with a player's decisions, dynamic quests that respond to skill levels, and co-created in-game content blur the line between designer and participant. Gaming is no longer just a one-way entertainment product—it's becoming a collaborative digital ecosystem.

- *Game Production*: AI autonomously generate levels, scripts, visual assets, and localizations and automate playtesting and debugging. This results in accelerated release cycles, reduced development costs, and tailored content at scale.
- *Live Operations*: AI adjusts game difficulty and in-game economies in real time; detects exploits, and flag harmful behavior. This results in real-time balancing, safer communities, and sustained player engagement.
- *Player Experience*: AI powers NPCs that learn from interactions and enable dynamic quests and responsive worlds. This results in personalization, immersion, and co-creative play which elevate player agency.
- *Web3 Economies*: AI acts as token managers, NFT traders, or DAO delegates within decentralized gaming ecosystems. This results in enabling player-owned economies and real-world income via gameplay.
- *No-Code Creation*: AI translates natural language into assets, game logic, or entire mini-games. This results in expands creative access to non-coders and accelerates user-generated content development.

This convergence introduces a new layer of intelligence to in-game economies. AI agents don't just respond to commands, they participate in the market. They can stake tokens, execute trades, manage digital portfolios, and fulfil smart contract objectives without human intervention. This marks the beginning of intelligent economic actors in play-to-earn systems. Players may find themselves partnering with AI co-creators who help them strategize, optimize gameplay, and even negotiate or bid on virtual assets. The gaming economy shifts from reactive participation to collaborative optimization.

Challenges and Gaps

As transformative as AI agents are, their widespread adoption reveals several critical gaps that the gaming industry must address:

1. *Narrative Coherence and Creative Integrity.* AI-generated quests and dialogue can drift in tone or logic without human guidance. The risk of incoherent or soulless stories looms. This will require AI narrative editors, style checkers, and human-led story oversight layers.
2. *Ethics and AI Safety.* Adaptive NPCs could inadvertently reinforce toxic behavior; autonomous agents in token economies could trigger unintended financial consequences. This will require clear ethical standards, AI governance tools, and real-time oversight mechanisms.
3. *Economic Balance and Fair Play.* Autonomous agents may destabilize in-game economies by exploiting arbitrage or dominating token markets. This will require anti-bot safeguards, dynamic inflation controls, and agent rate-limiters.
4. *Regulation and Accountability.* Who is responsible when an AI agent executes a trade or moderates content incorrectly? This will require regulatory frameworks for AI accountability and digital property rights in decentralized environments.
5. *Infrastructure and Data Access.* Multi-agent systems require significant computing and well-structured data resources that are not evenly distributed across the globe. This will require lightweight models, federated data access, and decentralized compute sharing protocols.
6. *Skills for the Future Workforce.* As AI takes over repetitive tasks, demand will surge for new roles: prompt engineers, AI designers, and economic simulators. This will require training programs, creative AI bootcamps, and updated game design curricula.
7. *Player Trust and Transparency.* Invisible AI systems can feel manipulative if players don't understand when or how AI is acting. This will require interface cues (e.g., "AI-generated"), opt-in systems, and transparency in agent actions.

In this emerging ecosystem, gaming is a platform. AI agents will enable games to become training grounds for real-world skills, on-demand workspaces, and participatory economies. Imagine earning tokens by debugging code with an AI partner, leading virtual teams in strategy simulations, or curating digital art for a DAO-based game guild. This is where AI agents can amplify human imagination and redefine the boundaries between work, play, and economic participation. As these technologies mature, the challenge is not whether AI can build better games, but whether the industry can design AI systems that serve players equitably, support creators sustainably, and foster creativity and trust in shared digital spaces.

The Ethics and Regulation of Addictive Game Design

The addictive potential of digital games has increasingly drawn ethical concern and regulatory attention worldwide. In 2019, the World Health Organization (WHO) officially recognized "gaming disorder" in the *International Classification of Diseases* (ICD-11), defining it as a behavioral pattern characterized by impaired control over gaming, prioritization of gaming over other interests and daily activities, and continued gaming despite negative consequences (World Health Organization [WHO] 2019). This recognition has catalyzed policy responses from governments, particularly in addressing youth gaming addiction.

China has implemented some of the most stringent regulations globally. In 2021, the Chinese government restricted online gaming for individuals under the age of 18 to three hours per week—one hour each on Friday, Saturday, and Sunday evenings—labeling excessive gaming as "spiritual opium" and a threat to national youth health (Yang 2021). These measures also include mandatory real-name registration, facial recognition for login authentication, and strict time limitations enforced by gaming companies, which are legally held accountable for compliance (Reuters 2021). South Korea, which previously enforced a "shutdown law" banning online gaming for under-16 s from midnight to 6 a.m., repealed the regulation in 2021 and replaced it with a system based on parental control tools (Park 2021; Chin 2021).

In anticipation of similar regulatory trends by 2035, some countries are already considering curfews, maximum gameplay durations per day, or compulsory in-game reminders. Game developers have begun to respond proactively by incorporating well-being features such as screen-time trackers, automated break reminders, and "healthy play" modes that reward players for pausing or engaging in real-world activities. Console platforms such as PlayStation and Xbox now include parental control settings that allow caregivers to manage time limits and restrict content access (Sony Interactive Entertainment 2022).

These emerging tools represent part of a broader shift toward ethical game design. Increasingly, there is pressure on developers to avoid manipulative design tactics such as daily login rewards or progression systems that encourage compulsive engagement. As a future-forward measure, some companies may establish internal ethics boards—mirroring AI ethics panels—to assess whether monetization and engagement mechanics might exploit vulnerable users.

One particularly contentious topic is the use of "loot boxes"—randomized, often monetized, in-game rewards that have drawn parallels to gambling due to their variable reward mechanisms. Belgium became the first country to outlaw paid loot boxes in 2018, categorizing them as a form of illegal gambling under national law (Belgian Gaming Commission 2018). Despite the ban, enforcement has proven difficult. Netherlands and China have introduced regulations requiring probability disclosures or limiting access to minors. In the United Kingdom, a 2022 government review stopped short of a legal ban but called on the industry to implement strong self-regulation to protect children and adolescents (UK Department for Digital, Culture, Media and Sport [DCMS] 2022).

Looking ahead to 2035, a fragmented regulatory landscape appears likely. Some jurisdictions may opt for outright bans, others may permit loot boxes under strict age restrictions and transparency requirements, while others could mandate clearly labeled opt-in mechanisms. To mitigate risk and avoid stricter oversight, industry trends may shift toward alternative monetization models such as "battle passes" or direct purchases, which are generally perceived as less predatory.

Monetization Ethics and Fair Play

Ethical concerns also surround monetization strategies beyond addiction. Players and regulators are concerned about fairness—for instance, "pay-to-win" mechanics (where spending money gives gameplay advantages) are widely criticized. Competitive game communities value a level playing field, so by 2030, it's likely that most successful games will avoid pay-to-win and stick to cosmetic or convenience items for monetization.

Another aspect is gambling in gaming—besides loot boxes, this includes real-money betting on Esports or casino-style mini-games within games. Regulators will keep a close eye on ensuring that gambling elements are kept away from minors and that games with such content are properly rated and partitioned. Some jurisdictions might require any game that simulates gambling (even with virtual currency) to carry adult age ratings.

Cheating and hacking also fall under an ethical umbrella, affecting fair play. While not a governmental regulation issue per se, game companies are employing increasingly sophisticated anti-cheat systems (sometimes kernel-level software, AI pattern detection) to ensure a fair environment. However, privacy concerns arise here too (some anti-cheat software is invasive on user systems). The law might become involved if, for example, anti-cheat measures are seen as violating privacy or if cheat sellers (who make and sell cheats) are prosecuted—there have been lawsuits and even arrests for selling cheats in some countries. By 2035, cheating in games might be a criminal offence in certain contexts (especially if tied to Esports betting fraud or large-scale hacking operations).

Consumer rights in the digital age also mean regulators might push for more transparency in terms of game odds (for random drops), clearer pricing (no hidden costs), and easier dispute resolution (like refunding accidental purchases made by children, as enforced in the Epic case). The industry is learning to proactively address these issues: for example, major platforms now often require password re-entry for purchases to prevent accidental buys by kids, and some have implemented spending caps or warnings for young users.

In conclusion, the next decade will see a solidification of the legal and ethical framework around gaming: what was once a "wild west" of new monetization and online behavior is becoming more regulated and standardized. We will likely have a set of best practices (some voluntary, some legally mandated) covering data privacy, community moderation, fair monetization, and health impacts. Gaming companies that adapt and lead in these areas (ensuring player well-being and trust) will build better reputations and long-term customer loyalty, whereas those that resist may face litigation, fines, or backlash from increasingly aware consumers. By 2035, a mature global gaming industry will be one where enjoyment and profit are balanced with ethical responsibility and compliance with worldwide norms and laws.

Moderation, Harassment, and Community Health

The issue of toxic behavior in online gaming—harassment, hate speech, and bullying—has long been a concern and will continue to demand focused intervention. As gaming communities grow in scale and diversity, ensuring that these spaces are safe and inclusive is both an ethical responsibility and critical for user retention. Recent developments indicate a trend toward more proactive moderation through advanced technologies. In 2023, Activision Blizzard partnered with Modulate to integrate an AI-powered voice moderation system known as "ToxMod" into *Call of Duty*. This system monitors real-time voice communications to distinguish between benign and harmful speech and is capable of identifying severe behaviors such as grooming or radicalization through longitudinal analysis (Minahan 2023). AI-driven moderators are expected to become a standard layer in community management, augmenting human moderators by automatically flagging or muting offenders.

Similarly, major developers like Riot Games and Ubisoft have launched the "Zero Harm in Comms" initiative, a joint research project aimed at developing AI that can interpret the unique linguistic and cultural nuances of gaming communication to mitigate toxicity (Siege.GG 2022). While AI-based moderation tools raise ethical and regulatory concerns, including data privacy, algorithmic bias, and false positives, their adoption is accelerating as the scale and complexity of online communities outstrip the capabilities of human moderation alone.

Regulators are also paying attention that there have been discussions in places like the EU about whether online platforms (including games) should be legally required to moderate hate speech and extremism. Large game companies may eventually be held to similar standards as social media under laws like the EU's Digital Services Act, meaning they must swiftly remove illegal content (e.g., threats, hate speech) once aware. By 2035, it's plausible that industry-wide codes of conduct backed by law or government pressure will exist, obligating games with user communications to implement robust moderation and reporting systems. We might also see age ratings factoring in the quality of a game's community moderation (for instance, a game could lose its certification if it doesn't control rampant abuse).

Selected Regulatory Responses

- *Data Privacy*: The European Union's General Data Protection Regulation (GDPR), enacted in 2018, established strict requirements for user consent, data protection, and transparency (European Commission 2018). In the United States, the Federal Trade Commission (FTC) has enforced children's privacy rules under the Children's Online Privacy Protection Act (COPPA). By 2030, global alignment around core privacy principles, such as data minimization, age verification, and bans on "dark patterns" is likely.
- *Toxicity and Moderation*: AI moderation tools are being adopted to address toxic behavior in games. In 2023, Activision introduced real-time voice chat moderation via AI in *Call of Duty* (Minahan 2023). Riot Games and Ubisoft launched the "Zero Harm in Comms" initiative to combat in-game harassment (Siege.GG 2022). Future legal frameworks may impose swift takedown requirements for hate speech and promote standardized community guidelines and enhanced parental controls.
- *Gaming Addiction*: The World Health Organization officially recognized "gaming disorder" in the International Classification of Diseases (ICD-11) in 2019 (WHO 2019). China implemented strict laws in 2021 limiting players under 18 to 2 h of online gaming per week (Yang 2021). South Korea's former "shutdown law" (2011–2021) restricted minors from playing online games overnight (Chin 2021). The trend suggests more countries will encourage education, provide optional healthy play features, and possibly regulate game time for minors.
- *Loot Boxes and Gambling:* Belgium ruled in 2018 that paid loot boxes constitute illegal gambling, forcing their removal from most games (Belgian Gaming Commission 2018). Other countries, including the Netherlands and the UK, have considered or implemented age restrictions or transparency measures (Zendle 2019). The ESRB and PEGI have introduced labeling such as "Includes Random Items" to promote self-regulation. By 2035, expect a mix of outright bans, 18+ gating, and mandatory odds disclosures.
- *Microtransactions and DLC*: Some countries are mandating odds disclosures for randomized in-game purchases, and regulators are scrutinizing potentially deceptive monetization models. Legal action may target misleading advertising of downloadable content or predatory pricing (Gebel 2022). By 2030, the industry is likely to adopt transparent pricing, avoid pay-to-win mechanics, and limit targeting of vulnerable groups.
- *Consumer Rights:* The European Union is exploring legislation to guarantee consumers the right to resell digital games and secure stronger refund policies

(European Parliament 2020). Platforms like Steam already offer no-questions-asked refunds under specific conditions (Valve 2023). By 2030, more consistent consumer protections for digital goods—including ownership rights and refund mechanisms—are expected across jurisdictions.

On the positive side, there's a push for healthy gaming communities. Features like content filters, voice transcription (for those who want text instead of voice chat to avoid slurs), reputation systems, and matchmaking that separates consistently toxic players from others will be more refined. Some games already penalize toxic behavior with chat bans or by matching toxic players only with each other; these systems will grow more sophisticated with AI analysis. Parental controls will also be more granular by 2030—parents might be able to restrict who their child can talk to in games, limit chat functions, or get reports on their behavior. All these measures aim to make online gaming spaces more civil and welcoming, which is essential as the gamer population diversifies in age and background. The culture is shifting such that toxicity is less tolerated; high-profile bans of well-known players/streamers for hate speech, for example, send signals that the community standards are tightening.

Conclusion

Artificial intelligence is fast becoming the core architect of dynamic, interactive, and adaptive virtual worlds. From procedural generation to emotion-aware NPCs and AI-powered voice synthesis, this chapter has demonstrated how AI is transforming not just the mechanics of games, but also their narrative depth, emotional resonance, and economic structures. These technologies enable personalized experiences, co-created storylines, and persistent game ecosystems that blur the boundary between designer and player, fiction and labor, entertainment, and education.

However, this transformation is not without challenges. The rapid infusion of AI into gaming raises important ethical, regulatory, and design questions. How can developers ensure fairness in adaptive difficulty systems? Who is accountable when AI agents autonomously participate in token economies? What safeguards are needed to prevent AI-generated content from replicating bias or manipulation? As games become sites of economic activity, social interaction, and even therapeutic practice, these questions demand rigorous oversight and inclusive design.

Looking ahead to 2035, the convergence of AI with other emerging technologies, such as decentralized systems, virtual and augmented reality, and biometric interfaces, promises to redefine gaming as a key arena for cultural expression, digital identity formation, and future of work experimentation. Yet this promise must be tempered by critical reflection. AI has the power to democratize game creation and enhance human creativity, but only if it is developed with transparency, inclusivity, and ethical responsibility.

In this new era of adaptive worlds, the central question is no longer *what games can do*, but *what kind of futures are being designed through them*. The challenge for developers, regulators, and players alike is to ensure that AI not only expands what is possible in play, but also safeguards what is essential in human experience—imagination, fairness, agency, and trust.

Cross-Chapter Insight

AI Dungeon exemplifies the fusion of AI and decentralized storytelling. This intersects with *Alethea AI* (Chap. 4), where generative avatars learn and earn. These AI integrations extend to *Neurable* and *NexMind* (Chap. 9), where AI interprets brain signals in real time. Creation-focused platforms like *Roblox* and *Fortnite Creative* (Chap. 10) are increasingly integrating AI tools for world-building. Together, these cases point toward a future of co-creation, where players and machines shape experiences collaboratively—and raise novel questions around authorship, agency, and bias.

Case Studies

Case Study: AI Dungeon by Latitude—Decentralized Storage in AI-Driven Narrative Gaming

Platform/Game Title: AI Dungeon
   Developer/Studio: Latitude
   Year Launched: 2019
   Core Technologies: GPT-based AI narrative generation, decentralized storage (IPFS)
   Genre: AI-generated interactive storytelling

Overview

AI Dungeon is a text-based adventure platform that allows players to co-create stories with an AI language model, initially GPT-2 and later GPT-3. Unlike traditional games with fixed narratives, AI Dungeon offers unlimited story possibilities shaped in real time by player input. The game quickly attracted a global user base and became a leading example of generative AI in gaming. To address concerns around censorship, content permanence, and user ownership, Latitude integrated decentralized storage protocols, notably IPFS, to preserve user-created adventures and align with Web3 principles.

Innovation

AI Dungeon broke new ground by combining generative AI with decentralized infrastructure. It allowed players to create, store, and revisit custom AI-driven storylines, pushing the boundary of player agency in storytelling. By storing user-generated content on IPFS, Latitude ensured stories could not be arbitrarily modified or deleted—offering resilience, privacy, and creator autonomy. The model signaled a move away from centralized content moderation and toward user-controlled creative spaces.

Impact

AI Dungeon set the standard for AI-assisted co-creation in gaming. Millions of stories were generated and shared many exploring complex or imaginative worlds that would be impossible to script manually. The game demonstrated the feasibility of decentralizing dynamic content at scale, making it a pioneering example of combining AI with Web3 storage solutions. Its success catalyzed broader interest in persistent AI worlds and decentralized narrative engines.

Challenges

As with many AI-first applications, AI Dungeon faced ethical and operational hurdles. Decentralized storage systems like IPFS introduced latency and retrieval complexity for real-time gameplay. Moderating inappropriate content, especially in procedurally generated and globally distributed narratives—proved difficult. Ensuring compliance with local laws while maintaining a censorship-resistant ethos required ongoing innovation in governance and filtering.

Lessons Learned

AI Dungeon illustrates the potential of decentralized storage to protect user creativity while supporting dynamic, AI-generated content. It also revealed the need for hybrid moderation approaches, blending AI filters with community governance. The platform proved that narrative persistence and creative freedom could co-exist in decentralized ecosystems, offering a template for future immersive AI games.

Future Outlook

Latitude is exploring new models for narrative AI integration, including modular storytelling agents, **NFT** ownership of storylines, and decentralized content economies. As AI and decentralized storage mature, games like AI Dungeon may evolve into persistent narrative Metaverses where stories, characters, and worlds live on-chain and are owned by their creators. This vision positions AI Dungeon at the frontier of narrative sovereignty in gaming.

References

Belgian Gaming Commission. (2018). *Research report on loot boxes in video games*. https://www.gamingcommission.be

Chin, M. (2021, August 30). China limits gaming for minors to three hours a week. *Engadget*. https://www.engadget.com

European Commission. (2018). *General Data Protection Regulation (GDPR)*. https://ec.europa.eu/info/law/law-topic/data-protection_en

European Parliament. (2020). *Digital content and consumer rights: Towards a new legal framework*. https://www.europarl.europa.eu

Gebel, M. (2022, October 18). Lawsuits and loot boxes: Why gaming's monetization model is under fire. *Business Insider*. https://www.businessinsider.com

Minahan, J. (2023, August 30). Call of Duty adds real-time voice chat moderation with AI. *SiliconANGLE*. https://siliconangle.com

Park, M. (2021, August 31). South Korea abolishes gaming 'shutdown law'. *WP Towson*. https://wp.towson.edu

Reuters (2021). China imposes 3-hour weekly limit for minors' online gaming reuters.com

Siege.GG. (2022, July 13). *Ubisoft and Riot announce "Zero Harm in Comms" to reduce in-game toxicity*. https://siege.gg/news/ubisoft-and-riot-announce-zero-harm-in-comms-to-reduce-in-game-toxicity

Sony Interactive Entertainment. (2022). *Parental controls on PlayStation consoles*. https://www.playstation.com

UK Department for Digital, Culture, Media & Sport (DCMS). (2022). Government response to the call for evidence on loot boxes in video games. https://www.gov.uk/government/calls-for-evidence/loot-boxes-in-video-games-callfor-evidence/loot-boxes-in-video-games-call-for-evidence

Valve (2023). Steam refund policy. https://store.steampowered.com/steam_refunds/

WHO (2019) https://www.who.int/standards/classifications/frequently-asked-questions/gaming-disorder

Yang, Y. (2021, September 1). Why China called online gaming 'spiritual opium'. *Reuters*. https://www.reuters.com

Zendle (2019). Dr David Zendle – Written evidence (GAM0022) Statement regarding loot boxes, video game-related gambling practices, and problem gambling. https://committees.parliament.uk/writtenevidence/83/html/

Chapter 9
Neural Gaming and the Brain–Computer Interface Frontier

Abstract "Neural Gaming and the BCI Frontier" explores how Brain–Computer Interfaces (BCIs) are ushering in a new immersive, mind-driven gameplay era. This chapter explores how BCIs enable direct communication between the brain and digital devices, turning thoughts into commands and reshaping how players interact with virtual environments. From enhancing accessibility for people with disabilities to unlocking deeper cognitive engagement and emotional responsiveness, neural gaming is at the cutting edge of human-tech fusion. Readers will learn how EEG-based systems, real-time neural signal processing, and neuroadaptive feedback loops enable next-generation gaming experiences. The chapter also examines the ethical considerations and data privacy challenges of accessing the brain's most intimate signals. As BCIs evolve, they offer profound implications for play and education, therapy, and human potential.

Keywords Brain–Computer Interfaces (BCIs) · Neural gaming · EEG signal processing · Neuroadaptive systems · Thought-driven interaction · Accessibility in gaming · Cognitive state detection · Neurofeedback · Machine learning in BCI · Ethical neurotechnology · Real-time brain interaction · Immersive AR/VR interfaces · Inclusive neurotechnology design · Human–machine symbiosis · AI-augmented gameplay

The Mind as the Controller

Brain–Computer Interfaces (BCIs) are enabling a new immersive, mind-driven gameplay era. This chapter explores how BCIs enable direct communication between the brain and digital devices, turning thoughts into commands and reshaping how players interact with virtual environments. From enhancing accessibility for people with disabilities to unlocking deeper cognitive engagement and emotional responsiveness, neural gaming is at the cutting edge of human-tech fusion. Readers will learn how EEG-based systems, real-time neural signal processing, and neuroadaptive feedback loops enable next-generation gaming experiences. The boundaries between the human mind and digital experience are reducing. With BCIs, players are no longer limited to physical controllers or even voice commands. Instead, thoughts themselves can become gameplay inputs. This chapter explores the science behind BCIs, their use in gaming, and the extraordinary possibilities they unlock, from cognitive enhancement to full neural immersion. The chapter also examines the ethical considerations and data privacy challenges of accessing the brain's most intimate signals. As BCIs evolve, they offer profound implications for play and education, therapy, and human potential.

BCIs enable direct communication between the brain and external devices, presenting transformative applications across medicine, gaming, automation, education, and neuroergonomics. While some BCIs involve surgical implants, gaming applications primarily rely on non-invasive methods like electroencephalography (EEG). These headsets detect and translate electrical activity in the brain's cortex into machine-readable signals. The BCI process includes signal acquisition, filtering, feature extraction, classification, and translation into digital commands. Companies such as Emotiv, OpenBCI, and Neurable have pioneered wearable EEG devices that bring this complex process into the hands of consumers.

Emotiv is a neurotechnology company that has been instrumental in making EEG headsets accessible to consumers, researchers, and developers. Their flagship devices, such as the Emotiv EPOC+ and Insight, allow for real-time monitoring of brain activity and have been integrated into a range of applications, including gaming, wellness, and education. In gaming, Emotiv's technology enables users to control gameplay elements through mental commands or facial expressions, providing a novel input modality that goes beyond traditional controllers. This type of interface enhances immersion by allowing players to influence game mechanics with cognitive and emotional states. Emotiv's SDK supports Unity, a popular game development engine, making it easier for developers to integrate BCI capabilities into interactive experiences (Emotiv 2023).

OpenBCI is an open-source neurotechnology company that empowers developers and researchers to create custom BCI solutions. Its products, such as the Ultracortex headset and the Cyton biosensing board, are designed to be modular and affordable. OpenBCI has become particularly attractive to indie game developers and academic labs seeking to build experimental or therapeutic gaming platforms. In 2023, OpenBCI partnered with Valve to explore the integration of BCI with virtual reality systems, suggesting future applications where brain signals could dynamically influence gameplay in VR environments. The company's commitment to open-source principles accelerates innovation in BCI gaming by allowing creators to tailor neural input systems to specific game mechanics or user needs (OpenBCI 2023).

Neurable is a Boston-based neurotechnology company focused on making brain–computer interfaces more intuitive and seamless, particularly in immersive environments. Its latest headset, the Neurable Enten, integrates dry EEG sensors into everyday headphones and is designed for real-time neuroadaptive applications. In gaming, Neurable's technology allows for hands-free control, enabling players to interact with digital environments using attention and intent detection. This opens possibilities for games that respond dynamically to a player's focus or emotional engagement, thus personalizing gameplay and enhancing accessibility. Neurable has demonstrated prototypes where players select objects or navigate virtual spaces purely through mental focus, hinting at future applications in both entertainment and Esports (Neurable 2021, 2023).

Cattan (2021) critically evaluated the current state of BCIs in gaming and concluded that, despite technological advances, BCIs are not yet ready for widespread consumer use. His paper highlights significant limitations across three key areas: low data transfer rates, high hardware costs and complexity, and inadequate game design integration. While research prototypes such as *Brain Invaders* have demonstrated the potential of EEG-based gameplay, real-world applications are hindered by the poor performance of low-cost headsets, lack of industry-standard middleware, and insufficient focus on aesthetics and user experience.

The paper emphasizes that the transfer rate for BCIs remains too low for effective input in fast-paced or traditional gameplay, making it difficult for BCIs to compete with existing interfaces like keyboards or game controllers. Additionally, the hardware is often either prohibitively expensive or insufficiently accurate, and development is fragmented across proprietary systems. Most BCI games developed in labs fail to meet the visual and design standards expected by mainstream gamers, leading to low engagement and replay value.

Cattan (2021) suggests that instead of competing with traditional inputs, BCI integration should be limited to novel mechanics that cannot be achieved otherwise, such as relaxation tracking or subtle emotional states. He calls for greater focus on user-centric design, standardization of tools, and middleware to make BCI development more accessible. Cattan concludes that BCI games are currently more suited to experimental and niche applications rather than mainstream entertainment and urges developers to treat BCIs as complementary rather than core technologies in gaming.

Aside from the stage of development, a recent study reports on a comprehensive review of the current state, trends, challenges, and potential threats of BCIs (Maiseli et al. 2023). The paper outlines the BCI architecture comprising signal acquisition, processing, and application and explores advanced features like thought decoding, memory extension, telepathic communication, and brain energy harvesting. The authors conducted a bibliometric analysis of over 25,000 BCI publications, revealing a significant surge in research, particularly from China since 2019, surpassing the United States. Despite growing applications, the paper warns of unresolved challenges including privacy, security, ethical concerns, safety (especially in invasive BCIs), limited affordability, and regulatory gaps. The study also highlights disparities in research output, with Africa contributing less than 1% of global BCI publications, urging inclusive global collaboration. The paper concludes that although BCIs hold immense promise to improve lives especially for those with disabilities, widespread adoption demands robust interdisciplinary research, global standards, ethical oversight, and expanded clinical trials to ensure safe, effective, and equitable implementation.

Current systems are primarily focused on measuring attention, relaxation, and basic intent, and the pace of innovation is bringing more nuanced control within reach. Yet, as access to brain signals increases, so do concerns around ethics and data privacy.

EEG-based BCIs use electrodes placed on the scalp to record brain activity. The signal is typically weak and susceptible to noise from eye movements, facial expressions, or muscle tension. Signal processing tools such as MATLAB and Python play a crucial role in the preprocessing and analysis of raw EEG data, which is often contaminated with noise and artifacts. MATLAB offers a comprehensive suite of built-in functions and toolboxes specifically designed for EEG signal filtering, artifact removal, and spectral analysis. Similarly, Python, through libraries like MNE-Python and SciPy, provides open-source frameworks for EEG data handling, including functions for event detection, time-frequency decomposition, and source localization (Gramfort et al. 2013; Virtanen et al. 2020). These tools enable researchers to transform noisy, high-dimensional EEG signals into interpretable features that are essential for downstream applications like brain–computer interfaces, clinical diagnostics, and cognitive neuroscience studies.

The key to gaming applications lies in real-time signal processing. EEG frequency bands such as alpha (relaxation), beta (active thinking), and theta (meditative state) are used to trigger in-game responses. With calibration, a player can learn to modulate their mental state to control game elements. The challenge is achieving sufficient signal fidelity and responsiveness without compromising user comfort or requiring excessive training.

BCIs offer a new dimension of immersion by enabling thought-driven interaction. In prototype games, players can move characters, launch attacks, or manipulate environments using attention levels or specific mental commands. Unity XR and WebXR toolkits support integration with BCI input to allow AR/VR games to respond to the player's cognitive state. They offer robust frameworks for integrating BCI input into immersive environments, enabling AR/VR applications to adapt dynamically to a player's cognitive or emotional state. These platforms provide cross-device compatibility and developer tools that facilitate the real-time mapping of EEG signals or other neural data to in-game responses, such as modifying difficulty levels, visual effects, or narrative flow based on attention or mental workload (Gürkök and Nijholt 2014; Bécue-Bertaut et al. 2021). By leveraging Unity's XR Interaction Toolkit or WebXR's browser-based capabilities, developers can create more personalized and responsive experiences that enhance immersion and usability, particularly in therapeutic, educational, or gaming contexts.

Emotional responsiveness adds another layer. Games that read frustration, boredom, or joy from brain activity can dynamically adjust narrative pace, difficulty, or soundtrack. Such adaptations enhance immersion by making the game world feel alive and attuned to the player's internal experience.

Moreno-Calderón et al. (2023) explored the development and evaluation of a multiplayer brain–computer interface (BCI) video game based on code-modulated visual evoked potentials (c-VEPs), aimed at enhancing accessibility for individuals with severe motor disabilities. The game is a BCI-adapted version of *Connect 4*, allowing two players to control gameplay through their brain signals, specifically using c-VEPs processed from EEG data. The research involved 22 healthy participants and assessed the system across individual and competitive multiplayer tasks. The c-VEP-based control system achieved a high average accuracy of 93.74% ± 1.71% with a command selection time of 5.25 s. Subjective evaluations using NASA-TLX and SUS questionnaires indicated low mental workload and high user satisfaction. Users found the system intuitive, responsive, and suitable for competitive interaction.

Compared to previous studies that used sensorimotor rhythms (SMRs) or P300 potentials, this study demonstrated superior performance in terms of accuracy, usability, and shorter calibration times. While the application showed strong potential, the authors noted the need to test with motor-disabled users and suggested improvements like early stopping algorithms and dry electrodes for greater user comfort. This study highlights c-VEPs as a promising control method for accessible, real-time multiplayer gaming and provides a benchmark for future BCI-based interactive systems.

In another study, Summers and Keizer (2022) reviewed the use of EEG-based brain–computer BCIs in video gaming. EEG devices detected electrical brain activity and can serve as either alternatives or supplements for traditional game controllers. When integrated with computers, they form BCIs that create a feedback loop between a player's brain signals and the game. The paper outlines the technical components of a BCI system, including EEG signal acquisition, relevant brain inputs, preprocessing techniques, and machine learning algorithms used for interpretation. It also examines the types of games developed using BCI technology, from entertainment to serious games. The authors highlight current technological, design, and usability limitations and suggest areas for future innovation to support broader adoption of BCI-enabled gaming.

Ahn et al. (2014) presented a comprehensive review of Brain–Computer Interface (BCI) games and surveyed the perspectives of nearly 300 stakeholders, including researchers, developers, and users. The study highlights the evolution of BCI games, focusing on EEG-based control paradigms such as motor imagery, P300, steady-state visual evoked potentials (SSVEP), and passive BCIs that read mental states. Survey results show broad optimism about the future of BCI and its applications, especially in prosthetics, rehabilitation, and gaming.

Key insights reveal a divide between researchers and developers. Researchers prioritize signal processing and sensor quality, while developers emphasize ease of use, platform compatibility, and user experience. Users and developers showed low interest in passive BCIs and whole-head sensor arrays, preferring minimal and comfortable hardware. The study identified three critical elements to scale BCI games commercially: (1) establishing standards, (2) enhancing gameplay design tailored to BCI's unique affordances, and (3) integrating BCI with other interfaces and systems. In conclusion, the paper calls for cross-stakeholder collaboration to bridge the gap between research innovation and consumer-ready BCI game products.

BCIs represent a promising frontier in gaming, enabling direct interaction between brain activity and digital environments. EEG signals, though inherently low-amplitude and prone to noise from artifacts such as eye movements or muscle activity, can be processed using robust computational tools like MATLAB and Python libraries (e.g., MNE-Python, SciPy) to extract meaningful features for real-time applications (Gramfort et al. 2013; Virtanen et al. 2020). In gaming, frequency bands such as alpha, beta, and theta are often mapped to in-game actions, allowing players to control virtual elements through cognitive state modulation. This immersive potential is further augmented through integration with AR/VR platforms like Unity XR and WebXR, which support adaptive environments responsive to neural inputs (Gürkök and Nijholt 2014; Bécue-Bertaut et al. 2021). Recent empirical studies demonstrate the viability of such systems; for instance, Moreno-Calderón et al. (2023) developed a multiplayer Connect 4 BCI game utilizing code-modulated visual evoked potentials, achieving over 93% accuracy with high user satisfaction and low cognitive load. These findings underscore the accessibility and responsiveness of EEG-BCI systems in competitive gameplay. Complementary reviews by Summers and Keizer (2022) and Ahn et al. (2014) affirm that while technological and design barriers persist—particularly regarding sensor comfort and calibration time—there is strong cross-sector optimism about BCIs' potential in gaming and beyond. Key factors for mainstream adoption include improved usability, standardized protocols, and the integration of BCI systems with broader digital infrastructures. As BCI-enabled gaming evolves, it offers not only novel interaction paradigms but also transformative applications in education, rehabilitation, and human–machine symbiosis.

Accessibility and Inclusion

One of the most transformative applications of BCIs lies in accessibility. For players with limited mobility due to conditions like cerebral palsy or spinal injuries, traditional input devices can be barriers. BCIs offer an inclusive alternative, enabling users to navigate menus, play games, or even control wheelchairs using mental commands.

Neurotech firms are partnering with rehabilitation centers and accessibility groups to develop custom BCI applications. These efforts not only democratize gaming but also expand opportunities for creative expression, communication, and social interaction for people with disabilities.

A groundbreaking study by Willsey, M. S.et.al. (2025) introduces a high-performance BCI capable of continuously decoding finger movements in a person with tetraplegia, enabling control over a virtual quadcopter in both structured and spontaneous tasks. Unlike traditional BCIs that often support only 2D cursor or robotic arm control, this system decodes four degrees of freedom: three independent finger groups and two-dimensional thumb movements. In tests, the participant, who had a C4 spinal cord injury, achieved real-time, precise control over a virtual hand and later used the decoded movements to steer a digital quadcopter through complex obstacle courses and randomized ring challenges. Performance metrics showed rapid task acquisition (up to 76 targets/minute) and successful multi-DOF navigation, outperforming earlier BCI studies.

Beyond technical achievements, the system significantly enhanced the participant's sense of enablement, recreation, and social connectedness, addressing commonly unmet needs among individuals with severe motor impairments. The study also confirmed that increased electrode channel counts correlate with improved decoding accuracy and that expanding decoding to more DOF doesn't degrade neural mapping for fewer DOF tasks. This work represents a leap forward in intuitive, fine-motor BCI control and suggests a future where people with paralysis can access immersive digital environments for both functional and recreational purposes.

Engineers at The University of Texas (2024) at Austin have developed a universal BCI that allows users to play video games, such as racing simulations, using only their thoughts. Unlike traditional BCIs that require time-consuming individual calibration, this new system uses machine learning to adapt quickly to different users without custom setup. By training a decoder on a simple task (balancing a digital bar), the system generalizes commands for more complex activities like steering in a game. This innovation could accelerate the clinical use of BCIs for people with motor impairments by removing technical barriers. The research involved 18 healthy participants and is viewed as foundational for broader applications, including wheelchair control and robotic rehabilitation. Future testing will focus on disabled users in real-world healthcare settings, with the ultimate goal of enhancing independence and quality of life.

Cognitive Enhancement and Neurofeedback

Gaming is also a fertile ground for cognitive training. BCI-based neurofeedback games encourage players to strengthen focus, emotional regulation, and working memory by rewarding desirable brainwave patterns. As players improve, the system adapts, creating a personalized training loop. Platforms like NeuroPype and OpenViBE provide powerful environments for developing real-time EEG applications by offering modular, user-friendly frameworks for processing and interpreting brain signals. These platforms support the integration of diverse signal processing techniques, machine learning algorithms, and visualization tools to enable rapid prototyping of brain–computer interface (BCI) applications. NeuroPype, a commercial platform, is designed for high-performance streaming and supports real-time classification of cognitive states, making it well-suited for neuroadaptive gaming and research (Intheon 2020). OpenViBE, an open-source alternative, is widely used in academic and clinical settings for designing BCI systems, thanks to its flexible architecture and compatibility with multiple hardware devices (Renard et al. 2010). Together, these platforms accelerate the development of applications that respond to neural input, fostering innovation in fields like neurogaming, rehabilitation, and cognitive training. Educational games for children with ADHD, mindfulness apps, and stress management tools are already using this approach to improve mental health and cognitive function.

AI-BCI Integration

Machine learning amplifies the potential of BCIs by enabling systems to predict intent and adapt to users over time. Using machine learning frameworks like TensorFlow and Keras, developers can train neural networks to classify brain states and predict user intentions based on EEG data. These tools offer high-level APIs and efficient computational backends that facilitate the rapid development and deployment of deep learning models for brain–computer interface (BCI) applications. By leveraging architectures such as convolutional neural networks or recurrent neural networks, researchers can capture both spatial and temporal patterns in EEG signals to detect cognitive states like attention, workload, or motor imagery with high accuracy (Lawhern et al. 2018; Abiri et al. 2019). TensorFlow's flexibility and scalability make it suitable for real-time classification in embedded systems or cloud environments, while Keras simplifies model building and experimentation, accelerating innovation in neurotechnology and interactive systems.

Reinforcement learning allows games to evolve in response to brain input, offering personalized experiences. For instance, an AI-driven BCI game might detect when a player is mentally fatigued and offers a break or lower the difficulty. Conversely, during moments of high engagement, the game might introduce new challenges. This bidirectional loop creates a truly adaptive gaming experience that evolves with the player.

Ethical Challenges

The power to access and interpret brain data comes with profound ethical responsibilities. Neural data is intimate, revealing not just intentions but potentially thoughts, emotions, and mental health status. Without proper regulation, BCI data could be exploited for commercial, manipulative, or discriminatory purposes. The key issues include:

Data Privacy: Who Owns Neural Data, and How Is It Stored or Shared?

Data privacy in brain–computer interfaces (BCIs) present significant ethical and legal challenges, particularly concerning the ownership, storage, and sharing of neural data. As BCIs collect sensitive brain signals that may reveal thoughts, emotions, or cognitive states, questions arise about who owns this information—the user, the device manufacturer, or the service provider. Currently, there is no universal legal framework governing neural data, leaving individuals vulnerable to potential misuse, especially in commercial or surveillance contexts (Ienca and Andorno 2017). Furthermore, the storage and transmission of EEG data must adhere to stringent data protection standards to prevent unauthorized access or breaches. This includes implementing secure encryption, anonymization protocols, and user consent mechanisms. As BCI technologies become more integrated into daily life, from healthcare to gaming, ensuring transparent data governance and user control over neural information is essential to protect cognitive liberty and personal autonomy (Wexler 2019).

Consent: Are Users Fully Informed of What Is Being Captured and How It's Used?

Informed consent is a critical ethical consideration in the development and deployment of brain–computer interfaces (BCIs), yet current practices often fall short of ensuring that users fully understand what neural data is being captured and how it will be used. Given the complexity and novelty of BCI technologies, users may not be adequately informed about the extent to which their cognitive states, emotions, or intentions are being monitored, processed, and potentially shared with third parties (Ienca et al. 2018). Unlike traditional biomedical data, neural data can reveal intimate aspects of an individual's mental life, raising the stakes for consent that are truly informed and voluntary. Moreover, the integration of BCIs into consumer products like gaming and wellness devices further complicates the consent process, as users may unknowingly agree to data practices buried in lengthy and technical terms of service agreements. Ethical BCI design must prioritize transparency, provide clear and accessible explanations, and offer users ongoing control over their data to uphold autonomy and trust (Haselager 2013).

Psychological Effects: Could Deep Immersion or Real-Time Feedback Cause Harm?

Brain–computer interfaces (BCIs), particularly when used in immersive environments such as virtual reality or neuroadaptive gaming, raise important concerns about potential psychological effects. Real-time neural feedback and deep cognitive engagement can alter users' emotional and cognitive states, sometimes leading to unintended consequences such as anxiety, dependency, or altered self-perception (Yuste et al. 2017). Prolonged use of BCIs, especially those providing continuous feedback on mental performance or emotional regulation, may also create pressure to "optimize" one's brain activity, potentially contributing to stress or reduced psychological well-being (Burwell et al. 2017). Additionally, users may experience disorientation or loss of agency if the interface responds unpredictably to subconscious neural activity, blurring the line between voluntary action and system-driven behavior. These risks underscore the need for psychological safeguards, user education, and ethical design principles to ensure that BCI applications enhance rather than compromise mental health.

Bias and Equity: Are BCIs Designed Inclusively, or Do They Favor Certain Brainwave Patterns or Demographics?

Bias and equity are growing concerns in brain–computer interface (BCI) design, as many current systems are not developed with sufficient consideration for demographic and neurodiversity. BCIs often rely on machine learning models trained on limited datasets that may predominantly reflect the brainwave patterns of specific populations—typically young, healthy, male participants from Western countries—thereby reducing performance accuracy for underrepresented groups, including women, older adults, and individuals with neurological differences (Thompson 2019). Such biases can lead to unequal access, lower usability, or even exclusion from BCI-enabled applications in areas like communication, gaming, and neurorehabilitation. Furthermore, physiological differences, including skull thickness, hair type, and baseline EEG variability, can influence signal acquisition and algorithm performance, reinforcing systemic inequities (Allison and Neuper 2010). To ensure fair and inclusive deployment of BCIs, developers must adopt equitable data collection practices, validate systems across diverse user groups, and embed inclusive design principles throughout the development lifecycle. Establishing neuro-rights and ethical standards is critical as BCI technology moves into the mainstream.

Conclusion: The Neural Horizon of Play

Brain–computer interfaces represent a radical evolution in gaming, from mechanical interaction to cognitive fusion. They unlock unprecedented immersion, accessibility, and personalization. They also open doors to learning, therapy, and self-discovery through games that respond not just to input, but to intention. As BCIs become more accessible and AI continues to enhance their intelligence, the line between thought and action will blur. But with that power must come care. The next generation of games won't just entertain; they'll think with us. And in doing so, they must honor not only our attention, but our agency, dignity, and inner world.

Cross Chapter Insights

Brain–computer interfaces in *Neurable* and *NexMind* introduce a new paradigm of neural interaction. These themes are echoed in *AI Dungeon* and *Alethea AI* (Chaps. 8 and 4), which embed adaptive, identity-linked agents into gameplay. Discussions of decentralized identity and user data sovereignty in *The Sandbox* (Chap. 2) and *Discord* (Chap. 10) also align with brain-linked authentication systems. As these technologies mature, ethics (Chap. 7), accessibility (Chap. 5), and skill development (Chap. 10) will become central to BCI's role in future gaming ecosystems.

Case Studies

Neurable—Brain–Computer Interfaces and the Rise of Neural Gaming Identity

Platform/Product Name: Neurable
  Company: Neurable, Inc.
  Year Launched: 2017 (initial research); 2021 (commercial BCI headphones)
  Core Technologies: Brain–computer interfaces (BCI), EEG sensors, neuroadaptive machine learning
  Application Domain: Neurogaming, identity-driven interaction, immersive environments

Overview

Neurable is a neurotechnology company developing non-invasive brain–computer interface (BCI) systems for real-world applications, including gaming, XR, and productivity. Its flagship product, the Neurable Enten headset, integrates EEG sensors into consumer-grade headphones, allowing users to control digital interfaces through cognitive states like attention and intent. In gaming, Neurable's technology supports a new form of player identity—one that is biometrically rooted in brain activity and capable of interacting with environments based on thought and attention alone.

Innovation

Neurable pioneered the integration of real-time neural data into digital interaction, enabling gamers to influence gameplay not by traditional input but by intention and focus. In immersive environments like VR and AR, this redefines identity and presence—making the player's brain patterns part of the input stack. Their AI models adapt dynamically to each user's brain signals, creating personalized experiences and opening new frontiers in identity-linked authentication and adaptive gaming interfaces.

Impact

Neurable's work has positioned BCIs as a credible input method for gaming and immersive experiences. It has inspired a wave of interest in neuroadaptive games, where challenges, narratives, and outcomes adapt to players' mental states. By potentially linking brainwave data with digital avatars or decentralized identifiers (DIDs), Neurable creates pathways for biometric identity in the Metaverse—offering new modes of access, verification, and engagement without relying on passwords or tokens.

Challenges

Widespread adoption of BCI in gaming faces several barriers. Hardware remains relatively expensive and niche, and continuous EEG monitoring raises privacy and ethical concerns. Data ownership and informed consent are crucial, especially when brainwave profiles could be used for personalization or monetization. There's also technical variability—signal quality and interpretation can differ by user, environment, and device calibration.

Lessons Learned

Neurable demonstrates that brainwave-driven identity and interaction are technically feasible and immersive. However, it highlights the need for clear ethical standards for neural data use. Integration with decentralized identity protocols—where users own and control their neural data profiles—could align BCI innovation with Web3 values of sovereignty, security, and self-custody.

Future Outlook

As BCI technology becomes more portable and cost-effective, its use in gaming and virtual identity will likely expand. Future iterations may integrate soul-bound tokens or DID-linked biometric traits, enabling secure, private neural authentication. Neurable's trajectory suggests that neural signatures could become the next frontier of decentralized identity, blending the body, brain, and blockchain in immersive digital ecosystems.

NexMind—Brain-to-Computer Control in Immersive Gaming Interfaces

Platform/Technology Name: NexMind
　Company: NeuroLeap Inc. (Malaysia)
　Year Launched: 2019 (research), 2022 (commercial product)
　Core Technologies: Brain–computer interface (BCI), electroencephalography (EEG), neurofeedback, real-time brain signal translation
　Application Domain: Neurogaming, immersive interaction, cognitive control systems

Overview

NexMind is a portable, non-invasive BCI headset developed to translate brainwave activity into real-time digital commands. Positioned at the intersection of neurotechnology and immersive gaming, NexMind enables players to interact with digital environments using cognitive intention alone—without physical controllers. Technology allows for mental commands like push, pull, rotate, and select, enabling a hands-free gaming experience that is particularly relevant in XR, VR, and Metaverse applications.

Innovation

NexMind offers an innovative neural interface with a machine learning brain decoding engine trained on user-specific EEG patterns. Through neurofeedback and adaptation, it builds a personalized BCI map, enabling intuitive game control based on focused mental tasks. Unlike traditional input methods, NexMind integrates mental state tracking (such as attention and calmness) into gameplay mechanics, laying the foundation for emotion-aware or adaptive game design. Its SDK supports integration with Unity and Unreal Engine, making it accessible to mainstream game developers.

Impact

NexMind represents a leap in human–computer symbiosis in gaming, especially in regions like Southeast Asia where it has catalyzed neurogaming startups and local research and development ecosystems. The headset has been piloted in AR/VR games, educational applications, and gamified meditation systems, illustrating how cognitive interaction can reshape gameplay, accessibility, and user engagement. It offers inclusive design benefits for players with limited mobility and opens new possibilities for adaptive gameplay in therapeutic and performance-based settings.

Challenges

BCI systems like NexMind face significant hurdles in mainstream adoption. Signal noise, muscle artifacts, and cognitive variability can affect performance. Calibration remains a user-intensive process. Real-time latency and bandwidth limitations in cloud-synced BCI environments can interfere with fast-paced gameplay. Moreover, ethical questions around neural data privacy and commercial use persist in the absence of robust data governance frameworks.

Lessons Learned

NexMind shows that intent-based interaction is not only viable but also enhances immersion and personalization in gaming. Neuroadaptive feedback mechanisms can improve user focus and retention, but data trust models and ethical AI protocols must be built alongside hardware. Decentralized identity solutions—where brainwave profiles are user-owned and selectively disclosed—could address future privacy concerns in neural gaming.

Future Outlook

As BCI headsets become more compact, accurate, and affordable, NexMind's platform may evolve into an open protocol for neuro-integrated Web3 gaming, allowing players to store, port, and monetize their neural profiles as NFTs or identity-linked credentials. The convergence of BCI, AI, and blockchain identity will likely shape the next phase of immersive, cognitive-first game design.

References

Abiri, R., Borhani, S., Sellers, E. W., Jiang, Y., and Zhao, X. (2019). A comprehensive review of EEG-based brain–computer interface paradigms. *Journal of Neural Engineering, 16*(1), 011001. https://doi.org/10.1088/1741-2552/aaf12e

Ahn, M., Lee, M., Choi, J., and Jun, S. C. (2014). A review of brain-computer interface games and an opinion survey from researchers, developers and users. *Sensors, 14*(8), 14601–14633. https://doi.org/10.3390/s140814601

Allison, B. Z., and Neuper, C. (2010). Could anyone use a BCI? In B. Graimann, B. Z. Allison, and G. Pfurtscheller (Eds.), *Brain–Computer Interfaces* (pp. 35–54). Springer. https://doi.org/10.1007/978-3-642-02091-9_3

Bécue-Bertaut, M., Poirier, F., and Baratin, L. (2021). Brain–Computer Interfaces and Human–Computer Interaction: Shared Perspectives for Evaluation. *Sensors, 21*(17), 5814. https://doi.org/10.3390/s21175814

Burwell, S. J., Sample, M., and Racine, E. (2017). Ethical aspects of brain computer interfaces: A scoping review. *BMC Medical Ethics, 18*(1), 60. https://doi.org/10.1186/s12910-017-0220-y

Cattan, G. (2021). *The use of brain–computer interfaces in games is not ready for the general public.* Front. Comput. Sci., 24 March 2021,Volume 3 – 2021. https://doi.org/10.3389/fcomp.2021.628773

References

Emotiv. (2023). *Neurotechnology for brain research, gaming, and performance.* https://www.emotiv.com/

Gramfort, A., Luessi, M., Larson, E., Engemann, D. A., Strohmeier, D., Brodbeck, C., ... and Hämäläinen, M. S. (2013). MEG and EEG data analysis with MNE-Python. *Frontiers in Neuroscience, 7,* 267. https://doi.org/10.3389/fnins.2013.00267

Gürkök, H., and Nijholt, A. (2014). Brain–computer interfaces for multimodal interaction: A survey and principles. *International Journal of Human-Computer Interaction, 30*(11), 788–801. https://doi.org/10.1080/10447318.2014.924986

Haselager, P. (2013). Did I do that? Brain–computer interfacing and the sense of agency. *Minds and Machines, 23*(3), 405–418. https://doi.org/10.1007/s11023-012-9289-4

Ienca, M., and Andorno, R. (2017). Towards new human rights in the age of neuroscience and neurotechnology. *Life Sciences, Society and Policy, 13*(1), 1–27. https://doi.org/10.1186/s40504-017-0050-1

Ienca, M., Haselager, P., and Emanuel, E. J. (2018). Brain leaks and consumer neurotechnology. *Nature Biotechnology, 36*(9), 805–810. https://doi.org/10.1038/nbt.4240

Intheon. (2020). *NeuroPype: Real-time biosignal processing platform.* Retrieved from https://www.intheon.io/neurotechnology

Lawhern, V. J., Solon, A. J., Waytowich, N. R., Gordon, S. M., Hung, C. P., and Lance, B. J. (2018). EEGNet: A compact convolutional neural network for EEG-based brain–computer interfaces. *Journal of Neural Engineering, 15*(5), 056013. https://doi.org/10.1088/1741-2552/aace8c

Maiseli, B., Abdalla, A. T., Massawe, L. V., Mbise, M., Mkocha, K., Nassor, N. A., Ismail, M., Michael, J., and Kimambo, S. (2023). Brain–computer interface: Trend, challenges, and threats. *Brain Informatics, 10*(20). https://doi.org/10.1186/s40708-023-00183-8

Moreno-Calderón, S., Martínez-Cagigal, V., Santamaría-Vázquez, E., Pérez-Velasco, S., Marcos-Martínez, D., and Hornero, R. (2023). Combining brain-computer interfaces and multiplayer video games: An application based on c-VEPs. *Frontiers in Human Neuroscience, 17,* 10435322. https://doi.org/10.3389/fnhum.2023.10435322

Neurable. (2021). *Enten: Brain-computer interface headphones.* Retrieved from https://www.neurable.com/

Neurable. (2023). *Everyday brain-computer interface technology.* https://www.neurable.com/

OpenBCI. (2023). *Open-source brain-computer interface technology.* https://www.openbci.com/

Renard, Y., Lotte, F., Gibert, G., Congedo, M., Maby, E., Delannoy, V., ... and Lécuyer, A. (2010). OpenViBE: An open-source software platform to design, test, and use brain–computer interfaces in real and virtual environments. *Presence: Teleoperators and Virtual Environments, 19*(1), 35–53. https://doi.org/10.1162/pres.19.1.35

Summers, C., and Keizer, S. (2022). Brain-computer interfaces in video games: A review. *Frontiers in Computer Science, 4,* 825077. https://doi.org/10.3389/fcomp.2022.825077

The University of Texas at Austin. (2024, March 29). *Universal brain-computer interface lets people play games with just their thoughts.* https://cockrell.utexas.edu/news/archive/9743-universal-brain-computer-interface-lets-people-play-games-with-just-their-thoughts

Thompson, D. E. (2019). Diversity and inclusivity in neurotechnology: Barriers and opportunities. *Neuroethics, 12*(3), 221–229. https://doi.org/10.1007/s12152-019-09401-1

Virtanen, P., Gommers, R., Oliphant, T. E., Haberland, M., Reddy, T., Cournapeau, D., ... and van der Walt, S. J. (2020). SciPy 1.0: Fundamental algorithms for scientific computing in Python. *Nature Methods, 17*(3), 261–272. https://doi.org/10.1038/s41592-019-0686-2

Wexler, A. (2019). Privacy in the brain–computer interface: Reconciling neuroscience and neuroethics. *Journal of Law and the Biosciences, 6*(1), 170–178. https://doi.org/10.1093/jlb/lsz007

Willsey, M. S., Shah, N. P., Avansino, D. T., Hahn, N. V., Jamiolkowski, R. M., Kamdar, F. B., Hochberg, L. R., Willett, F. R., and Henderson, J. M. (2025). A high-performance brain–computer interface for finger decoding and quadcopter game control in an individual with paralysis. *Nature Medicine, 31*(1), 96–104. https://doi.org/10.1038/s41591-024-03341-8

Yuste, R., Goering, S., Arcas, B. A. Y., Bi, G., Carmena, J. M., Carter, A., ... and Wolpaw, J. (2017). Four ethical priorities for neurotechnologies and AI. *Nature, 551*(7679), 159–163. https://doi.org/10.1038/551159a

Chapter 10
The Gamer's Edge: Skills for the Digital Century

Abstract "The Gamer's Edge: Skills for the Digital Century" explores how gameplay develops future-ready skills such as critical thinking, strategic decision-making, adaptability, digital literacy, and cross-cultural collaboration. From Esports teams that mirror startup dynamics to multiplayer environments that foster leadership and real-time communication, gaming has become a powerful incubator for twenty first-century talent. Readers will discover how games are used to train surgeons, teach coding, simulate corporate strategy, and prepare youth for jobs that do not yet exist. The chapter also highlights how gaming can bridge skill gaps in underserved communities, equipping them with tools to thrive in a tech-driven world. As automation and AI reshape industries, gamers may emerge as unexpected but essential leaders of the future workforce.

Keywords Artificial intelligence (AI) · Future of work · Gamified learning · Digital skills · Immersive Technologies · Web3 · Metaverse · Esports · Serious games · Tokenized economies · Digital inclusion · Skill-based education · Game-based workforce training · Lifelong learning · Human-AI collaboration

Introduction: Gaming as a Skills Incubator

Gaming is becoming a learning platform for many of the most in demand in today's digital economy. Whether it's mastering complex systems, leading teams, or adapting to constant change, gamers are cultivating habits of mind that mirror those of successful professionals. As automation and AI reshape industries, the competencies gained through gaming are increasingly relevant. This chapter explores how gameplay cultivates twenty first-century skills, prepares players for digital careers, and offers economic opportunity, especially for young people in underserved communities.

Gaming is creating new jobs for digital environments. These include game designers, narrative architects, and virtual world builders; streamers, Esports athletes, and influencers; 3D artists, avatar designers, and modders; community managers, DAO governors, and token auditors; AI avatar trainers, virtual educators, and digital event curators. Platforms like Roblox, Minecraft, and Fortnite have blurred the lines between gamer and creator. Roblox developers earned over $600 million in 2022 alone, showing that user-generated content can become a full-fledged digital career (Van Leugenhagen 2023).

With just a smartphone and an internet connection, individuals can participate in play-to-earn and contribute-to-earn models, access immersive education and skill-building, own digital property with appreciating value, and earn income from gaming guilds or digital labor. Gaming guilds, like Yield Guild Games, act as decentralized cooperatives and provide economic opportunities. They invest in NFTs and digital assets, renting them to players in return for revenue sharing. They enable players without capital to participate in Web3 games, share profits between players, the guild, and asset holders, and govern decisions through transparent, token-based DAOs. In the Philippines, Brazil, and India, thousands of players have earned real-world income through these structures.

As AI curates experiences and platforms gamify attention, the line between labor and leisure is increasingly blurred. Gamers now engage in a wide range of virtual labor, and terms like *digital labour*, *playbour*, and *gamified income* capture these emerging forms of work, where economic value is tied to presence, participation, and performance in virtual spaces.

Impact of AI and Automation

It is estimated that up to 300 million, full-time jobs globally could be automated (Deloitte AI Institute 2024), particularly roles in administration, customer service, data entry, and logistics. However, history offers a note of optimism, reflecting that 60% of jobs in the USA in 2018 did not exist in the 1940s (Brynjolfsson and McAfee 2017).

According to Eloundou et al. (2023), nearly 80% of the workforce may see at least 10% of their job functions impacted by generative AI technologies, and 19% may experience disruption to over half of their tasks. This shift highlights the growing need for creativity, data fluency, problem-solving, and collaborative skills; traits increasingly nurtured within immersive digital environments like games and virtual worlds. By 2030, over 700 million people are expected to inhabit digital spaces. These environments will give rise to jobs that blend entertainment, productivity, and social value; many of which are only now being imagined. New jobs are already emerging in AI governance, data science, cybersecurity, digital ethics, and immersive technologies. Fields such as telehealth, electric vehicle maintenance, and renewable energy installation are also expanding. Notably, roles that require human judgment and empathy, such as teachers, psychologists, healthcare providers, and creatives, are more resilient to automation.

Human Work in the Gaming Economy

Since 2015, global job skills have changed by 25%, with projections suggesting a 65% change by 2030 (World Economic Forum 2024). As industries transform, new roles are emerging that align closely with gaming mindsets. They include metaverse facilitators managing virtual events, education, and commerce, AI interaction designers shaping human–AI collaboration, gamified learning architects designing digital education systems, and neuroadaptive game designers creating responsive experiences using brain–computer interfaces. Currently, skills related to the digital economy are in demand, including AI-related skills (e.g., prompt engineering, machine learning, and data analytics), cybersecurity and digital ethics, communication, adaptability, and emotional intelligence, design and development for virtual worlds, and human–machine collaboration.

Gamers' comfort with systems thinking, digital spaces, and feedback loops uniquely positions them to lead in these domains. As remote work expands, the ability to collaborate in virtual environments will be essential.

In addition to formal skills training, games help develop valuable skills. Modern games demand more than reflexes. They require critical thinking, strategic planning, collaboration, adaptability, and real-time problem-solving. In fast-paced environments, players must analyze variables, anticipate consequences, and make quick decisions, skills directly applicable to fields like cybersecurity, emergency response, and financial trading.

Research shows that gamers often outperform non-gamers on tests of spatial awareness, multi-tasking, and decision speed. Role-playing and sandbox games foster creative thinking, while competitive genres like MOBAs (Multiplayer Online Battle Arenas) and battle royales develop situational awareness and pressure management.

Games like Roblox are rapidly evolving into platforms where players don't just play, they build, collaborate, and solve complex problems, effectively generating a verifiable, skills-based résumé through gameplay. Within Roblox Studio, users learn scripting, 3D modeling, game economics, and project management, often while working in globally distributed teams. These activities mirror real-world competencies such as coding proficiency, digital design, entrepreneurial thinking, and team communication. As Roblox continues to integrate analytics, badges, and creator dashboards, a player's in-game achievements, published games, monetization success, user engagement, and collaboration history can be tracked and showcased as tangible evidence of transferable skills. In the near future, these digital portfolios could serve as trusted, blockchain-verifiable credentials for employers or educational institutions seeking agile, creative, and tech-savvy talent. As an example, the digital skills portfolio that could be built through playing Roblox is shown below.

1. *Game Development and Scripting*
    - Developed interactive games using Lua scripting within Roblox Studio
    - Learned to apply programming logic, loops, conditionals, and functions

- Used modular coding practices to optimize game performance
- Integrated UI/UX features such as menus, health bars, and inventory systems

2. *3D Design and Environment Building*
   - Built immersive 3D worlds using Roblox Studio tools
   - Created terrain, architecture, lighting, and dynamic environments
   - Applied spatial design principles to guide player navigation and experience
   - Developed custom assets and textured objects using external tools (e.g., Blender)

3. *Game Design Thinking*
   - Balanced gameplay mechanics for challenge and engagement
   - Designed levels with progression, reward loops, and replayability
   - Applied feedback from player testing to improve the design
   - Experimented with genres including obstacle courses, simulations, RPGs, and tycoon games

4. *Data-Driven Optimization*
   - Used analytics tools to monitor player behavior, session time, and drop-off points
   - Iterated game features based on real-time engagement metrics
   - A/B tested monetization strategies (e.g., in-game passes, badges, collectables)

5. *Digital Collaboration and Teamwork*
   - Worked with remote team members on co-developed games
   - Participated in online game jams and creation challenges
   - Used shared platforms like Trello, Discord, and GitHub for coordination and feedback
   - Communicated project roles and timelines effectively in a virtual team environment

6. *Entrepreneurship and Monetization*
   - Created in-game economies using Robux and virtual items
   - Learned pricing strategies for game passes, avatars, and accessories
   - Managed developer products and payout structures
   - Marketed games through in-platform ads and player community engagement

7. *Community Engagement and Moderation*
   - Built and managed active game communities with thousands of players
   - Created rules, moderated behavior, and responded to user feedback
   - Used tools like Developer Console and group management settings for moderation
   - Fostered inclusive, respectful digital environments
   - Problem-*Solving and Adaptive Learning*

- Debugged scripts and solved gameplay logic issues
- Learned independently through tutorials, forums, and trial-and-error
- Applied creative solutions when tools or assets were limited
- Adapted games to meet player expectations and emerging trends

8. *Digital Literacy and Platform Navigation*
   - Gained fluency with a complex creation platform
   - Navigated asset libraries, publishing tools, and in-game economy systems
   - Understood concepts like file management, asset reuse, and cloud-based collaboration
   - Practiced safe digital behavior, identity management, and data protection

This portfolio demonstrates a powerful example of a future-ready skill set, which provides a foundation for careers in game design and development, UX/UI and interactive media, creative entrepreneurship, virtual world management, metaverse coordination, digital education, simulation, and storytelling.

Skilling for AI and Immersive Technologies

The world is entering a new era of intelligent workforces, where autonomous AI agents are rapidly transforming roles across sectors, from clinical pharmacy to human resources and hospitality. These AI agents can now reason, plan, and execute tasks with minimal human intervention, functioning as coordinated multi-agent teams that deliver accurate, scalable, and trustworthy outcomes (Deloitte 2024). This shift is a broader signal of workforce transformation, affecting how tasks are distributed, how decisions are made, and how value is created.

As organizations increasingly adopt AI agents to enhance efficiency and personalize services, the demand for human workers is shifting toward new hybrid roles. Professionals are now expected to interpret AI-generated insights, collaborate with digital systems, and supervise automated processes. For instance, while AI may manage data entry, inventory tracking, or initial customer queries, human workers are tasked with more complex judgment-based functions, such as ethical oversight, advanced problem-solving, and personalized engagement.

There will be multiple pathways to skilling and reskilling the workforce of the future. This evolution brings significant implications for skills training across all industries. Digital literacy, data analytics, and AI fluency are becoming essential baseline competencies. Moreover, domain-specific knowledge must now intersect with technical skills; for example, marketing professionals will need to interpret predictive analytics, while healthcare workers will need to evaluate AI-driven clinical recommendations.

In this context, education and workforce training systems must evolve rapidly. Traditional classrooms are giving way to immersive and adaptive learning environments powered by the Metaverse and AI. Technologies such as virtual reality, extended reality, and gamified simulations are creating new ways to develop both technical and soft skills. Immersive simulations allow learners to safely experiment, fail, and improve, making complex training more engaging, repeatable, and effective (Martin et al. 2023).

Already, institutions worldwide are pioneering this shift. The University of Nottingham (2025) has introduced digital health modules, while Monash University (2022) is using virtual reality for telepharmacy simulations. In the USA, Northeastern University is integrating machine learning and pharmacogenomics into its curriculum, and Taipei Medical University (2024) is exploring Metaverse-driven case-based learning.

These innovations are redefining education. In the Metaverse, learners can participate in avatar-based case studies, engage in collaborative problem-solving with peers worldwide, and receive real-time feedback from AI mentors. Blockchain-enabled systems may track credentials and incentivize lifelong learning through token-based economies, while decentralized platforms offer access to education beyond geographic and economic barriers (Nguyen and Pham 2023; Nadarasa 2023).

To prepare workers for the digital future, educational institutions must rethink curricula and pedagogy. This includes integrating AI ethics, data governance, digital consent, and algorithmic bias into core training, ensuring that graduates are equipped with the technological fluency, ethical reasoning, and adaptability needed to lead in a digitally intelligent economy (Bansal et al. 2022).

Ultimately, as AI agents become part of the mainstream workforce, the human role will evolve. Human workers will focus more on creativity, empathy, critical thinking, and oversight. Organizations that invest in digital upskilling, immersive learning, and cross-disciplinary education today will be better positioned to thrive in the intelligent, immersive, and decentralized economies of tomorrow.

The Uberization of Education and Skills Development

The "uberization" of education, on-demand, accessible, and personalized learning experiences will play a critical role in preparing people for the future of work. AI-powered personal learning assistants, immersive VR training, and blockchain-verified credentials are redefining lifelong learning (Martin et al. 2023).

The learning platforms and models will not mirror the past. Metaverse, Esports and games offer new pathways. Gaming offers an accessible gateway to skill-building for youth with limited access to traditional education or formal training. Mobile games, coding apps, and Esports leagues are being deployed by NGOs and schools to teach STEM, English, and digital citizenship. In regions like Sub-Saharan Africa, Southeast Asia, and Latin America, game-based learning helps bridge the digital divide. Initiatives that turn local game centers into training hubs are empowering young people with relevant, job-ready skills.

Learning by Doing: Education as an Immersive Experience

The Metaverse education market is projected to grow from $56.73 million in 2023 to $763.7 million by 2030, with a compound annual growth rate of 44.98% (Statista 2024). Experiential learning in the Metaverse allows students to safely simulate complex scenarios, such as virtual surgeries or engineering tasks, without real-world consequences. These environments foster not just technical skills but also collaboration, critical thinking, and resilience. Platforms must develop high-quality immersive content, train instructors and AI avatars, and build infrastructure to support engagement at scale.

In the evolving world of gaming and the Metaverse, education is being redefined, not as a phase of life, but as a continuous, interactive, and economically empowered experience. No longer limited to formal classrooms or static curricula, learning in the digital age is immersive, gamified, and personalized. It is taking place in virtual worlds where avatars learn, teach, and build careers. As Web3, artificial intelligence, and immersive technologies converge, the Metaverse is becoming not just a playground but a powerful engine for global skill development and economic inclusion.

Gamified education in the Metaverse leverages AR, VR, and AI to transform passive learning into active participation. Students no longer merely study subjects; they experience them. Through avatars and digital simulations, learners explore planetary systems in astronomy, perform virtual surgeries in medical training, or role-play as historical figures in social science modules. Real-time feedback and adaptive AI tutors ensure that every experience is personalized, just-in-time, and tailored to individual learning styles.

This immersive, experiential model is not just more engaging, it is more effective. It allows for competency-based progression, soft skills training, and multidisciplinary learning in a single, gamified ecosystem.

Learn-to-Earn: Turning Education into Economic Opportunity

In this new model, learning is no longer a sunk cost; it's a form of digital labor. Gamified education platforms reward learners with tokens, NFTs, or blockchain-based microcredentials for engaging in learning tasks. Completing a coding challenge, moderating a community forum, or winning a simulation game might earn a student verifiable credentials, each recorded immutably on-chain. These credentials can be stacked into personalized learning portfolios and used to gain access to employment opportunities, DAO participation, or exclusive content and mentorships. Education becomes a parallel economy, where progress is incentivized, credentials are tradable, and learners are compensated for their time and effort.

Tokenized Skills and Portable Digital Identity

In the Web3 Metaverse, skills are assets. Blockchain-secured microcredentials, such as NFTs or soulbound tokens, serve as verified indicators of what a learner has achieved. These can represent hard skills like programming, soft skills like leadership, or even behavioral traits like resilience or ethical decision-making, developed through interactive gameplay. This system enables learners to build portable digital identities that travel across platforms, ecosystems, and industries. A badge earned for mentoring peers in a gaming guild, for example, might serve as a qualification for moderating a DAO, managing an online community, or contributing to digital product development. It's a future where learning, play, and work are fully interconnected.

Reimagining Skills Training in the Digital Age

In this era of intelligent machines and immersive environments, the ability to learn continuously and adapt rapidly will be more critical than any static credential. The range of options for future skills training is rapidly diversifying:

1. *Immersive Virtual Platforms*: VR and AR technologies enable learners to inhabit simulated environments and learn through real-time feedback. Future doctors, engineers, and climate scientists can gain experience by performing virtual surgeries, managing smart grids, or mitigating digital disasters—all before entering the real world.
2. *AI-Powered Personalized Learning*: AI learning assistants will design adaptive curricula based on a learner's pace, interests, and goals. These platforms will recommend skills based on market demand, personalize pathways, and offer real-time mentoring. In essence, AI will become both tutor and talent scout.
3. *Community-Led and Peer-to-Peer Learning*: Decentralized autonomous organizations (DAOs) and online guilds are emerging as new educational institutions. Learners join global communities focused on areas like coding, content creation, and blockchain development. Participants co-create and co-teach, rewarded with microcredentials and tokens.
4. *Serious Games and Simulations*: Game-based learning is redefining how skills are acquired and measured. From scenario-based strategy games in business education to cooperative Esports challenges that develop leadership, these formats promote real-world readiness in a compelling, scalable way.
5. *Modular Credentials and Blockchain Verification*: Education will become unbundled. Instead of degrees, learners will earn verifiable microcredentials for specific skills. Blockchain will authenticate achievements across platforms, enabling the formation of lifelong learning portfolios.
6. *Corporate and Industry-Led Learning Hubs*: Tech companies, Esports platforms, and Web3 communities are increasingly becoming education providers.

Enterprises will not just hire talent—they will cultivate it through sponsored academies, hackathons, and mentorship ecosystems.

In this dynamic landscape, a diverse ecosystem of providers will contribute. Traditional institutions will have to evolve to survive, integrating digital tools, interdisciplinary coursework, and real-time analytics into their pedagogies. They will compete with private EdTech Firms with scalable, tech-forward delivery with platforms that combine gamification, data, and AI. Tech Companies like Microsoft, Meta, and Roblox are already creating training programs embedded in their platforms.

It will not just be the traditional institutions contributing to skills training. Web3 and Metaverse Communities will become participatory campuses, where members both learn and teach. NGOs and Development Agencies will adapt this approach and use mobile-first game-based learning to empower youth in underserved regions. Finally, individual creators and influencers will design niche courses and learning experiences, distributed via social and blockchain platforms.

The Reinvention of Universities and Colleges

Higher education will be forced to undergo a profound metamorphosis to stay relevant. The campus of the future will be:

- *Hybrid and Immersive:* With classrooms blending physical labs and VR Metaverses, learning will be active, experiential, and borderless. Stanford University blends in-person and VR classrooms through its Virtual Human Interaction Lab (Bailenson 2022). Embry-Riddle Aeronautical University uses extended reality labs for aviation maintenance training (ERAU 2023).
- *Modular and Stackable:* Rigid degrees will give way to personalized stacks of microcredentials, earned through a mix of academic study, industry training, and game-based simulations. Arizona State University and the University of Maine System offer stackable microcredentials and badges aligned to workforce needs.
- *AI-Augmented:* Intelligent tutors and learning analytics will optimize instruction, flag support needs, and connect learners to real-world mentors. At Harvard's massive CS50 course, the AI-driven "CS50 Duck" chatbot assists students with coding queries, doubling learning efficiency compared to in-class instruction online (Axios 2024). Similarly, research from the University of Puerto Rico presents "Iris"—an AI tutor that offers tailored prompts and feedback in computer science assignments, viewed as a complement to human teaching (Bassner et al. 2024).
- *Transdisciplinary:* Courses will blend coding with ethics, biology with systems design, and narrative storytelling with data science. UC Irvine's "Into the Metaverse" course unites students from psychology, art, business, and game design (Lee 2023). The H3ABioNet program in Africa integrates biology, programming, and systems design (H3ABioNet 2022).

- *Ecosystem-Centric:* Universities will partner with platforms, employers, NGOs, and gaming guilds to ensure curriculum relevance and learner impact. Technological University Dublin does partner with startup hubs through GROWTHhub (TU Dublin 2023). Stanford's SMILE project collaborates with local NGOs and global networks for scalable education (Patel et al. 2022).

To effectively prepare current teachers and educators for the digital age, a multilayered strategy is essential. This begins with comprehensive digital literacy training that equips educators with foundational knowledge in emerging technologies such as AI, gamification, and immersive tools like virtual and augmented reality. Professional development must evolve from one-off workshops to continuous, personalized learning journeys that reflect the rapid pace of technological change. Educators should be empowered to co-create digital content, navigate data dashboards, and facilitate interactive, student-led learning experiences within virtual environments. Peer mentoring networks, collaborative online communities, and access to on-demand microcredentials can further support skill development. Crucially, training must also address digital ethics, data privacy, and inclusive design to ensure technology use is equitable, responsible, and aligned with educational values. As frontline facilitators of future-ready learning, educators need not only tools but also time, mentorship, and institutional support to confidently lead in a digitally transformed world.

Immersive and Decentralized Education

Web3 and the Metaverse are redefining the nature of ownership, identity, and work. By 2030, over 700 million people are expected to inhabit digital worlds (Samala, 2025). In these environments, individuals will participate in virtual economies, own tokenized assets, and engage in decentralized collaboration. Web3 introduces a shift from corporate control to community-first models. Communities form around shared interests and operate through tokenized incentives and stakeholder participation (Nguyen and Pham 2023). Users own their data and assets via NFTs, which carry not just economic value but also digital rights. This opens up employment and entrepreneurial opportunities for digitally excluded populations. The open Metaverse, powered by blockchain and DeFi, is likely to fuel new forms of work where participants are not just users but stakeholders. As digital economies grow, so will the need for skills in blockchain governance, smart contract development, virtual asset management, and community moderation.

Education in the Metaverse is also becoming decentralized. Community-owned guilds and learning hubs are replacing traditional institutions. These self-organizing groups offer training in blockchain, digital storytelling, content moderation, and more. Learners are also contributors, creating content, co-governing the platform, and earning social or financial rewards in return. This peer-led model empowers learners to become educators, builders, and ecosystem stewards, flipping the top-down education model into one of collaborative knowledge economies.

Gamers are emerging as entrepreneurs, streamers, content creators, game designers, and community managers. These roles demand a combination of storytelling, brand development, platform literacy, and audience engagement. Modders create new game content, often developing portfolios that lead to careers in design and development. Streamers and influencers monetize content through subscriptions, sponsorships, and affiliate marketing. These self-taught digital professionals are redefining what it means to build a tech-enabled career.

Esports as Leadership Lab

Esports are fast becoming a leadership laboratory for the digital age. Esports will give players the opportunity to experience strategy, communication, defense, and execution. Success hinges on coordination, trust, and clear communication, all under pressure. Team captains lead reviews, analyze data, and assign roles. Coaches optimize group dynamics and individual performance. These experiences teach goal setting, peer feedback, iterative learning, and conflict resolution. The Esports ecosystem, including analysts, managers, and marketing professionals, mirrors the collaborative dynamics of agile tech teams.

Serious Games for Workforce Training

Beyond formal education, serious games will be central in workforce training and skill development. Many industries are already turning to simulations to train employees in a safe, cost-effective way—for example, pilot training has long used flight simulators (essentially a form of serious game). By 2030, there will be gamified training modules across sectors: emergency responders practicing disaster scenarios in a game, retail employees learning customer service via a role-playing game, or factory workers training on virtual replicas of machinery. This not only improves retention but also allows tracking of progress through game analytics. The military has used games for years (for training and recruitment), and this will continue with even more advanced VR war-game simulations by 2035. Soft skills like communication, teamwork, and leadership are also being taught through cooperative game scenarios. As the future of work demands continuous upskilling, employees might regularly engage with training games as part of their professional development.

One noteworthy area is AI and coding education, because understanding AI and programming will be important, many games will be created that teach these abstract concepts playfully (e.g., puzzle games that involve coding logic, or AI-driven games that let you tweak algorithms). Such approaches lower the barrier for people to enter tech fields by cultivating interest through interactive play rather than dry textbooks. In the same vein, future skills like critical thinking, creativity, and collaboration—identified as crucial by educational bodies—are naturally fostered in well-designed games.

A systematic review highlighted how serious games can develop "future skills" effectively when designed with clear pedagogical goals (Gurbuz and Celik 2022). The review of 32 serious game design approaches with a special focus on future skill development. It was found that 8 (25%) of these design approaches support at least one future skill, among which problem-solving, collaboration, and teamwork are the most commonly supported ones. It is also discovered that clear goals and interactivity, used in 6 (75%) and 5 (63%) of the eight design approaches, respectively, were the most commonly implemented game design elements. The study provides valuable insights for game designers, software developers, educational technology researchers, and engineering educators in various domains. They conclude that serious games offer a strong potential for developing future skills along with the twenty first-century learning ecosystem.

Serious games are now embedded in corporate and academic training. In medicine, surgical simulators help students refine precision and coordination. In law, legal scenario games develop analytical reasoning. Business schools use strategy games to simulate market conditions, risk management, and resource allocation. Coding games such as CodeCombat and Robocode teach programming logic in engaging formats. Games like Civilization are used in classrooms to teach history, diplomacy, and systems thinking. The controlled trial-and-error nature of games allows learners to take risks and build mastery without fear of real-world failure.

Playing games builds intuitive digital fluency. Gamers navigate interfaces, configure settings, interpret real-time data, and collaborate in online environments, with all core digital literacy competencies. They often troubleshoot systems, manage digital identities, and understand virtual economies. These skills transfer to workplace technologies from project management tools to data dashboards. Games foster a mindset of continuous learning and system exploration, these are traits vital for adapting to emerging tools in tech-driven industries.

Beyond formal education, serious games will be central in workforce training and skill development. Many industries are already turning to simulations to train employees in a safe, cost-effective way—for example, pilot training has long used flight simulators (essentially a form of serious game). In the future, gamified training modules will be ubiquitous across sectors. For example, emergency responders practicing disaster scenarios in a game retail employees learning customer service via a role-playing game, or factory workers training on virtual replicas of machinery. This not only improves retention but also allows tracking of progress through game analytics. The military has used games for years (for training and recruitment), and this will continue with even more advanced VR war-game simulations by 2035. Soft skills like communication, teamwork, and leadership are also being taught through cooperative game scenarios. As the future of work demands continuous upskilling, employees might regularly engage with training games as part of their professional development.

Global Access and Economic Inclusion

Perhaps most significantly, gamified education offers a lifeline to underserved communities. With only a smartphone and an internet connection, learners in developing regions can access world-class instruction, earn blockchain-verified credentials, and participate in global job markets.

Gaming today has evolved into far more than a source of entertainment; it now functions as a cultural operating system for the digital age. Within virtual worlds, players don't just compete or complete quests; they govern communities, enforce rules, and even engage in forms of virtual nation-building. This form of digital citizenship reflects a broader societal shift, where identity, responsibility, and participation extend beyond physical borders and into immersive, programmable environments.

At the heart of this transformation is a commitment to inclusive design; the creation of safe, diverse, and accessible gaming experiences that reflect the broad spectrum of players across gender, ability, geography, and culture. Developers are increasingly prioritizing environments where all users feel welcome, represented, and empowered to contribute. These design principles are not only ethical imperatives but also economic drivers, broadening market reach and deepening user engagement.

Gaming has also emerged as a launchpad for youth employment and entrepreneurship, particularly through Esports, digital asset creation, and decentralized governance. Players can build careers not only as competitors or content creators but as DAO leaders, virtual architects, and Metaverse educators. In this way, gaming acts as a career simulator and economic training ground, offering practical skills in digital finance, teamwork, and creative production.

Perhaps most transformative is the flow of value from virtual to real-world economies. Income generated through gameplay, whether via play-to-earn models, streaming, or digital asset sales, is increasingly being used to fund education, support families, and invest in real-world opportunities. Gaming has become a viable economic pathway, particularly for younger generations and those in regions underserved by traditional employment systems.

This potential is most visible in emerging markets, where gaming is bridging the digital divide. In Southeast Asia, Latin America, and Sub-Saharan Africa, mobile gaming is widespread due to affordable smartphones and internet access (GSMA 2022).

In regions where formal employment is limited, gaming is becoming an on-ramp to the digital economy. It fosters financial inclusion, digital literacy, entrepreneurship, and community leadership. Moreover, it introduces sustainability considerations through energy-efficient blockchains, ethical AI design, and attention-aware platform mechanics. These innovations ensure that the growth of the gaming economy can align with broader goals of environmental stewardship and social equity.

In summary, gaming is the foundation of a new cultural and economic logic. It is how a generation is working, learning, organizing, and building futures.

Navigating the Digital Skills Journey

Despite the promise of this new learning frontier, significant challenges must be addressed:

- *Access and Infrastructure:* Digital learning tools require reliable internet, hardware, and electricity. In underserved regions, the lack of infrastructure remains a barrier to participation.
- *Equity and Inclusion:* There is a risk that early adopters and affluent communities will monopolize opportunities. Deliberate efforts are needed to ensure equitable access across socioeconomic, gender, and geographic divides.
- *Digital Safety and Ethics*: With more learning taking place in decentralized, unregulated environments, protections around identity, data, and well-being must be enhanced.
- *Teacher Preparedness*: Educators may struggle to keep pace with the evolving digital education landscape. Ongoing support and digital literacy training are essential.
- *Resistance to Change:* Institutions steeped in tradition may resist the unbundling of degrees or integration of immersive learning models. Policy, accreditation, and funding reforms are required.
- *Over-commercialization:* The gamification of education risks reducing learning to transactional behavior unless carefully balanced with intrinsic motivation, ethics, and social purpose.
- *Recognition of Non-Traditional Credentials:* There is still hesitation among employers and educational institutions to recognize game-based or community-issued credentials. Standards and frameworks for verification must be developed.

Addressing these challenges will require collaboration between governments, educators, technologists, and communities. Only then can the promise of game-powered, immersive education be fully realized for all learners.

Parenting Challenges

For parents, the future of work may feel both exciting and overwhelming. The skills their children will need to thrive are shifting rapidly. But parents can play a proactive role by:

- *Exploring Digital Tools Together*: Co-play games that teach logic, design, or language. Platforms like Roblox Studio or Minecraft Education offer a gateway to creativity and code.
- *Supporting Passion Projects*: Whether it's modding games, launching YouTube channels, or joining online competitions, these projects cultivate initiative, digital fluency, and entrepreneurial thinking.

- *Encouraging Portfolio-Building:* Help children track their digital accomplishments, such as games built, challenges completed, or skills learned. These will increasingly count toward job and college applications.
- *Demystifying Emerging Careers:* Discuss how roles like game developers, Metaverse architects, and digital community managers connect to real-world impact and income.
- *Promoting Healthy Digital Habits*: Balance screen time with reflection, set learning goals, and ensure online safety while encouraging exploration.

Gaming as a Blueprint for Future Readiness

To thrive in this new era, individuals must embrace continuous learning, develop both technical and interpersonal skills, and participate in the co-creation of equitable digital systems. Organizations must invest in ethical AI deployment, workforce retraining, and inclusive innovation. Education systems must pivot toward immersive, flexible, and relevant training.

The future of work will be shaped not by AI alone, but by how humans adapt, respond, and collaborate with it. AI agents and multi-agent systems are already revolutionizing industries, but it is human ingenuity, ethics, and resilience that will define the next Chapter of labor. This is not a time for passive observation. The transformation of work is underway. Those who act now to reskill, innovate, and lead with purpose will help shape a more just, sustainable, and prosperous future.

Gaming is evolution in action. It is where many young people are developing the mental models, social skills, and digital literacies they need to thrive. The future workforce will be built not in rows of desks, but in networks of players, creators, coders, and collaborators. As the world embraces immersive technologies, AI augmentation, and decentralized systems, the responsibility for skills development will be shared across institutions, industries, and individuals. We must empower learners—and especially young gamers—with opportunities to explore, create, and earn through learning. The edge they gain in virtual worlds may well become the foundation of success in the real world. In this century, those who play lead and those who learn through play may just be writing the next Chapter of work itself.

Gaming is a platform for exploration, experimentation, and skill development. Players build adaptive minds, lead teams, navigate complexity, and create value in digital spaces. As work becomes more dynamic and technology is more embedded in daily life, these capabilities will be essential. Gamers are not the passive consumers of yesterday's stereotypes. They are the problem-solvers, collaborators, and innovators of tomorrow. This will be a generation ready to shape the digital century.

Cross-Chapter Insights

Platforms like *Roblox*, *Fortnite Creative*, *Discord*, and *Reddit* empower users as creators, moderators, and community architects. These skills echo the economic models of *YGG* (Chap. 4), the education strategies in *Minecraft* (Chap. 6), and the identity protocols discussed in *Neurable* (Chap. 9). Technical innovation tools like *Moralis* and *Alchemy* (Technical Annex) enable the infrastructure for skill-building in Web3 and gaming. Across these case studies, a new generation is not just playing games—but learning, earning, and building through them.

Case Study

Roblox—A Universe of User-Generated Worlds and Digital Creativity

Game/Platform Name: Roblox
 Developer/Publisher: Roblox Corporation
 Year Released: 2006 (full platform maturity by 2016)
 Genre: User-generated game platform/sandbox/Metaverse
 Technology Stack: Roblox engine, Lua scripting, proprietary cloud infrastructure, cross-platform support (PC, mobile, Xbox)

Roblox is a game creation platform enabling users to design, publish, and monetize interactive 3D experiences. Powered by a vibrant user base of creators, Roblox became one of the most culturally significant platforms for digital youth, education, and the Metaverse movement.

Innovation

No-code/low-code development tools using Lua for scalable experience creation
 Virtual economy driven by Robux, convertible into real-world currency for developers
 Avatar customization and a digital fashion ecosystem
 Roblox Studio provides comprehensive tools for game logic, asset import, and user interaction
 Immersive events, including virtual concerts, brand activations, and education partnerships

Impact

User Base and Engagement
Over 70 million daily active users as of mid-2025
 2.4 billion hours of engagement per month
 Majority of users are under 18, especially popular among Gen Z and Alpha

Economic and Developer Impact
In 2023, creators earned over $680 million collectively
    Top developers-built studios with full-time staff and multimillion-dollar revenue
    Digital fashion and item sales generate billions of Robux in peer-to-peer commerce

Cultural and Educational Reach
Adopted in schools via Roblox education for game-based learning
    Hosts real-world brand activations (e.g., Nike, Gucci, Netflix) and virtual concerts (e.g., Lil Nas X)
    Influences youth culture through virtual identity, expression, and storytelling

Challenges and Controversies

Content Moderation: Vast volume of UGC poses moderation challenges, particularly for child safety
    Developer Exploitation: Critics argue the platform underpays creators relative to value captured
    Data Privacy and Regulation: Ongoing scrutiny over child data and COPPA compliance
    Platform Saturation: Discoverability and success rates have declined due to the influx of new creators

Lessons and Legacy

For Developers: Roblox proves that user-generated platforms can scale into billion-dollar ecosystems—but require ethical monetization and content curation.
    For Players: Offers a gateway into digital creativity, collaboration, and online community building.
    For Policymakers: Roblox necessitates child-first regulatory models, especially for virtual economies, safety, and digital labor rights.

Future Outlook

Growing use of AI-assisted creation tools to lower barriers for new developers
    Global expansion into non-English-speaking markets
    Deeper integration with education and enterprise training
    Greater governance and moderation tools to support safe, inclusive spaces
    Roblox remains one of the most influential platforms shaping the digital generation's understanding of creation, commerce, and community in virtual environments.

Discord: From Gamer Chat to Digital Third Place

Overview

Game/Platform Name: Discord
Developer/Publisher: Discord Inc. (founded by Jason Citron and Stan Vishnevskiy) **Year Released**: 2015
Genre: Social communication platform (originally gamer-centric)
Technology Stack: WebRTC, Electron, React, Go, Rust, and proprietary infrastructure; supports bots, webhooks, and API integrations.

Discord launched as a free voice, video, and text chat app for gamers frustrated with existing VoIP tools like TeamSpeak and Skype. It quickly evolved into a digital hub for communities beyond gaming, including education, fandoms, music, and startups, becoming a critical infrastructure for virtual presence and decentralized social spaces.

Innovation

Frictionless, high-quality voice chat optimized for low-latency gameplay.

Persistent, multi-channel servers (not one-time chatrooms) allowing ongoing community building.

Bot-friendly architecture enabling automation, moderation, and mini-games.

Community-as-platform model: users build and moderate their own "servers" with extensive permissions and integrations.

Digital identity flexibility through avatars, handles, and nicknames per server.

Community-first monetization: Nitro subscriptions, not intrusive ads.

Decentralized governance tools empower server admins and moderators as micro-leaders.

Impact

User Adoption and Demographics
Over 750 million registered users globally (as of 2025).

Core audience: 13–35-year-olds, with heavy adoption by gamers, streamers, and Gen Z creators.

Expanding into education (e.g., study groups), crypto communities, indie developers, and fan cultures.

Economic Value Generated
Raised over $1 billion in funding, with valuations peaking at $15 billion.

In-app Nitro subscriptions are a core revenue stream, supporting emojis, server boosts, and custom features.

Case Study 191

Cultural/Social Influence
Became the "third place" of the digital age—a space for casual hangouts, niche communities, and mental health support.

Widely used by DAOs, **NFT** communities, Esports teams, YouTubers, and fandoms as a default collaboration layer.

Geographic Reach
Global reach with particular strength in the USA, Brazil, India, Germany, and Southeast Asia.

Challenges and Controversies

Moderation at Scale
Decentralized server control means moderation standards vary—leading to issues with harassment, hate speech, and disinformation. Discord has invested in AI moderation tools, community guidelines, and trust and safety teams, but enforcement remains complex.

Association with Toxic Subcultures
Discord has at times been a platform for extremist groups, piracy, and doxxing. Public scrutiny in events like the 2017 Charlottesville rally forced the platform to adopt stricter content policies.

Monetization Tensions
Balancing user-centric design with business growth has led to debates around privacy, ads, and platform neutrality.

Lessons and Legacy

Discord transformed from a niche gamer tool to a foundational layer of digital social infrastructure. It exemplifies how communication platforms can evolve into multi-community ecosystems where governance, identity, and economy are shaped from the ground up. Its journey signals a future where platforms enable creation—not control—and where gaming logic (voice chat, co-presence, avatars) underpins next-gen online interactions.

Reddit—The Front Page of the Internet and the Rise of Decentralized Communities

Platform Name: Reddit
   Developer/Publisher: Founded by Steve Huffman and Alexis Ohanian, currently owned by Reddit, Inc.

Year Released: 2005
Platform Type: Social news aggregation, content rating, and discussion website**Technology Stack:** Python, PostgreSQL, Amazon Web Services (AWS), mobile (iOS/Android), web-based PWA.

Reddit is a user-driven content platform where individuals can post links, text, images, or videos, and communities—called "subreddits"—organize discussion around virtually any topic. It is structured around upvotes/downvotes and community moderation, giving rise to a dynamic, self-regulating ecosystem of discourse.

Innovation

Decentralized Community Governance: Reddit's subreddit structure enables niche, self-governed communities with distinct norms and moderation.

Karma and Voting System: Visibility is democratized through upvotes/downvotes, incentivizing quality and relevance.

Open API and Mod Tools: A robust ecosystem of bots and moderator tools supports decentralized content governance.

AMAs and Real-Time Public Figures: Reddit pioneered the "Ask Me Anything" format, fostering direct, unfiltered communication between celebrities, politicians, and users.

Impact

User Adoption and Demographics
Over 73 million daily active users as of 2024
  Largest audiences from the USA, UK, Canada, and India
  Particularly strong among Millennials and Gen Z
  Popular subreddits span r/science, r/worldnews, r/MadeMeSmile, and r/WallStreetBets

Cultural Influence
Originator of viral trends and memes
  Played pivotal roles in social and political movements (e.g., GameStop short squeeze 2021)
  Hosted influential AMAs with figures like Barack Obama and Bill Gates

Economic Value
Valued at $10 billion during 2021 funding round
  IPO filed in 2024
  Subreddits like r/WallStreetBets have influenced financial markets via collective action

Challenges and Controversies

Moderation and Misinformation: Community-led moderation can allow hate speech and misinformation to flourish if unchecked.

Monetization Tensions: API pricing and advertising strategies have prompted widespread user protest.

Platform Governance: 2023 API changes affected third-party apps, triggering blackouts and platform-wide dissent.

Privacy and Data Ethics: Concerns around AI training data, tracking, and data commodification persist.

Lessons and Insights

For Developers: Empowering decentralized communities can drive platform vitality, but governance and tools must evolve to prevent harm.

For Users: Reddit proves the potential of community self-governance and the power of collective digital voices.

For Policymakers: Reddit highlights the tension between free expression and content moderation, data ethics, and financial influence in digital spaces.

Future Outlook

Maintaining community trust and open access

Evolving moderation practices through AI and human collaboration

Balancing decentralization with content integrity and platform stability

Continued expansion of Reddit's role in financial, political, and cultural ecosystems

Reddit stands as a case study in how decentralized communities can co-create culture, drive market movements, and challenge traditional media and governance structures.

References

Axios.AI. (2024). *The future of AI agents and the labor market.* Axios. Retrieved from https://www.axios.com/newsletters

Bailenson, J. (2022). *The Metaverse classroom.* Stanford University. https://vhil.stanford.edu

Bansal, S., Garg, C., Padappayil, R. P., & Kumar, S. (2022). Virtual reality and the future of medical education: Embracing immersive learning for real-world impact. Medical Education Online, 27(1), 2043264.

Bassner, P., Frankford, E, Krusche, S. (2024). Iris: An AI-Driven Virtual Tutor for Computer Science Education

Brynjolfsson, E., and McAfee, A. (2017). *Machine, platform, crowd: Harnessing our digital future*. W. W. Norton and Company.

Deloitte AI Institute. (2024). *How AI agents are reshaping the future of work*. https://www2.deloitte.com

Eloundou, T., Manning, S., Mishkin, P., & Rock, D. (2023). *GPTs are GPTs: An early look at the labor market impact potential of large language models*. OpenAI. Retrieved from https://openai.com/research/gpts-are-gpts

Embry-Riddle Aeronautical University. (2023). *VR aviation labs take off*. https://erau.edu/news

GSMA. (2022). Mobile internet connectivity report. https://www.gsma.com

Gurbuz, S.C., & Celik, M. (2022). Serious games in future skills development: A systematic review of the design approaches. *International Journal of Serious Games*, 9(2), 1–19. https://doi.org/10.17083/ijsg.v9i2.431

H3ABioNet. (2022). *Building capacity in bioinformatics through interdisciplinary systems learning*. H3ABioNet. Retrieved from https://h3abionet.org

Lee, S. (2023). *UC Irvine and the cross-disciplinary future of the Metaverse*. University of California, Irvine. Retrieved from https://uci.edu/metaverse

Martin, D., Lee, S., & Thompson, R. (2023). *The role of immersive technologies in workforce training and AI fluency*. Journal of Educational Technology, 12(1), 45–59. https://doi.org/10.1109/JET.2023.0581234

Monash University. (2022). *Virtual reality clinical skills laboratories*. Faculty of Pharmacy and Pharmaceutical Sciences.

Nadarasa, D. (2023). Social prescribing in the Metaverse: A new frontier for primary care practice. Journal of Medical Internet Research, 25, e45231.

Nguyen, A. Q., & Pham, D. T. (2023). Decentralised healthcare in the Web3 era: Opportunities for clinical trials and patient engagement. Frontiers in Blockchain, 6, 1174512.1174512. https://doi.org/10.3389/fbloc.2023.1174512

Patel, R., Sharma, T., & Tanaka, M. (2022). *SMILE: A model for mobile education partnerships*. Stanford University. Retrieved from https://smile.stanford.edu

Samala, A.D., Rawas, S., Rahmadika, S. et al. (2025) Virtual reality in education: global trends, challenges, and impacts—game changer or passing trend?. Discov Educ 4, 229. https://doi.org/10.1007/s44217-025-00650-z

Statista. (2024). *Metaverse education market size worldwide from 2023 to 2030*. Statista. https://www.statista.com/statistics/1122479/metaverse-education-market-size

Taipei Medical University. (2024). Immersive learning in pharmacy education: Exploring the Metaverse. TMU Digital Education Initiative.

Technological University Dublin. (2023). *GROWTHhub innovation partnerships*. https://tudublin.ie

University of Nottingham. (2025). Digital health curriculum and AI integration in pharmacy. School of Pharmacy.

Van Leugenhagen, P. (2023, September 5). *Roblox earnings: Takeaways*. Yondr Agency. Retrieved from https://www.yondr.agency/insights/roblox-earnings-takeaways

World Economic Forum. (2024). *Future of Jobs Report*.

Chapter 11
Infinite Playgrounds: Gaming and the Architecture of Tomorrow

Abstract "Infinite Playgrounds: Gaming and the Architecture of Tomorrow" the concluding chapter reinforces the core theme that gaming is no longer just entertainment, its infrastructure reshaping systems, not just sectors. It provides a thematic synthesis of chapters, including technology and infrastructure; skills and work; equity and access; economy and value creation, governance, and ethics. It highlights the macro shifts that will define the next decade, such as from player to creator, from centralized to decentralized platforms, from content consumption to skill accumulation, and from physical workspaces to gamified virtual labor. The chapter outlines strategic imperatives for policymakers, for educators, for developers and tech platforms, and for parents and young people. It reiterates key risks like surveillance, addiction, inequality, and environmental costs and emphasizes the need for inclusive governance, transparent systems, and digital well-being. Finally, it ends with an optimistic vision for the future, where gameplay becomes a portal to meaning, belonging, and purpose and agency, and opportunity flow from games to society.

Keywords Gaming futures · Immersive technologies · Digital credentials · Gamified learning · Web3 and decentralization · AI agents · Brain–computer interfaces · Platform governance · Play-to-earn economies · Ethical design · Digital well-being · Youth empowerment · Metaverse ecosystems · Global inclusion · Civic simulation

Gaming at a Turning Point

This book has tracked the evolution of gaming from an entertainment pastime to become the infrastructure for learning, work, culture, and identity. The key thematic clusters emerging from the book include:

- *Technology and Infrastructure*: AI agents, BCIs, Web3, Immersive platforms.
- *Skills and Work*: Gamified learning, Digital credentials, Esports careers.

- *Equity and Access*: Gaming in the Global South, Inclusion in digital futures.
- *Economy and Value Creation*: Play-to-earn, Creator economy, Tokenization.
- *Governance and Ethics*: Data privacy, Moderation, Community-led models.

Gaming is reshaping global systems of learning, labor, identity, and value. From brain–computer interfaces and AI agents to tokenized economies and immersive education, the convergence of gaming with frontier technologies signals a structural transformation. Below are seven interrelated macro shifts that will define the next era of digital civilization.

From Player to Creator

The traditional divide between game developers and players is dissolving. Platforms like Roblox, Fortnite Creative, and Minecraft Education enable players to build, code, and monetize user-generated content (UGC). In this participatory culture, creation is the new gameplay—and with interoperable platforms, players become world-builders, storytellers, and entrepreneurs. Education systems must support creative computation, digital storytelling, and design thinking from an early age.

From Centralized Control to Decentralized Ownership

Web3 and blockchain technologies are driving a shift from platform-owned assets to user-owned economies. NFTs, smart contracts, and DAOs (Decentralized Autonomous Organizations) allow gamers to own digital property, govern communities, and earn from their contributions. This challenges the extractive monetization models of traditional gaming platforms. New models of platform governance and interoperable asset portability will be essential for sustainable digital economies.

From Content Consumption to Skill Accumulation

Games are evolving into skill simulators and credential engines. As learners complete coding challenges, manage in-game economies, or design virtual worlds, they acquire verifiable skills. These can be captured via digital portfolios or blockchain-based microcredentials, recognized by employers and educational institutions. Credentialing frameworks must evolve to accommodate play-based and performance-based evidence of learning.

From Physical Workspaces to Gamified Virtual Labor

With the rise of the Metaverse and AI-driven virtual platforms, work is becoming increasingly digital, distributed, and gamified. Gamers are now streamers, DAO governors, digital asset designers, or AI curators—roles once unimaginable. "Playbour" (play + labour) is now a serious form of economic activity. Labor policies, digital rights, and income protections must be updated to reflect these new forms of work and value creation.

From Educational Institutions to Learning Ecosystems

Traditional schooling models are being redefined. Immersive simulations, AI mentors, modular credentials, and game-based learning are creating decentralized, lifelong learning environments. Learning is becoming continuous, interactive, and embedded in virtual communities and global guilds. Universities and training systems must reimagine curricula as adaptive, experiential, and learner-led ecosystems.

From Attention Economies to Trust Economies

Gamified platforms currently thrive on capturing user attention and monetizing engagement. However, rising awareness of surveillance capitalism, digital addiction, and platform fatigue is prompting a shift toward trust-centric design—where well-being, autonomy, and data dignity are prioritized. Ethical design, consent-based data governance, and transparency will be competitive differentiators in future platforms.

From Entertainment to Civic Infrastructure

Gaming is increasingly being used for civic simulation, peacebuilding, climate adaptation, and public education. As governments, NGOs, and citizen groups turn to game-based systems for engagement, problem-solving, and training, gaming has become part of our public and institutional infrastructure. Cross-sector partnerships must harness gaming for social good—embedding resilience, participation, and problem-solving into gameplay.

With this extraordinary power comes risks and responsibilities, which have been outlined in the book, including surveillance, addiction, inequality, and environmental costs. This demands the need for policy makers to focus on inclusive governance, transparent systems, and digital well-being through human-centered design. Building the infrastructure of tomorrow is not without risks.

Policymakers need to be ready to recognize digital credentials and user-generated content portfolios and regulate to ensure safe, ethical, and inclusive gaming environments.

Educators need to recognize and embrace game-based, modular, and immersive pedagogies and build capacity for AI and Metaverse integration.

Developers and Tech Platforms should build equitable economies and open-source tools and embed ethical design and user sovereignty.

Parents and Youth need to understand games as ecosystems of growth and encourage balanced, creative, and collaborative digital practices.

A Vision for the Future

What Is the Future We Want to Build Through Gaming?

A world where gameplay becomes a portal to meaning, belonging, and purpose. Where skills, agency, and opportunity flow from games to society. Where to play is to prepare, to create is to contribute, and to connect is to grow. A world where gaming is inclusive infrastructure, a means of participation, learning, and livelihood. It is community-led, interoperable, and driven by digital agency.

A world that is collaborative, ethical, and ecologically aligned. It is possible to envision a future in which gaming is a regenerative force. Game worlds are designed not just to entertain but to cultivate empathy, critical thinking, and ecological awareness. Attention is no longer monetized but protected; digital well-being metrics are embedded into platform design. Gamers earn tokens for climate-positive actions, community stewardship, and co-creation of public digital goods.

Gaming guilds form the backbone of a new civil economy, where knowledge, care, and creativity are the most valuable currencies. Players become digital citizens, builders, and guardians of inclusive futures.

The trajectory the world takes will depend on the regulation of immersive platforms;how inclusive infrastructure and education systems become whether developers design for addiction or for agency and how innovation is balanced with equity and ethics. Gaming is not destiny. It is design. The future of gaming will be shaped not just by developers or governments, but by the collective choices of players, educators, investors, and communities.

These shifts are part of a systemic transformation where gaming is becoming a foundational layer of digital society. Understanding and shaping these dynamics will be critical not only for game designers and technologists, but for policymakers, educators, and communities. Those who anticipate and align with these shifts will help shape more inclusive, ethical, and empowering digital worlds.

Technical Companion

Why Blockchain Matters for Gaming

Blockchain introduces a new paradigm for the gaming industry with new technological and economic features that distinguish it from traditional infrastructures. The first is digital ownership, where players can own NFTs of in-game assets like skins, weapons, and virtual land, enabling direct peer-to-peer trade and secondary markets. Second is interoperability. Digital assets built on blockchain standards (e.g., ERC-721 or SPL tokens) can be used across multiple games or Metaverses, provided they share compatible ecosystems. Third, community governance is made possible through Decentralized Autonomous Organizations (DAOs) which allow players to participate in key game decisions, such as voting on updates, and community funds. Finally, blockchain's transparency and security ensures that game logic, player rewards, and transactions are recorded immutably on-chain. This minimizes fraud and enhances trust, especially in competitive or asset-heavy games.

Key Blockchain Features Critical for Game Developers

Several blockchain characteristics are vital for building popular games.

High Throughput (Transactions Per Second—TPS): Real-time multiplayer games demand high-speed interactions. Platforms like Solana (up to thousands of TPS) and Polygon (over 30 TPS) are optimized for such performance, unlike Ethereum Layer 1, which processes only 15–30 TPS.

Low Transaction Costs: For games involving microtransactions—like NFT trading, minting, or pay-per-action—transaction fees must remain minimal. Layer 2 solutions (e.g., Polygon) and alternative Layer 1 s (e.g., Solana) offer fees typically under $0.01 per transaction.

Smart Contract Languages: Game developers should choose programming languages based on project needs. Solidity (used in Ethereum) offers flexibility and fast prototyping, especially for NFTs and DeFi-based gaming. Rust (used by Solana) provides better performance and memory safety, ideal for high-volume or AR/VR-integrated games.

Scalability Solutions: Technologies like zk-Rollups, sidechains, and state channels help scale blockchain games without overloading main nets. These solutions support more users and smoother gameplay without compromising decentralization.

Security Auditing Tools: The use of libraries and auditing services like OpenZeppelin, CertiK, and ConsenSys Diligence is essential for securing smart contracts. This is especially important in games where bugs can lead to economic exploits or loss of player assets.

Blockchain Consensus Mechanisms

Every blockchain has a consensus mechanism for adding new blocks to the chain. The main blockchain mechanisms used on the platforms described below are proof-of-work (PoW), proof-of-stake (PoS), and proof-of-history (PoH).

Proof-of-Work

Proof-of-work was the first consensus mechanism used on the Bitcoin blockchain. The aim of the Bitcoin platform was to provide for financial transactions that are computationally impractical to reverse, thus protecting buyers and sellers from fraud and implement the possibility of peer-to-peer transactions without the third-party authority (Nakamoto 2008a, b).

Network participants in Bitcoin have to solve complex arithmetic puzzles to calculate the alphanumeric codes, called hashes. If a puzzle is solved successfully and the number meets the network's difficulty, the person who solves the puzzle gets a new Bitcoin. As this process is computationally complex, it is very difficult to tamper with code of a blockchain. To modify a past block, an attacker would have to redo the proof-of-work of the block and all blocks after it and then catch up with and surpass the work of the honest nodes (Nakamoto 2008a, b). However, the proof-of-work consensus mechanism is slow to support thousands of transactions per second which are required by decentralized apps.

Proof-of-Stake

PoS is a more environmentally friendly, secure, and sustainable alternative to PoW. However, because this consensus system favors entities with a higher number of tokens, PoS has drawn criticism for its potential to lead to centralization.

Prominent PoS platforms include Ethereum (ETH), Cardano (ADA), Solana (SOL), and Tezos (XTC). In September 2022, the Ethereum-based cryptocurrencies transitioned to the proof-of-stake protocol, which became known as The Merge event (Statt 2022). Under the new protocol, miners stake at least 32 Eth as a deposit for the right to approve new transactions. Then, the validator receives the right to install the validation software on their node (Lighthouse, Prysm, or Teku), which automatically validates user transactions. The role of the human validator is confined to ensuring the uptime, maintaining updates, and monitoring logs. Validators are rewarded for their participation, so they are financially motivated to provide high level services. If one of the validators tries to corrupt the system, they lose the staked Eth (Buterin 2022). The process is less time and energy-consuming, and it allows the network to be used for microtransactions and processes more transactions for the same time.

Proof-of-History

Proof-of-history principle was introduced by Anatoly Yakovenko, the founder of Solana (Yakovenko 2018). Yakovenko's proof-of-history is a sequence of computations that can provide a way to cryptographically verify the passage of time between two events (Yakovenko 2018). The PoH mechanism generates a sequence of hashes that prove the time passed. Each hash works like a tick of an imaginary cryptographic clock. Since the hashes are programmed in sequence, you can see exactly how much time has passed between transactions. This way, a user can see that no transaction was tampered with. PoH allows to synchronize multiple PoH generators and achieve horizontal scaling. According to Yakovenko, by periodically synchronizing the generators, each generator can then handle a portion of external traffic, thus the overall system can handle a larger number of events to track.

Major Blockchain Platforms

Ethereum

Vitalik Buterin outlined the aim of Ethereum was to be the superior foundational protocol to allow other decentralized applications to be built on top of instead of Bitcoin, giving developers more tools to work with and benefit from Ethereum's flexibility and scalability (Buterin 2022). Ethereum became a foundation for digital ownership, NFTs, play-to-earn models, decentralized game economies, interoperability between games, and building decentralized autonomous organizations with voting systems.

One of Ethereum's greatest achievements in the domain of Web3 was the introduction of smart contracts. According to Buterin, smart contracts execute themselves without any need or any opportunity of human intervention (Buterin 2022).

Although first developed for financial applications, smart contracts became a powerful means to code almost anything.

In gaming, smart contracts are used to distribute rewards automatically based on gameplay or ensure that NFT creators receive royalty payments each time an NFT item is resold. In DAOs, Ethereum smart contracts are used to code tamper-proof elections or decision-making processes, managing community-owned wallets, automating proposals.

In other words, the Ethereum platform, the Solana programming language, and smart contract technology, working on their basis, enabled multiple use cases for blockchain-based applications.

At the same time, Ethereum is the Layer 1 blockchain platform. It is the base platforms, transactions are recorded, validated, and stored permanently. It is also the layer where consensus mechanisms like proof-of-work or proof-of-stake take place.

This leads to multiple limitations, one of which is the limited throughput. Ethereum can handle approximately 15–30 transactions per second, while the growing popularity of Ethereum-based apps requires faster traffic. The increased traffic contributes to the higher price; during congestion, simple transactions can cost transactions can cost $20–$100. Since Layer 1 blockchain like Bitcoin or Ethereum hindered the development of the blockchain community due to the lack of flexibility and scalability, Layer 2 solutions like Polygon were created.

Polygon

Polygon is a Layer 2 blockchain platform that works based on Ethereum. Its purpose was to unload the Ethereum main net while keeping the operations secure. Since the Ethereum platform became too complicated for millions of users, Polygon was built to enable a more inclusive and equitable environment for NFT creators, communities, and collectors. This way, the platform enabled individuals to build decentralized applications, mint unique assets, and participate in global economies without gatekeepers (Sabry 2025).

Here's how it works: as a user submits a transaction, the transaction goes through the Polygon PoS chain for the verification. The Polygon PoS chain has its own validators and quicker PoS time. Then, the Polygon chain posts a snapshot of its state to Ethereum. This way the system maintains the security level of the Ethereum platform while taking the load of minor transactions off it. This way, Polygon achieves lower costs and faster transactions (Lacity 2020).

For example, Polygon's average transaction processing time is more than 32 transactions per second, with a typical transaction fee equaling less than $0.01 (Reiff et al. 2024).

Since 2023, Polygon has implemented a new feature, called Zero-Knowledge Rollup. After a user submits a transaction to the Polygon zkEVM chain, the chain bundles thousands of such transactions to create zero-knowledge proof. The proof is sent to Ethereum, proving all the transactions happening, without disclosing the details of these transitions.

This means that Polygon has massive scalability compared to Ethereum, which invites numerous users to the platform.

Since Polygon is compatible with Ethereum, users can easily migrate from platform to platform with minor changes.

Solana

Solana is another blockchain platform that prioritizes speed and is designed to remove the bottlenecks of other platforms. Solana's design uses algorithms other than those of other platforms, allowing it to remove performance bottlenecks caused by other kinds of software.

Anatoliy Yakovenko, Solana's creator, states that in the ideal conditions Solana's architecture can allow for more than 710,000 TPS (transactions per second) on a standard gigabit network (Yakovenko 2018). In practice, Solana processes 3574.16 TPS. The transactions on Solana are also comparatively cheaper, as its average cost per transaction is $0.00026 (Solscan n.d.). To compare, the price of a transaction on Ethereum is around $0.30 (Etherscan n.d.).

While offering greater flexibility and lower transaction cost, Solana brings to life decentralized apps with frequent user interactions, or the ones that require high amounts of microtransactions like in gaming and NFT exchange.

Solana's speed makes the platform the best option for the development of real-time applications like games or decentralized social networks (like Dialect, DriP), as it allows processing functions without lag.

As mentioned, Solana's enhancements, compared to other platforms, are possible through its architecture.

Solana's blockchain operates on the proof-of-stake (PoS) and the proof-of-history (PoS) consensus model. While the PoS model allows validators to verify transactions based on how many coins they hold, the PoH adds timestamps to every transaction, making the validation processes much faster (Yakovenko 2018), as they are automated.

In Solana's architecture, every transaction gets a timestamp that can guarantee that the data was created sometime before the next hash was generated in the sequence (Yakovenko). This way the data cannot be tampered with as any change receive another timestamp as the original.

Compared with Ethereum, which is the second largest blockchain network after Bitcoin (Coinmarketcap n.d.-a, b). Solana has a smaller community and following. Yet, speed and flexibility make it a favorite platform for various applications. Major platforms like Phantom (wallet) and Magic Eden (NFTs) are built on Solana proving its viability.

Overall, Solana has the fastest throughput and near-zero fees, making it suitable for real-time games and fast DeFi. Ethereum remains the base layer for security and decentralization but relies on Layer 2 s for scalability. Layer 2 s like Arbitrum and zkSync bring scalable, low-cost computation with Ethereum-level security. Finally,

Polygon offers Ethereum Virtual Machine compatibility with low fees, widely used for gaming and NFTs.

Smart Contract Languages

Smart contracts are essential to blockchain technology and have made the development of Decentralized Applications (dApps) possible (Benetollo et al. 2024). Smart contract languages are programming languages created to code self-executing smart contracts. Developers use them to program the agreement terms that should trigger contract execution.

Each language has distinctive language-specific features, such as usability, programming style, safety, and security, which also define its area of implications. For example, the Solidity syntax is considered lighter, especially for people coming from the JavaScript environment, so many developers prefer it to build DeFi, NFTs, and DAOs which require shorter development time.

However, Rust is considered a more secure option than Solidity (Sharma 2024). Rust is better suited for use cases where high performance, safety, and concurrency are needed. Examples include building blockchain networks and cryptographic libraries.

Smart contract languages tend to be associated with specific platforms. For example, Solidity is defined as a language used for Ethereum, Rust for Solana, Aiken for Cardano, (Py)TEAL for Algorand, Move for Aptos, and SmartPy for Tezos (Benetollo et al. 2024).

As the blockchain community tried to explore the full potential of Dapps, NFTs, and other blockchain applications, more smart contract languages appeared. Some target functionality and simplicity of coding, presenting syntax and architecture that make it easier to understand the code and spot mistakes. Others focus on security. Altogether, they signify the constant movement towards a more efficient and secure crypto space.

This section outlines the main smart contract languages currently available and explains how they differ from each other.

Solidity

Solidity is the first and, hence, the main smart contract language for blockchains compatible with the Ethereum Virtual Machine (EVM), which includes Ethereum, Avalanche C-Chain, Hedera, and others (Solidity n.d.). The primary language enables the creation of Decentralized Autonomous Organizations (DAOs), blockchain-based games with features like asset ownership and in-game economies and NFTs.

Being close to general-purpose programming languages like JavaScript, C++, and Python, Solidity is relatively simple for developers experienced in these languages. Solidity is used to set the rules and logic for smart contracts on Ethereum and other platforms like Hyperledger Fabric blockchain. It is the language that introduced the smart contract and the one used to create the first smart contract architecture (Jones 2024).

The basic structure of a Solidity contract includes functions, state variables, and modifiers. Functions define the contract's behavior under certain conditions (e.g., the transfer of an asset). State variables store the essential data (the user's assets). Modifiers control the execution of functions, for example, restricting access to specific addresses. Such architecture ensures that the contract is only executed under safe conditions.

However, Solidity has been found to have vulnerabilities, which led to several major breaches of the Ethereum platform in the past (Quantum Risk n.d.). Solidity is primarily used for dApps, decentralized finance, NFTs, and innovative logistics solutions. This language codes loans, investments, and currency exchanges in DeFi projects or asset transfers in gaming. It is also the basis for platforms like OpenSea and Rarible, which provide an environment for creating, selling, and buying NFTs.

Solidity is widely used in Web 3 gaming, where the rules are coded in Solidity to verify immutability and transparency. This language is used to create decentralized worlds where players own and exchange lands and assets coded as NFTs. It is also used for collecting items, such as trophies, and for play-to-earn gaming models, where players earn rewards, such as cryptocurrency.

Rust

Rust is a general-purpose programming language that has been used for coding smart contracts. Its main advantage over Solidity is greater flexibility, which allows it to be used for a wider variety of blockchain applications. Since its release in 2015, Rust has been one of the most popular languages on Stack Overflow (Developer Survey 2023).

Rust is a smart contract language used by many non-Ethereum blockchains, such as Solana and Polkadot. Rust language's toolset is still limited, which limits some use cases. Rust code is known to be lightweight and easy to edit. Also, Rust codes contract conditions in small types (type being a structure for organizing data), which makes Rust data very compact. As a result, Rust code runs fast, making this language suitable for performance-critical operations.

Another feature that makes Rust different is the futures. The futures in Rust encapsulate pending results of time-consuming operations. The result becomes available once the operation is resolved. This allows Rust to handle complex and asynchronous operations in situations where multiple network-level requests are made and may not resolve immediately (Sharma 2024).

Rust is known for its built-in memory safety feature. Every value has a single owner, who is responsible for allocating and dealing with memory for a certain operation. When an owner goes out of scope, Rust calls out the destructor functions that automatically clear memory space. As a result, Rust doesn't collect garbage code and prevents memory leaks, where memory is allocated but never dealt with (Sharma 2024). This makes Rust code less prone to errors and security vulnerabilities, which is why it is often preferred for banking apps coded on blockchain.

Rust's concurrency feature allows writing code that can handle multiple tasks simultaneously. Running multiple tasks simultaneously makes it a useful language for building complex game engines that require low latency. Rust is the main language for the Solana platform. It is also used in other blockchains, such as Polkadot and Near. This language is effectively used to develop smart contracts, Solana dApps, and NFTs, solving various Web3 blockchain tasks. Due to the memory safety and concurrency features, Rust has become perfect for apps requiring multiple tasks to be run in real time, so it is used for augmented and virtual reality applications.

Move

Move is another popular language used in building smart contracts on blockchain. It is used on multiple platforms and is developed on the basis of Rust. Developed by Facebook's Diem (former Libra) project, its key purpose is to provide flexibility and safety. Move provides all the safety features of Rust but also is lighter and more simple to learn which makes it a preferred choice for many blockchain applications (Sharma 2024).

One of Move's key features is the so-called must-move semantics, which ensures that resources (tokens) are never replicated or lost (The Move Book n.d.). Move is also chain-agnostic, meaning it can code different blockchains. Move's resource-oriented programming introduces a novel approach to managing digital assets, making it simpler to drive state changes.

Web3 Development Libraries

In Web3 development, a library is a reusable collection of code that helps developers interact with blockchain networks, smart contracts, wallets, and dApps more easily.

If a user has a gaming website that allows the collection of NFT trophies, they need several technology sets to make it work. First, users need smart contract languages like Solidity, Move, or Rust to code NFTs. Second, users need a website to let gamers select a personage, perform actions, make payments, and buy or sell NFTs. Finally, users need technology that connects the website with the game's secure blockchain.

Web 3 libraries are specific software packages that allow interaction with blockchain nodes (Snow 2023). For example, they allow us to send ether from one account to another, read wallet balances or smart contracts states, invoke smart contracts, dynamically display blockchain data, create user identities inside the games, etc.

Technical Companion 207

Yet, the features described vary across libraries as the development community continues to explore new ways to make Web 3 libraries better.

Three main Web 3 libraries such as Web3.js, Ethers.js, and Hardhat are explained below.

Web3.js

Web3.js is a library collection that allows interaction with a local or remote Ethereum node using HTTP, IPC, or WebSocket (Ethereum Foundation n.d.-c). Web3.js was developed by the Ethereum foundation and is maintained and supported by them.

Web3.js works like a jQuery library that makes Ajax calls to the web server and reads and writes to the Ethereum blockchain. Web3.js is used to connect dApps to users' Ethereum wallets, send tokens between users, and update a website or app's UI when a new token is minted. In a DAO network, Web3.js can be used to vote, as it calls the smart contract method. Web3.js code is heavy, which makes it less suitable for low-latency front-end apps. Yet it is useful for developers who want to build a well-supported and well-documented library (Snow 2023).

Ethers js.

Ethers js. is also a JavaScript Ethereum library developed and maintained by Canadian developer Richard Moore and releases in 2017 (Announcing ethers.js 2017). Ether js has a smaller library size than Web3.js. The Ethers.js bundle takes 400 KB, while the Web3.js bundle takes 1.4 MB. This means the architecture of Ethers.js makes it easier and faster for developers to create, deploy, and test dApps.

Ethers.js connects users with their online or hardware wallets, checks how much data a user owns on their wallet, sets and reads DAO contracts, authenticates users, and deploys NFT collections (Ethereum Foundation n.d.-b).

Hardhat

Hardhat is another library including useful development tools that speed up the process of coding, testing, and debugging the app. Hardhat also provides wider opportunities for smart contract development, testing, and debugging (Hardhat n.d.). Hardhat can also compile, test, and deploy smart contracts. It is also used to create back-end scripts and test environments. Hardhat is most often used to write contracts, test game logic and rewards, and simulate real-world cases. In DAOs, Hardhat codes governance, voting, and fund management rules.

In gaming, Hardhat is used for minting swords, characters, or skins in games, writing and compiling contracts, running tests for minting, transferring and burning trophies, and deploying games to testnets and main net. It is also used to code game logic, such as PvP battles and in-game currency rewards. It also allows testing and debugging games in real time, so it is useful for developers who want to build complex Web3 apps (Snow 2023).

Wallet Integration Technologies

Smart contract libraries are foundational for integrating with digital wallets, which are software applications or hardware devices used to store and manage a user's digital assets. Digital wallets give users direct control over their funds, allowing them to transfer assets without controls, approvals, or permissions. They store access to digital assets on different blockchains (Baker 2023). This allows a user to connect to different blockchain platforms, apps, games, and DAOs. The security of the funds is the responsibility of crypto wallet users. For example, in the case of password loss, a user gets locked out of their wallets and has no access to their contents.

Digital asset wallet providers implement complex encryption rules to ensure the technology is secure. The wallets have public and private keys. Public keys are strings of code that signify a wallet address. They are comparable to classic bank account numbers and are used to let others identify a user's wallet/account and transfer funds to accounts. They can be freely shared with others. Private keys work as secure passwords that keep accounts safe.

Types of Crypto Wallets

There are two major types of parts of digital asset wallets. Hardware wallets are physical devices, comparable to USB sticks that securely save your keys offline. In the blockchain community, such wallets are also known as "cold" wallets as they work without access to the internet and are impossible to hack without physical access.

Software wallets or applications are installed on desktop or mobile devices. They are also known as "hot" wallets as they are more convenient to use every day and can be accessed from any device. Online wallets store private keys online and can be accessed from any device. These wallets are more prone to threats, as they can still be hacked remotely.

The most popular online crypto wallets are MetaMask, TrustWallet, SafePal, Coinbase Wallet, Electrum, and Tangem Wallet.

These wallets operate similarly, but they differ in features, support assets, ecosystems, and use cases. For example, MetaMask is focused on Ethereum or EVM-compatible DeFi and is available as a browser app with a mobile version. SafePal is a mobile app with a hardware key, so it is considered safety centered. Unlike MetaMask, it offers multi-chain support, allowing users to buy NFTs from different blockchains. Trust Wallet is a mobile-first app that supports multiple blockchains and is optimized for beginners, while Coinbase's wallet is optimized for the users of the respective cryptocurrency.

Wallet Integration

Wallet integration connects digital wallets with other blockchain-based applications, systems, or services. It is not a single technology but rather a set of different approaches for connecting crypto wallets with decentralized apps, games, blockchain platforms, or Point-of-Sale systems. MetaMask, ConnectKit, WalletConnect, and Coinbase Wallet SDK are the most popular wallet integration technologies.

The Coinbase Wallet SDK is a specialized tool for connecting the Coinbase Wallet to dApps. It can only be used with the Coinbase Wallet and has some limitations (Coinbase n.d.-a, b).

WalletConnect is a protocol that facilitates secure and convenient connectivity between crypto wallets, blockchain platforms, decentralized apps, and other networks (WalletConnect n.d.). WalletConnect allows users to link wallets and dApps using QR codes and URL links. Before WalletConnect was created, users had to switch between wallets supporting decentralized applications built on different blockchains. WalletConnect standardized communication between wallets and dApps, allowing users to connect multiple wallets and dApps and enhance communication between them. This way, integrating dApps and other blockchain solutions with cryptocurrency wallets allowed for creating more user-friendly interfaces.

Decentralized Storage

Decentralized storage technologies allow data storage without relying on centralized servers. Decentralized storage is often used to securely store sensitive information, like files with financial or medical data. It is also used in gaming and DAOs. NFTs and blockchain-based games use decentralized storage to hold metadata and digital assets. In DAOs, decentralized storage solutions are used to store proposals, voting outcomes, discussion threads, and other information. It is also used to store DAO constitutions, codes of conduct, contributor agreements, project plans, working documents, etc. Its safety and security make it a means for storing and using DAO documents like Gitcoin Passport or Proof of Humanity.

Decentralized storage differs in how the data is stored, split, and distributed, how nodes communicate, whether they use payment structures and incentives. Some platforms provide temporal storage. For example, Arweave charges users once for lifetime storage. Other platforms offer limited storage, which keeps data only until paid.

Decentralized storage works by distributing data across a network of distributed nodes. In decentralized storage, data is split into smaller chunks. These chunks are then encrypted and distributed among different nodes (computers or servers) of the network so that no single node keeps all of the data. When a user needs the data back, the system locates the necessary file using metadata, downloads and decrypts the information, and then reassembles the file.

The most common decentralized storage services are IPFS, Arweave, Filecoin, and Storj.

IPFS (InterPlanetary File System) is a peer-to-peer distributed system, meaning that the files get distributed between the computers (nodes) joining the network (IPFS n.d.). When data is split into chunks, every chunk of data receives a cryptographic hash by which it is later retrieved. The system ensures content integrity, meaning that every content change drives the hash change. IPFS allows version control so that users can track the changes that their documents undergo, and this also means that data in the document can be replaced with newer versions.

Arweave serves a similar purpose to IPFS, yet it has a different business model. In IPFS, data is stored as long as someone pays for the storage, while Arweave users buy out the lifetime storage (Arweave n.d.). In Arweave, data is immutable once written. There are also differences in how data is hashed. In IPFS, each data chunk receives a hash. Arweave saves data as separate blocks linked by hashes. While the service is secure, users receive the benefit of limitless storage. In decentralized gaming worlds and DAOs, this feature allows users to store assets permanently, ensuring the stability and immutability of the data records.

Filecoin is an IPFS-based decentralized storage solution that allows users to rent out their unused hard drive space to those who need storage. The users providing storage receive incentives in the form of FIL tokens.

Storj is often compared to the decentralized version of Dropbox or AWS. Storj uses a network of nodes (individual computers, where the owner of every computer provides the storage space) that are operated in a peer-to-peer fashion (Storj n.d.).

Blockchain Governance Tools

Blockchain governance systems allow users to perform multiple actions: propose changes, run votes, enforce rules in blockchain-based projects, and make decisions. This class of tools enables the growth of community-driven games and DAOs. Community members participate in rule-making, decisions about the in-game economy, voting on treasury spending, and granting DAO memberships (Green 2025).

Blockchain governance tools can be split into two categories: on-chain and off-chain (Reijers et al. 2018). The on-chain governance tools code all the decisions made. Users vote with the help of smart contracts, and every proposal and vote are recorded on-chain. On-chain tools enable automated voting—if a proposal gets passed, it is immediately implemented. Voting in on-chain systems is often token-weighted; users with more tokens have more voting weight, which can lead to the centralization of power. Off-chain governance systems work differently. Decisions are discussed in informal discussions, meetings, and forums, and voting is coded to the blockchain.

Decentralized platforms like Aragon or Snapshot were built to enhance these processes and make self-governance faster and more straightforward.

Aragon provides tools and frameworks to help communities govern themselves without centralized authority. With a play-and-plug interface, Aragon simplifies access to DAOs for non-technical users, lowering the barriers people face when joining decentralized communities. On Aragon, discussion proposals are submitted on-chain, and voting is also recorded and stored on-chain. Once the proposal is passed, smart contracts automatically execute the decision. This solution offers more control and security since everything, from role assignments and permissions in gaming to treasury controls in DAOs, is on-chain (Aragon n.d.).

Snapshot is an example of an off-chain governance tool. The participants record the proposals on the network, which are then encrypted and stored in blocks. The voting happens off-chain, and the result is also stored off-chain. The decision is then coded on the blockchain (Snapshot n.d.).

Decentralized organizations often use different governance tools simultaneously. For example, DAOs use Snapshot for off-chain voting, which is faster and simpler to organize and allows Aragon to execute the voting results.

Digital Assets and Tokenization

Token Standards and Evaluation

Tokenization standards are a set of rules that enable the creation and management of digital assets (Krishnan 2023). These rules are written down in technical documents that define the methods of research, development, and innovation developers must follow when creating new tokens.

ERC-20

The first tokenization standard on Ethereum was ERC-20 (Ethereum Request for Comments 20). It was proposed by Fabian Vogelsteller in November 2015 and became the primary standard for creating fungible tokens. A fungible token is always equal in value to another token of the same kind and can be interchangeable with it. For example, fiat currency, in which every dollar note has the same value. The implementation of the ERC-20 standard made token interoperability possible; it allowed transferring tokens from one account to another, getting an account's current token balance, getting the total supply of tokens available on the network, and approving token spending. In this way, fungible tokens became the basis of stablecoins (USD Coin, Tether), governance coins (Uniswap, Aave), and initial coin offerings (ICOs) for new blockchain projects.

ERC-721

In 2018, the founders of CryptoKitties created an Ethereum Improvement Proposal, where they presented the ERC-721 standard for non-fungible tokens (Entriken et al. 2018). The ERC-721 token standard deploys one smart contract for each NFT. For example, in CryptoKitties, each CryptoKitty is a separate ERC-721 token with specific properties, which make it one-of-a-kind and non-interchangeable with other tokens of the same class.

ERC-721 tokenization standards enabled the tokenization of unique digital artworks, social media posts, in-game collectibles, gaming characters, cartoon characters, etc. However, the ERC-721 was unable to conduct batch transfers. To transfer multiple NFTs under the ERC-721 standard, the system has to initiate a separate transaction for each transfer since each NFT is separate contract, resulting in high transaction costs when minting or trading.

ERC-1155

ERC-1155 is the tokenization standard for contracts that manage multiple token types. A single deployed contract may include any combination of fungible, non-fungible, or other configurations (e.g., semi-fungible tokens) (Ethereum 2025). The key difference between the ERC-721 and ERC-1155 is that the latter allows storing several tokens under one smart contract and sending them as a batch, including fungible and non-fungible ones. The ERC-115 standard decreases the cost and time required to complete the transaction by allowing multiple tokens to be sent in one batch transfer.

ERC-1155 also allows the creation of an unlimited number of NFTs under the same contract. In addition, ERC-1155, smart contracts are linked to multiple URIs and do not store additional metadata (such as file names), making them more flexible for creating large volumes of NFTs.

The key features of ERC-1155 are:

1. Batch transfers: ERC-1155 allows sending multiple assets in a single call.
2. Batch balance: Getting the balance of multiple assets in a single.
3. Batch approval: This feature allows approving or managing multiple token types in a single transaction.
4. Hooks: Hooks refer to special functions that allow a smart contract to react to token transfers. This includes acknowledging and accepting transfers, notifying when a transfer fails, and reverting tokens, if the case, to protect users' assets.
5. NFTSupport: According to this rule, if a transfer contains only one asset, the system treats it as an NFT.
6. Safe transfer rules: ERC-1155 has a prescribed set of rules to ensure transfer safety (Ethereum Foundation n.d.-a).

ERC-1155 simplified the way games introduce complex player inventories or asset collections. The standard allows a player to hold multiple assets in an inventory coded as one smart contract, receive or send various reward types in one transaction, and mix multiple tokens to create new items.

In marketplaces, this standard enables multi-asset listings and faster and more cost-effective trade. ERC-1155 also supports semi-fungible tokens, or objects that behave like fungible tokens and then convert into NFTs, such as tokenized concert tickets that are interchangeable before the person buys them and become non-fungible once redeemed.

In dApps, the ERC-1155 allows the granting of various user roles within one smart contract and rewarding users with multiple assets (like fungible points and non-fungible badges) in one transaction. An e-commerce dApp can use ERC-1155 to bundle products and services under one contract and send them in one transaction. An educational dApp can combine payment for the monthly subscription (fungible), study reward points (fungible), and a certificate of completion (non-fungible) as one contract.

Future Token Standards

While ERC-721 launched the NFT economy, ERC-1155 allowed for more flexibility and laid the foundation for wider NFT adoptions. The Ethereum platform contains over one hundred ERC proposals (Improvement Proposals n.d.), each presenting new functionalities. For example, in the same year, the ERC-1155 was issued, the ERC-998 standard was also proposed. It allows for composable NFTs or an architecture where one NFT can hold other tokens. In gaming, it is embodied in the form of NFT avatars, which own wearable NFTs and in-game currency.

In 2020, the EIP-2981 was proposed, allowing users to include on-chain royalty info for NFTs presenting digital artists a consistent way to define royalties. The protocol is supported by marketplaces like Rarible and OpenSea.

Further evolution came with ERC-6551 in 2023, which introduced NFTs that can own assets. In this standard, each NFT gets a smart wallet, which is also coded as NFT. This improvement has applications in DAOs and gaming in the form of autonomous characters.

Cross-asset tokenization, enabling fractional ownership of real-world commodities, like real estate, stocks, and bonds, will likely bridge the gap between traditional financial markets and blockchain-based decentralized financial systems (Woodrum 2024).

Similarly, for decentralized identity solutions, Vitalik Buterin et al. proposed the concept of tokenizing identities in the work "Decentralized Society: Finding Web3's Soul" (Buterin 2022). Buterin proposes soul-bound tokens (SBTs) which are non-transferable tokens tied to a person's identity. The Ethereum community has developed several standards for tokenized identities. The ERC-1238 and ERC-5484, for example, create conditions for building non-transferable or revocable tokens. The ERC-3643, while focusing on the tokenization of securities, standard can also be used to code an on-chain Identity system (Lebrun et al. 2021).

Tokenization of conventional intellectual property and banking securities, certificates of ownership, and further institutional adoption of blockchain are also trending ERC-3643 was created to meet the unique challenges of security tokens. The standard features the possibility of token pausing and freezing, which allows for responses to changes in the status of the token or its holders. Yet, new standards like this are likely to appear in the future.

The growing number of standards and new features they implement intensify the development of cross-platform integration tools and the rise of marketplaces where users can trade and exchange their assets for other tokens or real-world currencies, building bridges between Web3 and real-world economies. These are summarized below.

- **ERC-20**—Fungible token standard. Supports one token per transfer. Commonly used for cryptocurrencies, governance tokens, and utility tokens. Offers low gas cost per transfer.
- **ERC-721**—Non-fungible token (unique) standard. Supports one token per transfer. Used for NFTs such as art, collectibles, virtual land, and gaming items. Has higher gas cost per token.
- **ERC-1155**—Semi-fungible/mixed token standard. Supports batch transfers. Common in gaming for fungible and non-fungible assets, as well as digital collectibles. Enables gas-efficient batch minting and transfers.
- **ERC-6551**—Non-fungible + smart wallet standard. Treats an NFT as a wallet with programmable features. Used for smart NFTs, on-chain identity, and composable game characters. Gas cost depends on underlying operations.

Smart Contract Architecture

To ensure each NFT is unique and guarantee NFT ownership, each smart contract has a list of attributes that define it. These attributes can be split into primary functionality, properties, and token interface (Griffin 2022).

The first part defines the token's key functionality or what it can do within its environment. For example, if the token is an in-game asset, these rules define how it can progress in the game.

The second part includes the assets' properties, including the name and ID, the "owner," the "location," and the "avatar." The property owner defines who stores and tracks the NFT. The location represents where a token in question is located in the game or reference to other objects.

The metadata contains special details about the NFT which are not stored in the properties. This includes information about the name, image, creator, creation time, and image ID.

The smart contract interface contains data on how different applications interact with an NFT. For example, for a game character, this part of the code defines the power level for a character.

NFT Market Places

An NFT marketplace is a platform where you can create, buy, and sell NFTs (Joo et al. 2023). One of the first marketplaces was OpenSea, created right after the launch of CryptoKitties in 2017. The platform makers saw the potential of NFT ownership and trade and created a software product to simplify that process for the end users. Most popular NFT marketplaces are coded on the Ethereum blockchain or Ethereum-compatible platforms like Arbitrum or Optimism.

NFT marketplaces are decentralized. The NFT marketplaces display all product collections worldwide. This means that if an NFT product enters the platform, it becomes visible on other marketplaces since each platform scans the blockchain universally (Joo et al. 2023).

NFT marketplaces like OpenSea, Rarible, Magic Edem, or Zora provide free access to their software development kits (SDKs) to encourage ecosystem growth. Based on this open-source documentation, developers worldwide can create marketplaces using the marketplace backend without needing to deploy custom smart contracts.

The most used open-source SDKs used in Web 3 are the OpenSea SDK and Rarible protocol.

OpenSea SDK

The OpenSea SDK is a software development kit that allows developers to build a native marketplace for non-fungible, fungible, and semi-fungible tokens (OpenSea SDK 2021). Using the free-to-access and developer-friendly SDK, developers can build native NFT marketplaces without deploying smart contracts or backend order books. OpenSea SDK employs Web3.js to bridge the applications with the blockchain to create and fulfill the NFT orders. By integrating OpenSea SDK in their code, developers can fetch assets, make offers, listings and selling items, run crowd sales, fetch orders, buy items, collect offers, and transfer items or coins (ProjectOpenSea n.d.-a, b). The advanced features allow users to schedule future listings, buy NFTs for other users, use ERC-20 tokens for payment instead of Ethers, run private auctions, and listen to events (Project OpenSea n.d.-a).

Initially, OpenSea was a multi-million project attracting $427 million in funding over seven rounds (OpenSea IPO 2022). The first round of investment, which set the project live just after the release of CryptoKitties, raised USD two million (Finzer 2018). The company's opening of access to its SDK contributed to the development of NFT trade. Numerous specialized NFT and gaming marketplaces, such as Footbattle, Decentraland, and Etherland, have been built using the OpenSea SDK.

It has also been used in dApps to enhance user experience such as by building lists of a dApp owned NFT collectibles. There are limitations in that OpenSea SDK is intended only for integration with the OpenSea backend and doesn't allow employing its own smart contract or making changes to the platform's core.

Rarible Protocol

Rarible Protocol powers both Rarible.com and thousands of community marketplaces. At its core, it's a decentralized toolset that simplifies how developers can build NFT applications on Ethereum, Polygon, Immutable X, and Tezos (Rarible Protocol n.d.). The Rarible Protocol offers developers tools and building blocks for developers to create and deploy. These include custom marketplaces, NFT aggregators, minting platforms, in-game trading features, and DAO governance tools (voting tokens).

Rarible Protocol allows developers to create their own NFT marketplaces with custom logic using Rarible's smart contracts and APIs. Rarible Protocol allows building applications that operate on different blockchains, which presuppose features like NFT minting, order management, royalties' system management, and others. The Rarible SDK and APIs allow developers to build the NFT experiences they want without building everything from scratch, lowering the entry level for developers interested in NFTs

Cross-Chain Interoperability

Cross-platform integration tools in blockchain refer to technologies that enable communication and interaction between different blockchain networks. These tools allow assets and data to be transferred and utilized across various platforms, enhancing interoperability and creating a more connected blockchain ecosystem.

The cross-platform integration allows in-game collectibles to be sold on marketplaces or reused in other games. For example, as Epic Games closed its Paragon game in 2018, it released its assets for free, allowing gamers and studios to use them in Unreal Engine games. The offer included heroes, custom animation blueprints, additional skins for distinct character variants, base meshes, textures, VFX and animation cycles, and dialogues (Unreal Engine n.d.-a).

In another example, the Shrapnel game, built on the Layer-1 blockchain, can connect to Ethereum-based marketplaces to trade on NFT-based assets, like skins. This is possible due to the use of cross-platform bridges like LayerZero or Axelar.

Cross-platform integration can be implemented through various means, including bridges, cross-chain messaging protocols, Ethereum standards, multi-chain NFTstandards, Web3 wallet APIs, decentralized storage solutions, APIs and SDKs, and Layer 2 solutions.

Cross-chain bridges are critical infrastructural components that connect blockchains like Ethereum with Solana, Binance Smart Chain, and others. They rely on on-chain smart contracts and off-chain validators to attest and relay messages representing locked, minted, or redeemed assets or more general-purpose instructions to be executed on target chains (Johnson 2025).

Sending NFTs through the cross-chain bridges involves locking assets on the original chain and minting equivalent tokens on the destination chain. This way, one blockchain sends the other information on which token to mint.

This takes several steps. For example, sending an NFT from Solana to Ethereum looks as follows:

1. A user has to deposit tokens into the Solana bridge contract. The bridge contract then puts the contract into escrow.
2. The lock event generates a verifiable receipt.
3. Off-chain relayers observe this event and submit proof to the Ethereum bridge contract.
4. Following the cross-chain validation rules, the Ethereum bridge contract validates the proof.
5. As verification passes successfully, equivalent wrapped tokens are minted on Ethereum. They represent the assets locked (Johnson 2025).

The reverse operation takes place to redeem the assets back to the source platform. So, this is a reversible operation, often referred to as lock-and-mint (Themistocleous 2025), as the asset gets locked on the origin blockchain and can return there. In contrast to this principle, the burn-and-mint technique presupposes that the original asset is burned on the source blockchain and minted on the target one.

As illustrated, a blockchain bridge is a communication mechanism between two blockchains designed to move data and assets. The exchange of messages between blockchains is achieved through cross-chain messaging protocols. The cross-chain messaging protocols work similarly to bridges:

1. A user or protocol sends a message on the source blockchain.
2. The messaging protocol verifies it.
3. The message is relayed and executed on the target blockchain.

Another means to enable interoperability is the Ethereum standards like ERC-721 and ERC-1155. These standards offer an architecture that lets NFTs be used in different Ethereum and Ethereum-compatible blockchain applications.

Solutions like multi-chain standards create means to connect isolated non-compatible blockchains. For example, LayerZero, an omni-chain protocol, allows smart contracts on different chains to communicate with each other (What is LayerZero n.d.) LayerZero is used for the development of apps like Stargate Finance, which enables native-asset swaps, like USDC and USDT, across Ethereum, Avalanche, BNB Chain, Polygon, Arbitrum, Optimism, and more. It is also the basis for Omni X, an omni-chain NFT platform operating on Ethereum, Polygon, BNB, Arbitrum, and others that allows for cross-platform NFT minting and trading.

Web3 wallet APIs are also an example of technology that enables interoperability as wallets are originally made to allow access to multiple blockchains from a single interface.

Immutable X

Immutable X is a Layer 2 Ethereum solution designed specifically for NFTs and gaming. It was created to streamline the development of games and in-game assets while keeping the security standards of the Ethereum Layer 1 (Immutable X n.d.)

While surpassing the limitations of Ethereum Layer 1, Immutable X achieves the high throughput of Ethereum transactions by facilitating thousands of transactions per second. It suits building complex multi-character games supporting a huge number of players. Currently, Immutable has onboarded over 440 games (Immutable 2024).

One of the key features of Immutable X is the Immutable Passport, a single sign-on (SSO) wallet and identity layer that users can use across different games on the platform. This feature allows users to log in once to use multiple games and apps on the chain. Interoperability is now possible for users of Immutable and the platform has implemented zero-knowledge EVM, which is compatible with Ethereum Virtual Machine (Immutable 2024). ZkEVM supports the Immutable passport and wallet across games and has prerequisites for supporting these features for games built on other blockchains in the future.

The assets and tokens minted on zkEVM are simpler to bridge to other EVM chains like Polygon's zkEVM. Tokens can be seamlessly transitioned between the two blockchains with the help of an additional connector: Polygon's AggLayer, a solution to unite Layer 1 and Layer 2 blockchains. Immutable X enhancements move the platform towards complete interoperability in the future and allow integration of dApps, games, and wallets that already work on Ethereum, Arbitrum, and Optimism with the Immutable zkEVM ecosystem, which is also a high level of interoperability.

Enjin and Multiverse

Enjin was a gaming platform founded in 2009. In 2017, the company joined blockchain development to release their cryptocurrency Enjin (ENJ) and start a powerful platform supporting the development of blockchain games, applications, wallets, etc.

One of the key features of Enjin products is the focus on creating a unified ecosystem for blockchain assets. Enjin pioneered the idea of the multi-chain multiverse in 2021. After the topic of Metaverses hit the mainstream, Enjin creators proposed the idea that a Metaverse should be decentralized and blockchain-based. (Franklin Tan 2021) Practically, this creates the ability to transfer digital items (like weapons, skins, or avatars) across multiple games or virtual environments built on the Enjin platform.

To simplify game development, Enjin has launched its own blockchain, Enfinity Blockchain, designed specifically to create NFTs that can move between blockchains. They have also created a new standard of tokens, Paratokens. This standard allows tokens from other blockchains like Ethereum or Binance Smart Chain to work on Enfinity.

Currently, there are over 700 games on the platform, yet not all the games support cross-compatible NFTs. The games that participate in the Enjin Multiverse have shared NFTs (like weapons, pets, skins, or badges), which can be used across multiple games.

Layer 2 Solutions and Gaming Integration

The important condition for the growth of tokenization is the availability of development tools and platforms that allow users to create, exchange, and trade NFT tokens, such as games, dApps, marketplaces, etc. Numerous resources offer no-code NFT builders with drag-and-drop functionality and intuitive interfaces for minting and distributing NFTs. Examples include services like NittyKit, DropChain Labs, and NFT. Kred, Arianee, and LaunchMyNFT.

Marketplaces like OpenSea and Rarible Mint automatically submit items like images, videos, or 3Ds once the NFT purchase is confirmed. Such resources allow users to launch non-fungible tokens (NFTs) without needing to write any code, as they include prebuilt smart contracts.

Two platforms helping developers build up and scale tokenized apps are Alchemy—the provider of the decentralized developer platform that provides powerful APIs and node services to build blockchain apps; and Moralis—which can be described as a full-stack dApp builder, which provides users with the prebuilt backend, SDKs, cross-chain support and other services.

Moralis—Streamlining Web3 Development

Moralis is a leading web3 development platform that offers everything a user needs to create, launch, and grow great decentralized applications (dApps) in one place (What Is Moralis n.d.).

The platform is focused on providing backend infrastructure to dApps while supporting integration with various front-end networks, such as Angular, React, NextJS, and Python. This means that developers have flexibility working with different front-end technologies, while the backend part, like managing blockchain data, is handled with the help of Moralis tools.

Unlike traditional backends, which require substantial custom development to interface with blockchain nodes, construct complex indexing services, and maintain synchronization states, Moralis provides a unified API layer that encapsulates these processes (Johnson 2025).

Besides APIs (Token APIs, Wallet APIs, DeFi APIs, NFT APIs, etc.), Moralis also offers software development kits, IPFS integration, and a prebuilt backend for over 30 chains, including Ethereum, Polygon, Binance Smart Chain, Arbitrum, Optimism, Avalanche, Fantom, Cronos, and Gnosis. Using Moralis, developers can create various games and dApps with minimal backend work. Moralis enables the functionality that allows gamers to mint and trade NFTs in-game, display collectibles in user dashboards, or redeem NFTs for products or discounts.

All of these are done with a simplified development interface, which reduces time-to-market and lowers the entry barrier for developers unfamiliar with blockchain backend protocols. This way, the growth of Moralis revolutionizes Web3 by providing a community with means to further app and NFT development and tokenization.

Alchemy—Infrastructure for Web 3 Development

Alchemy is a platform that provides blockchain infrastructure and developers tools to build and scale applications on various blockchain networks, including Ethereum. It offers a suite of APIs, developer tools, and infrastructure services that simplify interacting with blockchains and building decentralized applications.

Alchemy acts like an interface that enables a decentralized app to interact with the other blockchain. Alchemy provides APIs, developer tools, and infrastructure for low-latency data delivery. This allows developers to build fast and scalable applications with optimized performance.

Alchemy provides a basis for token creation and smart contract deployment across different blockchains and tools for developing highly performant decentralized applications. It integrates easily with token contracts for minting and transfers, fully supports most common token standards, and presents the basis for cross-chain NFT deployment.

Alchemy and Moralis are examples of the growing pool of development platforms providing infrastructure and tools to create decentralized apps, games, and marketplaces. Since services like these simplify interactions with the blockchain backend and smart contracts, developers worldwide experience lower barriers to creating tokenized games and NFT assets, which promotes the development of the NFT-based economy and Web 3.

Regulatory Tech for Compliance and Security

The responsibility for due diligence rests on individuals who may lack the necessary expertise (Williams 2025). Companies like Chainalysis and TRM Labs help businesses provide regular checkups regarding compliance and risk management, as well as provide investigations in case of incidents.

Chainalysis

Chainalysis is a blockchain data platform that provides software, services, and research to government agencies, exchanges, financial institutions, and cybersecurity companies (Chainalysis n.d.-a, b). Chainalysis offers a range of services that include network analysis, wallet analysis, asset analysis, profile analysis, and process analysis.

For example, Chainalysis can scan entire token ecosystems to identify risks and compliance with regulations, assess deposit and withdrawal patterns to detect fraud, and visualize illicit networks.

The tool's real-time analysis functionality empowers the fraud detection system to continuously monitor on-chain activities and identify potential fraud instances as they occur. This alleviates the burden on in-house tech and legal professionals, who often lack the skills and means to monitor the network 24/7.

Using Chainalysis, companies can ensure compliance with anti-money laundering (AML) regulations, laws for countering the financing of terrorism (CFT), and other relevant regulations.

Chainalysis operates based on blockchain analytics, big data infrastructure, and machine learning. The system operates full nodes for each blockchain. A full node is a computer or server that holds the complete history of the blockchain ledger. This allows Chainalysis to independently verify every transaction on the blockchain using machine learning algorithms. Chainalysis immediately validates and records every new block added to the blockchain on its full node. After this, data about these operations goes to the internal analytics pipelines, where it is indexed, analyzed, and sent back to customer-facing products.

The client-facing services on Chainalysis include crypto investigations and crypto compliance tools (Chainalysis Products n.d.), which present findings to clients based on their task type.

Crypto investigation tools like Reactor, Wallet Scan, and Rapid check instances like illicit operations on crypto wallets or fraudulent activities associated with certain profiles, among others.

Crypto compliance tools like KYT, VAPS Risking, Sentinel, and Address Screening allow businesses and organizations to ensure safe operations on the blockchain. Address screening provides a risk assessment for any address before sending or receiving funds, and VASP (Virtual Asset Service Provider Risking) assesses the risk profiles of other crypto businesses, allowing the selection of a reliable partner.

TRM Labs

TRM Labs solutions target crypto crime and fraudulent activities to help businesses, financial institutions, and governments fight fraud, money laundering, and financial crime (TRM Labs n.d.). TRM operates full nodes on various blockchains, such as

Bitcoin, Ethereum, Solana, etc., to check operations in real time. Using machine learning and addressing external data sources, the system provides risk assessment and detection of illicit businesses and activities, sending the findings further to customer-facing tools. Their customer-facing tools help customers identify the risk profiles of crypto partners (TRM Entity Risk), run real-time wallet address risk (TRM Screening API), investigate hacks (TRM Forensics), and more.

Artificial intelligence and infrastructure development promise further sophistication and development of blockchain compliance tools, offering businesses a secure ecosystem that works within the regulatory framework developed to protect customer rights.

Gaming Economy Technology

Creator Economy—Technologies Supporting Play-and-Earn Gaming

In Web3, creators can showcase and sell their products on platforms such as OpenSea, Rarible, Flixxo, Theta, Content Box, LBRY, and You42.

On You42, creators can sell their content with direct peer-to-peer transactions using the platforms ERC-20 token and U42 token (You42 Inc. n.d.), and on Theta, viewers can receive rewards for sharing their free bandwidth and resources and participating in the network. This way, they generate traffic and contribute to a highly stable node architecture (Theta Token n.d.).

Another decentralized platform is Flixxo, which enables content creators to establish direct relationships with advertisers by eliminating intermediaries from the process, while also allowing them to receive direct payments from consumers within the same business model. However, they lack the developed infrastructure and some advanced features of Web 2 creator platforms to reach an audience and scale.

Traditional Web2 creator tools (Patreon, Ko-fi, Kickstarter, Twitch, Gumroad, BuyMeACoffee) excel in providing a seamless interface, access to large audiences, and extensive feature sets, and become an integral part of centralized gaming. Platforms like Patreon, Ko-Fi, or Twitch, for example, enable creators to establish their own shops and engage with fans through chat services like Discord. Web2 platforms have matured developer tools, allowing for advanced functionality such as auction leave streaming, creating bots, dashboards, reward systems, and other gaming features.

The obvious benefits of Web3 decentralized creator platforms and their Web2 feature-rich counterparts prompted developers to seek complementary use cases. For example, there are games that utilize the Twitch API to stream NFT auctions within the blockchain game. As a result, the creator economy utilizes a combination of Web2 and Web3 tools to achieve faster growth, greater flexibility, and more independence.

Blockchain-Based Creator Economy Platforms

Blockchain platforms present content creators with the ability of direct monetization, transparent content ownership, reduced platform fees, and community governance. Smart contracts are used to mint NFTs and handle subscriptions, royalties, memberships, licensing agreements, tipping or rewarding creators, and community voting.

A creator has to connect to the platform via a digital wallet, upload digital content for NFT, add metadata, choose a blockchain to mint the NFT on, and mint the content as an NFT. Some platforms offer lazy minting, i.e., minting NFTs, as someone is interested in buying them. Creators can select from various blockchains (Ethereum, Polygon, Solana, etc.) based on the platform they are using. This way, on platforms like OpenSea, Rarible, Zora, Foundation, Magic Eden, etc., creators can both mint and sell their NFTs on the platform.

For example, on Zora, there are a full set of tools to build a game, including Zora SDKs such as the Protocol SDK, Coins SDK, and Zora Dev Kit, which connect the app's backend and frontend. Zora Protocol SDK allows coders to deploy NFT contracts for minting, listing, auctioning, and selling NFTs (Zora NFT n.d.). The Coins SDK allows for managing token collections (Zora Labs n.d.). ZDK, which supports TypeScript and React development, simplifies building the app's frontend (ZoraOS Devs n.d.).

Zora API structures NFT data, such as metadata, sales, or collections, to bridge it with UI components like search, filters, and statistics. There is also a Zora Starter App, a ready-made app on Next.js, which anyone can clone and customize. The feature set of the Zora Starter App includes wallet connections, NFT uploads, metadata creation, and minting. Although it is not a no-code solution, like some other platforms offer, it is a developer-friendly template that simplifies work with JavaScript tools.

Web 2 Creator Platforms

Creator platforms help gamers promote games and increase visibility of their products among larger audiences. They help gamers shape communities that can further support gamers with donations. Streaming games on platforms like Twitch directly influences their sales and popularity.

The Web 2 creator platforms don't allow creating NFTs or making blockchain transactions. Instead, they provide webhooks to tie blockchain apps to their functionality, such as live streaming, auctions, chat integration, subscriptions, tipping, drops, and more. This way, they make it possible to also sell NFTs or receive tips in cryptocurrency.

Developers can integrate their games and products into creator platforms via third-party solutions, thereby experiencing the full benefits. This way, gamers, developers, and creators can present and sell NFTs, stream auctions or games, and enjoy the rich interface for interacting with the audience while receiving payments.

For example, Patreon is a platform that directly connects creators and their fans (Patreon n.d.) by allowing each creator to run a shop on the platform, interact with fans through chats, comments, and emails, and collect analytics on chat preferences. Patreon invites game developers and gamers to join the platform for creating communities around their games (Unreal Engine n.d.-b). Developers and gamers can sell early access to games and features, exclusive NFTs (skins, armor, jewelry, characters), behind-the-scenes content (development diaries, design documents), game currency, bonus tokens, private community access, tutorials and workshops, discounts, and pre-orders. In other words, gamers and communities receive various possibilities to grow their audience.

Platforms like Patreon support payments though the integration with credit/debit cards payment systems, PayPal, Apple Pay, Google Pay, Venmo, and direct debit. In case of NFT trade or payment in cryptocurrency, Patreon can allow transactions between the blockchain wallets of creators and buyers. To integrate Patreon accounts with blockchain wallets of creators and buyers, third-party tools like Collab, Land, and Unlock Protocol are used. To verify that buyers (patrons) are qualified for membership to Patreon or for receiving specific rewards from creators, Patreon monitors blockchain events and statuses (NFT transfer, token holdings) with the help of dedicated Patreon APIs. Additionally, Patreon provides numerous APIs that enhance the experiences of creators and developers by expanding the platform's features (Patreon Documentation n.d.).

Another solution, Ko-fi SDK, helps developers integrate Ko-fi functionality into their products and websites. For example, developers can integrate a "Support Me on Ko-fi Button" in their games to collect donations. Ko-Fi is a Patreon alternative with lower fees, allowing for the collection of in-game tips for selling digital products (Ko-fi n.d.). Its functionality enables creators to more effectively manage donations, memberships, commissions, shop alerts, and other key aspects.

Another platform helping gamers showcase their games and art and connect with fans is Twitch. Primarily, it is a streaming platform, but with the help of Twitch Extensions, users can connect to their games, or blockchain wallets to display real-time data (e.g., current power or in-game asset levels). Twitch APIs enable game developers to implement features such as starting polls, creating predictions, generating stream clips, scheduling broadcasts, obtaining game analytics reports, and more (Twitch API n.d.-c).

Twitch APIs also enable users and creators to integrate chat and chatbot functionality, allowing them to communicate during real-life events. The EventSub feature, connected to games through webhooks, enables creator subscribers to receive notifications for various events (e.g., a broadcaster going live, a broadcaster gaining a new subscriber, etc.) (Twitch Developer n.d.-b).

To increase audience engagement, game developers can run Twitch Drops campaigns. Twitch Drops enable game developers to grant in-game rewards to the

Twitch community when streamers play the game (Twitch Developer n.d.-a). Game developers often use NFTs to run such drop campaigns. This requires linking viewers' wallets to their Twitch accounts, which is possible with the help of third-party solutions, such as Oath for Twitch identification and MetaMask or WalletConnect for integration with a Web3 wallet. When the Drop condition is met, a smart contract triggers the reward distribution directly to the viewer's wallet.

Platforms like Twitch, Ko-fi, Patreon, and other open-source developer tools provide blockchain game developers with the ability to build features that increase engagement. Additionally, they simplify monetization options, enabling users to receive additional rewards through subs and tips. Also, these streaming platforms provide a seamless gaming experience and ease of implementing the features described.

Blockchain technology supports the development of monetization features; however, there are challenges that include scalability, latency, and user experience friction. Layer 2 blockchain solutions, that are actively being developed, promise more seamless and feature-rich creator platforms.

Decentralized Identity Solutions

Decentralized identity technology allows users to identify themselves across various blockchains without sharing sensitive personal information or relying on centralized databases. Users can interact with different parties through verifiable credentials, fostering a trustless environment where privacy and security are inherently built into the identity network (Williams 2025).

The technology behind decentralized identity solutions follows distinct sets of rules, such as the W3C DID standard and the W3C Verifiable Credentials standard. In 2022, W3C (World Wide Web Consortium) issued a protocol for creating decentralized identifiers that enable verifiable, decentralized digital identities. This protocol defines a standardized way to create, resolve, update, and deactivate decentralized identifiers without relying on a centralized registry (Decentralized Identifiers 2019). DID works as a unique name for a decentralized identity and also as a link that connects with the decentralized identity profile, like that on a Ceramic Network, where the data about the person is stored.

In 2025, W3C also issued a Verifiable Credentials Data Model setting rules for verifying decentralized identities. The protocol sets rules for Web users, allowing them to issue, hold, and verify credentials digitally (Verifiable Credentials 2021). The digital credentials serve as proof of identity or achievements, like a driver's license or university diploma.

The two standards provide a common language and framework that allows developers to build interoperable decentralized identity solutions across different blockchains.

A decentralized identity solution should also have features like user control and ownership, selective disclosure, interoperability, tamper-proof storage, and portability. There are multiple services online, allowing developers to build decentralized identity solutions with the features described above and solve other tasks related to their management. Ethereum Name Service, Ceramic Network, Sovrin, and Hyperledger Indy are the most popular ones.

Ceramic Network

The Ceramic Network is a decentralized, open-source protocol that sets standards for managing dynamic, mutable, and composable data on Web 3 (Ceramic n.d.). While most blockchains deal with immutable data that cannot be changed once recorded, Ceramic's focus on mutable data makes the platform a usable environment to create user profiles, content feeds, and reputation systems.

A decentralized user profile contains information like names, achievements, credentials, and social links. In terms of gaming, there may be information about achievements, guild memberships, experience, and ratings. Logically, this information changes through time.

On a classical blockchain, each update requires rewriting the whole document using smart contracts. Ceramic allows every user to create a special document, an account, where all achievements and other information are recorded (Ceramic Documentation n.d.). This document is stored on the Ceramic Network, which consists of decentralized nodes (computers). Since Ceramic is not a blockchain-based solution, all accounts are stored off-chain. Each time a change happens, Ceramic generates a document state hash and anchors it on-chain. The document itself is off-chain, and it is stored in a way that only its owner can make changes, and each change is proved with a hash so the history of changes can be proved. This combination makes decentralized identities flexible but also secure. Ceramic anchors the documents to the Ethereum main net (Ceramic Roadmap n.d.), but users can connect to other blockchains, such as Bitcoin, Avalanche, NEAR, and Moonbeam (Polkadot parachain) on desire.

An account on Ceramics can be seen as an extension of a digital wallet ID. A Ceramic account stores more data (achievements, ranks, or in-game ownership records). Since a Ceramic account is integrated with a wallet, it is not uncommon in Web 3 gaming to use a wallet ID to access a Ceramic account to make changes.

To create a Ceramic account using a wallet ID, Ceramic uses the DID protocol, which they adapt for blockchain in the form of the PKH DID method (Identifiers n.d.). The PKH DID method natively supports blockchain accounts. It is a decentralized Identifier (DID) from a wallet's public key hash and links the Ceramic account to that wallet. To create a Ceramic account, a player has to connect their wallet to the Ceramic Network, create a profile document on Ceramic, and receive a unique DID, which can be used across Web 3 to prove achievements.

Ethereum Name Service

The Ethereum Name Service, or ENS, is the decentralized naming protocol that is built on the Ethereum blockchain. It adheres to open-source standards and is based on a set of decentralized smart contracts that translate blockchain addresses into human-readable names (ENS Support n.d.).

The system transforms complex cryptographic addresses with human-readable names. Each name is saved as an NFT and has a memorable format, e.g., yourname.eth. Using ENS, in-gaming identities are easier to recognize, remember, and share.

ENS is an Ethereum-based solution but can be used across different games and chains. ENS enables cross-chain naming of long addresses such as crypto wallets, content hashes, metadata, and even smart contracts in the wider blockchain ecosystem (ENS Support n.d.). ENS allows a limited interface for storing data, so it cannot store profile data, like the Ceramic Network. Its core function is working as a user's identity pointer, allowing a gamer to use it as a unique, recognizable name across various blockchains.

Payment Gateways for GameFi

Payment gateways act as a bridge to connect earnings in GameFi and real-world finance. A payment gateway is a service that processes digital transactions, acting as a middleman between buyers and sellers. It ensures that payments made online go swiftly and securely (Williams 2025).

Payment gateways connect both centralized finance solutions and blockchains in different ways, allowing users to deposit and withdraw user crypto, track on-chain balances, monitor transactions, and interact with smart contracts.

Payment gateways are usually Web 2 solutions. They present centralized services, storing data in traditional infrastructure and databases. Users' accounts are managed by the service provider, not independently by users, like in blockchain. Such systems are built on a private backend and not on the decentralized network and store the wallet key information.

Some, like Circle, were built with the purpose of processing blockchain payments and issuing stablecoins. So, such applications have APIs for minting and burning tokens, providing on-chain payments, and interacting with wallets and smart contracts. Others, like Stripe, were built specifically for Web 2 services. Although, later in their evolution, they implemented crypto-friendly features like payouts in USDC, on-ramping to crypto wallets, and NFT checkouts, so they can also be integrated in decentralized gaming. Web 2 payment gateways work as an important element of Web 3 and Web 2 economy, enhancing flexibility in both.

For example, users can buy NFTs on a marketplace like Curios with their credit card if they don't have blockchain-based assets in their wallets, using Curios integration with Stripe. Avalanche-based games like DeFi Kingdoms or Shrapnel have implemented a fiat-to-crypto widget to streamline the in the game user experience.

Circle

Circle products and infrastructure are designed to support and accelerate the use of blockchain-based earnings in real-world finance. Circle started as a company providing blockchain-based financial services. In 2018, the company issued a USDC stablecoin, which is a digital currency completely backed up by the US dollar assets at a 1:1 ratio.

The USDC Circle Reserve Fund is held at The Bank of New York Mellon and is managed by BlackRock, so it is not a decentralized network (Circle Reserve Fund 2024). Yet, USDC is often used as a currency in blockchain games, decentralized communities, and marketplaces. Being compatible with blockchains like Ethereum, Solana, Avalanche, Polygon, Base, and more, Circle allows gamers, traders, and creators to exchange their earnings in different cryptocurrencies into USDC or EURC.

The integrations with Web 3 applications are executed by Web3-native APIs for accepting payments (Circle Payment API), sending USDC to wallets or bank accounts (Payouts API), interacting with smart contracts on-chain (Smart Contract APIs), and managing wallet accounts (Accounts APIs).

Despite the high level of centralization and its custodial nature (Circle holds control over the funds in the wallets on behalf of users), the Circle development resources are valued in the blockchain community for high-quality bank-grade development tools, like off-ramping from USDC to USD via bank wires or APIs, auditability, cross-chain USDC transfers, and programmable payouts. Circle is used for cases like AAA blockchain RPG paying streamers in USDC or large game studios needing tools for USDC payrolls.

Coinbase Commerce

Coinbase Commerce is a cryptocurrency payment platform from Coinbase, an American cryptocurrency exchange. Coinbase Commerce offers an open-source protocol that helps to unify and simplify crypto payments. It enables a consistent experience for all users, irrespective of their platform or wallet choice (Coinbase n.d.-a, b).

As Coinbase is primarily the cryptocurrency exchange, the key feature the Coinbase API allows is exchanging hundreds of currencies into USDC for further use in the blockchain environment.

Coinbase Commerce APIs and SDKs offer the basis for the development of different tools and features like the integration with wallets and processing payments. Their infrastructure of tools and services is wide and includes, among other things:

1. Wallet API—the API helps create wallets and automate on-chain actions.
2. Onramp API/SDK- allows users to fund their on-chain apps from fiat and crypto balances. One of the key features of Onramp API is the Guest Checkout, which

allows users from certain locations to deposit money in games, dApps, etc., without a Coinbase account.
3. Offramp API/SDK—features allowing users to cash out their on-chain earnings into fiat currencies.
4. On-chain Reputation API—enables users to check a wallet address, ENS, or Basename for activities and receive a score between −100 and + 100, indicating its on-chain reputation.
5. Webhook SDK—the open-source documentation allowing developers to create webhooks and receive on-chain notifications.
6. Smart Contract Event SDK—offers instruction on how to retrieve smart contract events or manage smart contracts using the CDP SDK (Coinbase Commerce n.d.).

Unlike Circle, which operates with USDC and EURC, Coinbase Commerce allows accepting payments in different tokens, including BTC, ETH, USDC, DAI, LTC, etc. Coinbase is non-custodial in its nature, providing users full control over their crypto assets. It also offers simple crypto-payment buttons and other tools, so it is perfect for streamlining integration within blockchain products.

Stripe

Stripe is a classical Web 2 payment processing provider. Yet recently, they built features allowing blockchain platforms to pay gamers in USDC on Solana, including on-ramping to crypto wallets, NFT checkouts, recurrent payments, and subscriptions.

While games use Stripe to process regular payments in fiat currencies, blockchain games, and NFT marketplaces resort to Stripe to let users buy NFTs from their credit cards without MetaMask integration and gas fees. This lowers the entry barrier to customers who are new to cryptocurrencies and don't have crypto wallets.

Stripe helps build features like recurrent payments purely on-chain. Therefore, Web3 games that need this feature use Stripe integration. Examples may include DAOs and gaming guilds, which collect regular payments (e.g., monthly fees). Stripe also makes it possible to implement recurrent payments from regular credit cards. Another Stripe feature attractive to the GameFi industry is immediate global payouts.

Stripe provides numerous open-source APIs and SDKs that enable Stripe functionality in blockchain apps, games, and marketplaces. They include Onramp API, Quotes API, Stripe Checkout, Payment Intents API, Wallet API, etc. (Stripe API n.d.).

Built on the basis of Web 2 technologies, the payment gateways are an important connection between GameFi and real-world finance. They enable users to accept payment or acquire assets seamlessly. In blockchain gaming, they lower the entry barrier for people with no previous experience in blockchain-based technologies. Additionally, with the abundance of open-source SDKs and free-to-access APIs, these solutions streamline building new games and apps, which allow gamers, creators, and gig workers to receive payments in real-world currencies without delays and around the world.

Guild Software

Guilds were formed to address the high cost of purchasing tokens required for games. Since individual gamers find it hard to overcome the entry barrier to join new games, they may become guild members to benefit from their access. Gaming guilds acquire access to different games with the purpose of sharing them later with the guild members. For example, Yield Guild Games states it aims to seek yield across the Metaverse by purchasing assets from popular blockchain games like Axie, The Sandbox, and League of Kingdoms (Egliston 2025). This gives the guild the ability to grow the community and maximize the returns of their play-to-earn business models by allowing more players access to more games.

Technologically, gaming guilds have to provide various sets of features relating to guild, asset, and activity management. Blockchain technology and self-executing smart contracts, with their traceability, provide the basis for the features described.

Guilds like Yield Guild Games, Merit Circle, Guild Fi, Unix Gaming, Astra Guild Ventures, and Google Games Guild use smart-contract-based DAOs to intermediate the process of leasing assets (and paying out returns to those who lease their assets) (Egliston 2025).

To lease assets, pay out returns, and automate these processes, guild software requires wallet integration (MetaMask, WalletConnect, etc.) and role-based access control via NFTs or Soul-Bound Tokens.

To decide which players will get the lease and to distribute leased items among the guild members, guild software requires decentralized identity features (DID). These may include on-chain and off-chain profiles, reputation scores, and the means for anonymous or pseudonymous participation with verified credentials.

On-chain profiles, as public ledgers of a person's blockchain activity, allow a user to connect to different wallets and blockchain platforms and use one identity through various games and platforms. Some guilds prefer off-chain profiles, which record part of the identity information off-chain (in a centralized storage or another decentralized network) for flexibility and gas-saving.

Managing guild membership requires introducing membership tiers (Initiate, Contributor, etc.) and NFT gating for access and privileges.

Decentralized governance also requires NFTs or guild tokens to run the voting. Likewise, smart contracts are used to guarantee automated interest payouts on crypto asset loans.

Treasury management is achieved through treasury dashboards with real-time analytics. To ensure gamers and investors have an interest in the long-term success of the project, token vesting features are needed. Running a guild requires sophisticated sets of tools that both guarantee the principles of decentralization on the one hand and allow for a high level of flexibility and scalability to boost the guild development on the other. Some established gaming communities like that of Yield Guild

Games have developed complex systems that allow players across the Metaverse to build guilds of their own, following the model of Yield Guild Games.

Yield Guild Games Protocol

Yield Guild Games issued their Concept Paper in September 2024 (Protocol) with the aim of facilitating seamless coordination among gaming groups. Using this document, any gaming community can create guild software of their own.

According to the product team at YGG, Guild Protocol is a global standard for guild-related interactions, designed to optimize scalable opportunities through verifiable and transparent transactions recorded on-chain (Building with the YGG 2024). This means that the product is aimed at reaching audiences worldwide. It is possible because the protocol is open-source and has a modular structure. Each module represents a set of features and can be used as a model for a modular decentralized application (modular dApp). The modules can be combined either to create dApps or add features to the existing dApps.

The protocol's modular libraries and tools allow to develop functionality in the following categories:

1. Guilds—The features of this module allow for creating a guild, inviting people, and setting up management dashboards. Each member of a guild can have a membership badge coded as an NFT. Each guild is structured as a DAO, with the ability to create smaller DAOs, called SubDAOs, for specific games and regions. The guild is governed using token-based voting with YGG tokens (ERC-20). The YGG token is also used for payment for services and unlocking exclusive perks.
2. Treasury—The Treasury module provides features for setting up a guild wallet to store points, assets, and rewards. It also has an integration with a payment system for trading. The multi-signature (multi-sig) wallet works as a bank account for the guild. The smart contract operating multi-sig wallets prescribe the number of keys in the wallet (e.g., five) and the minimum number of keys to approve the transaction (e.g., three). The functionality also allows users to assign wallet roles as owners, signatories, and administrators.
3. Quests—Setting up multiple quests, managing quest lifecycle and content. The functionality also allows following the progress of the quest for validation and iteration. The functionality also allows assigning tasks within quests, and there are different types of tasks possible, e.g., game testing, user acquisition, etc.
4. Campaigns—The features needed for launching promos, landing pages, and rewarding systems.
5. Identity—An achievement system to build reputation and tie it to identity profiles. Each achievement is represented in the form of an NFT badge, which also serves as a certificate of completion. In the YGG, soul-bound tokens are used to track achievements and track reputation, so each NFT earned is permanently linked to the member's wallet.

Operations—Setting up chats, bots, and tools for management and collaboration (Guild Protocol 2024).

Technologically, Yield Guild Protocol is based on Ethereum, leveraging smart contracts for YGG tokens (ERC-20) and NFTs (ERC—721, ERC—1155). But it also has sidechain integrations that may be used by developers for cheaper and faster transactions (Polygon, Ronin, XPLA).

Smart contracts are used to automate scholarships or, in other words, rent NFTs, split revenues (e.g., x% to the gamer and y% to the guild), make stakes, and distribute awards.

YGG DAOs and SubDAOs are also governed by smart contracts, allowing token holders to influence decision-making (treasury spending, partnership decisions, allocation of resources, launching SubDAOs) with voting with the help of ERC-20 tokens. The more tokens a member holds or is ready to stake, the greater their influence is.

It is also important to mention that YGG is multi-chain by design, allowing it to support different popular games regardless of the blockchain they are built on. It supports token bridges, allowing users to transfer YGG and NFTs from Ethereum to other blockchains like Polygon or Ronin.

This way, the Guild Protocol provides the infrastructure to facilitate collaboration between guilds, presenting possibilities for gamers to transfer their achievements and reputation built on-chain between different games like Illuvium (Immutable X), Axie (Ronin), and The Sandbox (Ethereum).

According to the Guild Protocol, with the growth of groups coming together on-chain, the Guild Protocol becomes the coordination layer to aggregate guilds of the world, facilitating new economic opportunities for all members based on the reputation that they have developed through community-based activities (Guild Protocol 2024).

Other Guild Games Protocols

Besides Yield Guild Games Protocol, several other solutions help gamers with guild formation and integration of their communities in Web 3. These include:

DAOhaus: A platform offering features for creating and managing DAOs. It is built on the DAOhaus protocol, which is open-source and flexible, allowing users to fork and build solutions on top of the protocol. The DAOhaus SDK enables users to create DAO apps of their own with a plethora of functionality, like DAO overview, proposal forms, members list, and more (DAOhaus Developer Docs n.d.).

Common: This platform offers a comprehensive set of features for on-chain communities to discuss, vote, and fund projects. They include integrated forums, on-chain and off-chain voting, treasury management, and support for multiple communication channels. All these features are accessible through open APIs, code bases, and scripts (Common n.d.). Although the platform is not built on blockchain, it integrates with Ethereum, Polkadot, and Solana chains for on-chain proposal creation and voting, wallet integration, etc.

XDAO: It is a multi-chain platform for creating and managing decentralized autonomous organizations. As it provides tools for groups of people to control and manage shared assets, build communities, and facilitate investments into mutual funds, it can also be a solution to build gaming guilds. XDAO supports Ethereum and a range of other blockchains, including Polygon, Avalanche, Fantom, Aurora, Moonbeam, Moonriver, Astar, Shiden, and others (xDAO n.d.).

There are also many other open-source solutions powering GameFi guilds to build and scale guild software. The availability of easy-to-access protocols, SDKs, and APIs supports guild growth and makes guilds more transparent and adaptable, which caters to the growth of the Web 3 gaming economy.

Mobile Game Development

Network Infrastructure

New connectivity technologies, like 5G, Starlink, and edge computing, enhance mobile gaming by delivering significantly lower latency, which improves responsiveness in real-time multiplayer games. Starlink and other low Earth orbit satellite services enhance connectivity in areas with low connection, increasing accessibility to high-end games. These technologies provide high-speed connections, supporting cloud gaming and large game downloads.

Low earth satellites are systems of satellites that circle around the Earth at lower altitudes, between 500 and 2000 km (TechTarget 2019). Thanks to the lower altitude and higher density of equipment, LEO satellites provide better internet connectivity. For example, while traditional geostationary (GEO) satellites provide a high latency (500–600 ms) internet connection, LEO satellite connection latency is only between 2 and 20 ms. This makes them suitable for real-time applications like online mobile games in areas with a lack of terrestrial connectivity.

SpaceX's Starlink is the market leader in the LEO domain, which makes technology often associated with the company. Yet, there are other service providers, including OneWeb, Amazon (Project Kuiper), Telesat, ViaSat, and Hughes.

5G technology, or the fifth-generation technology, is the new standard for telecommunications networks launched by cell phone companies in 2019 (Flinders and Smalley 2024).

5G networks occupy the same radio frequencies as their predecessors, 3G, 4G, and 4G LTE networks, but with the help of several tweaks, they provide faster connectivity in areas with dense populations.

The enhancements are possible as 5G networks operate on a wider range of bandwidths than 4G and 3G networks. Their radio spectrum resources are expanded from the sub-3 GHz specification used in previous networks to 100 GHz and greater (Flinders and Smalley 2024).

This tweak expands the capacity and throughput of 5G networks, allowing for more devices to be connected to a single network at once. This specification also provides faster speeds, which improves the quality of mobile apps, like games, when many users are on the same network, like in a crowded urban environment.

Edge computing allows devices in remote locations to process data at the "edge" of the network. This is done either by the specific device integrated into the local infrastructure or a local server. When data needs to be processed in the central data center, only the most important data is transmitted, thereby minimizing latency (Microsoft n.d.-c).

Edge computing uses small, distributed data centers or servers placed near end users. Often, edge computing devices are placed in local ISP hubs, cell towers, or even on-premises. In terms of gaming, edge nodes may handle matchmaking, physics calculations, or video rendering closer to the player. This reduces game latency, meaning the game responses happen faster and feel immediate. It is especially important for mobile gaming, as technology offloads complex processing tasks from the user's device. Thanks to this, gamers have high-quality graphics and performance on less powerful hardware. Such services are provided by a range of companies, including Amazon Web Services (AWS), Microsoft Azure, Google Cloud, and companies like Cloudflare and Akamai.

Low-spec Game Optimization

Sometimes, computer-hungry games are not supported on lower-spec hardware, which becomes an issue in terms of game accessibility.

Therefore, game developers resort to game spec optimization or making a game run smoothly on computers and mobile devices with limited hardware capabilities. There are various techniques and services that allow game developers to achieve this effect.

For example, developers often implement user settings to cater to player preferences. This ranges from simple tweaks, such as turning shadows off or adjusting resolution, to complex imaging configurations (Williams 2025).

The strategies developers use for optimizing low-spec games vary. It can involve using lower-resolution textures, simplified 3D models with fewer polygons, limiting visual effects, or reducing the use of lighting and shadows, optimizing code and assets for faster load times, and including adjustable graphics settings.

Some game development tools are designed to meet optimization needs. For example, Godot's game engine is lightweight, and it can run on a variety of hardware, including older or less powerful computers and consoles (Godot n.d.).

Additionally, Godot allows compressing and reducing textures during imports, which reduces VRAM usage.

Games built on Godot support dynamic resolution scaling, allowing for adjustments to the resolution during gameplay. When performance drops, the resolution is automatically lowered, allowing gamers to balance visual quality and performance.

Another feature supporting game optimization is that building games on Godot supports LOD rendering. LOD stands for the Level of Detail. It is a technique in development that allows for the reduction of complexity in 3D models as they move farther from the player's viewpoint, which is referred to as the camera.

The logic of LOD is as follows: when an object in the scene is far away from the camera (player's viewpoint), the amount of detail is reduced, but the number of triangles used to render the details remains the same. LOD allows the reduction of the number of triangles in the object as the distance from the camera increases, so not only do smaller details become invisible, but they also become uncoded (Unity Documentation n.d.-a).

In Godot, the LOD rendering is set on the stage of coding, which improves the application's performance on older versions of computers or mobile devices.

At the level of project export (uploading files into a standalone game), Godot allows customization of the files, for example, to exclude high-resolution assets, strip debug info, or compile minimal exports.

Another game framework that enables the development of games for low-spec devices is Cocos2d-x. Cocos2d-x is a game engine based on C++, which makes apps built on the platform lightweight by default.

The platform is optimized to use less memory, as it allows for fine-grained allocation and deallocation of memory resources, enabling developers to select features without including default features, unlike other platforms. Also, Cocos2d-x doesn't have an in-built editor or 3D tools, which means fewer background processes.

With these and other features (asset size reduction, minimal RAM usage, and efficient rendering), Cocos2d-x is well-suited to target mobile platforms, such as low-end Android devices and other devices with lower CPUs and memory requirements for graphics.

Platforms like Cocos2d-x and Godot enable the creation of games that can run on a wide range of devices from the outset. Yet, they are not the only technical solutions with toolsets for low-spec game optimization. Several other engines and frameworks can be suitable, including Defold, LÖVE, and GameMaker.

Mobile Game Development Technologies

Mobile game development technologies have grown rapidly in the last decade, progressing significantly to low-code and no-code solutions, enabling individuals with limited technical backgrounds to build applications from scratch.

Platforms like Buildbox, GameMaker Studio 2, GDevelop, and FlutterFlow offer drag-and-drop development interfaces, breaking down code into building blocks that come with the necessary prebuilt functionality. For example, Buildbox allows users to create backgrounds, characters, objects, or actions with just a few clicks. Special effects like particles, lights, and trails can be simply dragged to the scenes or attached to a character (Buildbox n.d.). These solutions enhance development cycles and increase the speed-to-market of the game, powering the mobile gaming market.

Enterprise-grade game development also offers new tools and possibilities not available a decade ago. Smartphone games can handle graphics and gameplay of console quality. High-resolution displays enable detailed visuals, and advanced processors and GPUs facilitate complex game mechanics and smooth performance on mobile devices.

The development of game engines like Unity and Unreal Engine enables the optimization of gaming performance across various devices, including mobile. Being lightweight, these solutions enable the creation of games of varying complexity.

While high-end technologies enable more advanced player experiences, the growth of generative artificial intelligence solutions, such as Sora, Midjourney, Stable Diffusion, DALL-E, and Adobe Firefly, shortens product design cycles.

The ability to visualize game concepts with high precision in the early stages of game development gives game creators the ability to elicit precise feedback from gamers and make more informed design choices.

In parallel cloud gaming technologies are developing, allowing people to play high-end video games remotely without owning special devices.

The mobile game technology landscape encompasses a range of developing branches, including mobile development platforms, connectivity solutions, cloud services, and adaptive technologies, which enable users to play traffic-hungry games in lower bandwidth and speed conditions.

Developer Resources

Today, multiple services make coding games easier by providing comprehensive sets of prebuilt functionalities to facilitate the creation of ready-made products. For example, Unity, Unreal Engine, Buildbox, GameMaker Studio 2, Cocos2d-x, Solar2D, and AppGameKit.

Using pre-made resources frees developers from having to code the game's backend and frontend from scratch, allowing them to concentrate on the game's logic and dynamics. For example, Unity provides resources for building such feature sets as 2D/3D characters and animation, AR, VR, 3D world-building, engineering, gameplay, and storytelling on mobile (Unity n.d.-d).

While building a game in Unity, developers work in the Unity Editor, where they can visually arrange objects and scenes. The editor is the visual tool that enables developers to build games in a "what you see is what you get" fashion (Geig 2022). This method enables users to see the properties of the selected items (positions, occlusion, background, projection) and enhance them with the help of buttons, without coding for each feature separately.

A developer can assign prebuilt functions, such as physics, animations, and input handling, to developed objects or create custom ones by coding them in C#. For example, to make an object fall in Unity, developers can use the prebuilt Rigidbody component, which allows the object to be affected by physical forces within the game, such as pushing, gravity, collisions, and more. Without this component, the object will not react to reality (Unity n.d.-b). The component performs the calculations for the object's motion according to the rules set by the developer. It includes how a character will move, slow down after reacting to an outer force, and more. In this way, developers don't have to create custom code to calculate object movements and other kinetic properties.

While a developer sets properties on objects and scenes and assigns functions to perform, Unity handles the backend connections. The platform offers various tools and documentation for developing, testing, and debugging features, all of which are already on-site. Additionally, it has a growing community where developers can discuss bottlenecks, which simplifies the development process. Unity has integrated the popular scripting tool Bolt to offer no-code game building. At the same time, Unreal Engine has introduced the Blueprint Visual Scripting system, described as a visual programming language based on a graph of interconnected nodes (Unreal Engine n.d.-c). Each node represents some of the actions, events, or variables that developers select to comply with the game without writing code.

Google's Flutter is another platform frequently used for game development. It is based on the Dart programming language, optimized for speed and quality. Flutter is most often used for developing cross-platform applications (working on Android, iOS, and Windows Mobile).

Although not traditionally a game development platform, Flutter offers game-focused packages that are suitable for various game designs. For example, the Flutter Casual Games Toolkit provides a base for the code, with prebuilt integrations for services such as Ads, IAP, Firebase, Google Play, and Game Center (Flutter Casual Games Toolkit n.d.), which simplify and accelerate game development.

Its branch service, Flutter Flow, transforms Flutter's possibilities into a drag-and-drop interface. Flutter Flow enables developers to create games without having to code everything from scratch. As a low-code platform, Flutter Flow is a go-to resource for prototyping and creating simple games. For customization, a developer can also add more features and widgets by utilizing Dart code.

GameMaker Studio 2 also offers a visual interface for selecting scripts and incorporating them into a game, but it allows developers to add custom code for more complex game logic.

While developers are building games, either with the help of a no-code solution or by enhancing the base with custom features, each system compiles everything into a single, runnable application based on a specific programming language, architecture, and a proprietary set of features.

Some engines offer high-end graphics, while others are lightweight and support better game performance in areas with low-speed connections. These peculiarities of the game engine side influence the choice of the platform for development.

Game Engines

Game engines are software solutions that stand behind game functionalities like rendering 2D and 3D graphics in real time, handling visual effects (lighting, shading, shadows, textures), simulating real-world physics (gravity, collision detection), building believable relations between objects (bouncing, falling, breaking), controlling characters behaviors, game rules, triggering UI events, and organizing game environments, levels, and assets.

The features described are built using different programming languages and engine architecture solutions, which influence performance, visual effects, gaming speed, and other factors.

For example, Unity primarily uses C#, which is not a performance-oriented programming language; however, it is more developer-friendly, resulting in faster development cycles and better code optimization. Using C# makes Unity more beginner-friendly and is optimized for mobile because of its architecture.

For example, Unity uses the IL2CPP solution, which compiles C# code to C++ and then compiles the resulting C++ code into native machine code, making Unity the best solution for cross-platform mobile development (Unity n.d.-a). Mobile games created with Unity can be easily deployed on Android, iOS, Windows, consoles, and more.

Unreal Engine relies on C++, which supports high-end graphics. In terms of mobile game development, Unreal is used to develop AAA video games that can be scaled for mobile (Epic Games n.d.). To solve the issues with battery, drain and memory usage, Unreal apps require optimization.

Game Maker 2 uses the proprietary Game Maker Language created specifically for game development. The Game Maker Language properties allow to enhance a game's runtime performance. Since it manages memory automatically, games avoid garbage collection, and that reduces performance bottlenecks. It also comes in two versions: GML Visual and GML Code. The first variety allows users to "write" code visually by placing blocks of code, while the second option offers manual code writing (YoYo Games n.d.).

Godor's game engine is based on GDScript, C#, and C++. As an open-source product, Godot architecture allows for a higher level of customization than the ones described above, which makes this platform perfect for experimentation.

In other words, game engines like Unity, Godot, and Unreal Engine define what can be done with any object, scene, or character inside the game. The more developed the engines are the more realistic and highly performant the games become.

Advancements in GPU and CPU, such as multi-threading and parallel processing (the ability of a processing unit to perform several computing tasks simultaneously), enable engines to handle more data at once, allowing for dynamic lighting and physics simulations in real time. This laid the groundwork for the rise of cinematic-quality games, such as Genshin Impact, Wuthering Waves, and Call of Duty: Mobile.

Most modern game engines support realistic graphics and physics, creating immersive gaming experiences. By streamlining development with tools for rendering, scripting, animation, and cross-platform deployment, game engines empower developers to innovate more rapidly, pushing the gamification universe forward.

Graphic Tools for Game Development

The visual side of game development is supported by a range of tools, including Adobe Substance Painter, GIMP, Adobe Illustrator, Blender, Maya, ZBrush, and others.

These tools have undergone incredible evolution over the last 20 years, enabling more realistic visuals and faster design cycles. Modern tools offer photorealistic graphics, real-time lighting, reflections, shadows, realistic motion, and facial capture integration, among other features. For example, Substance Painter allows designers to paint directly on 3D models with real-time PBR preview. The application features a user's viewport, allowing designers to see how the product changes in progress, including all effects such as lighting and shadows (Adobe n.d.). The platform also allows the recomputing of any design at any time, as it records all brushes and strokes. Besides a wide variety of dynamic brushes and projection tools, Substance supports advanced material creation typically used in AAA video games, including the simulation of real-world material behaviors such as sheen, anisotropy, clear coat, and subsurface scattering.

Examples of materials and asset designs created with the help of Substance Painter can be seen in games like Horizon Zero Dawn, Call of Duty, and Cyberpunk 2077.

3D gaming design is simplified by a variety of dedicated tools tuned for the peculiarities of #D art. Blender is a popular tool for creating in-game assets and animation. It is used for the entirety of the 3D pipeline—modeling, rigging, animation, simulation, rendering, compositing and motion tracking, even video editing, and game asset creation (Blender n.d.).

Blender offers advanced features such as sculpting, rigging, and rendering and is simple to integrate with other game design tools. Advanced designers utilize the Blender API for Python scripting to create new design tools and possibilities for Blender. As a result, this product is, by nature, an open-source platform, the development of which is driven by a huge community of designers.

The industry standards for animation in gaming are set by tools like Autodesk's Maya. Maya provides a variety of animation tools that allow it to bring game objects to life. The algorithm uses skeletal rigs to create realistic character movements (climbing, fighting, and stealth sneaking) (Autodesk n.d.).

Maya algorithms, based on forward kinematics and inverse kinematics, ensure a smooth and realistic-looking motion. Forward kinematics (FK) means that each joint movement of the character moves one by one (rotating the shoulder, then the elbow, and then the arm). Inverse kinematics (IK) presupposes the motion of one part of an asset (e.g., the arm), and the motion of the connected parts is calculated automatically.

With FK and IK features, designers don't have to calculate the object motion, as this is done by the program. They should only control and rigs to create natural, complex motion quickly. The photorealistic animation effects of Maya are used in AAA games and videos.

Generative AI

Generative AI (genAI) offers powerful capabilities for code, image, and video generation. AI features have become present in most of the game development tools. GenAI services, such as Midjourney, DALL-E, Sora, and ChatGPT, are widely used to streamline ideation, prototyping, and development.

Generative AI models for text-to-image generation are based on diffusion models. Diffusion models are trained to generate images using a two-step process: forward diffusion and reverse diffusion (Lawton 2025). In the first process, the image is gradually distorted by adding noise in small steps. In the second process, the model learns to reverse nosing and restore the image to resemble the original used for training. This way, the model learns to generate visuals.

Diffusion models are the basis of all text-to-image AI tools, which have gained much popularity and broad applications. Starting from concept art, where these tools help designers select between different potential variations of a character's look or an asset design, generative AI is widely used to generate visuals for in-game use. For example, genAI can create detailed 2D portraits and full-body designs for player characters and non-player characters, as well as scenic environments such as landscapes or urban settings. Additionally, it can add stylized or photorealistic surface details and architectural variations to enhance world-building with the help of text prompts.

There are numerous game-specific AI services that can be used for automating various tasks, from generating visuals to creating whole game levels and controlling non-player character behavior. Rosebud AI, Layer AI, Leonardo AI, Meshy AI, Promethean AI, Skybox AI, Scenario, Adobe Firefly, and DeepMotion are AI tools for asset creation, which allow for generating hyper-realistic characters, assets and scenes from text prompts, building 3D models, and 360-degree environment. Tools like Cascadeur automates character posing, making characters change positions faster and more intuitive. Game ideation and research are simplified with tools like Ludo.ai.

Sora, the video generation product from Open AI, also has the potential to change how the games are developed. Sora can generate videos from text prompts, and these videos are further used as game scenes or other assets. The tools find various applications in the prototyping stage. For example, game developers can use Sora for visualizing game mechanics or other game elements. Sora can be potentially added to game engines to generate adaptive game environments in real life.

The concept of using generative AI to influence game dynamics was used in God's Innovation Project GIP), developed by Nair et al. (2025). The god genre of games is a genre where players take roles of deities and are granted supernatural abilities such as terrain manipulation and weather control. Classically, these "superpowers" come from the pre-coded menu and are strictly regulated by the rules of the game. In the GIP, the players are allowed to shape the gaming world according to their own vision with the help of text prompts. For example, a player has to collect a certain number of "words," the in-game assets, which can be further used to generate new terrains.

Developers have restricted the players from composing their prompts using only words in a word bank. When the number of words needed is collected, players engage in terrain formulation using prompts. The terrain in this game is not only a visual background but an active environment with movement restrictions, strategic positioning, and resource availability, so it is an element of game mechanics.

The experiment doesn't just prove the possibility of AI integration into game mechanics but also high user engagement in such types of games. It is also an example of an emerging field where players can use text-based prompts to influence game mechanics and devise their own winning strategies. Including generative AI into game mechanics, granting players more power to influence their gaming world, will become a prominent feature in the future of gaming.

Cloud Platforms

The rise of cloud technologies, such as cloud storage and cloud computing, has influenced the domain of gaming as well, giving rise to the phenomenon of cloud gaming.

In its essence, cloud gaming is a technology that allows streaming video games directly across the internet, eliminating the need for downloads and saving storage space (Microsoft n.d.-b).

Instead of running the game on a local computer or console, gamers can access the game online while the game itself is stored on the remote server. Such games as Fortnite, Call of Duty: Warzone 2.0, Grand Theft Auto V, and Apex Legends can be played on the cloud.

In cloud gaming, games are run on remote servers with powerful CPUs powering high-end game engines. In conditions of good internet quality, this technology allows gamers to play computing-hungry games even if their devices can't support them technically. Also, cloud gaming removes the need to download or install the games on gamers' devices, thus saving time and memory.

Cloud computing is not only the means to host and run games, but it also provides an environment for game development, testing, and deployment.

Platforms like Unity Cloud, Unreal Cloud, Amazon GameLift, and Unreal Pixel Engine Streaming provide tools and features like browser-based editors, version control, and collaboration software for remote teams to build, test, and manage games without needing powerful local hardware. They mark a comprehensive shift in game development methods.

Previously, software development architecture was mainly monolithic, meaning one application was a huge bundle of interrelated code, and changing one element could trigger changes in all the applications. This method was not convenient in terms of speed and resource management; it was slow and only allowed one part of the development team to work on the project at once.

Cloud computing offers a different approach. Thanks to uploading software to the cloud, different teams could access the same code at the same time. This led to a shift in the architectural approach. Instead of using monolithic architecture, developers broke applications into separate pieces of code or microservices, allowing several teams to work on their solutions simultaneously. Since microservices were united but strongly tied to each other, changes in one feature didn't lead to changes in the other.

Examples of microservices in gaming can be leaderboards, gamer accounts, game inventory, matchmaking, chats, payment systems, and analytics. Each of these services can be developed separately, and all of them can be developed simultaneously by different team members. This approach shortens development cycles and allows for troubleshooting and debugging without stopping game streaming in case bugs appear after the launch.

The leading platforms providing cloud services dedicated to gaming are AWS GameLift, Azure PlayFab, Google Cloud for Games, and Edgegap.

These platforms allow game developers to deploy, operate, and scale dedicated game servers where they can develop and launch session-based multiplayer games.

For example, Amazon GameLift Servers is specifically designed for hosting and scaling multiplayer game servers, which makes it different from general-purpose Amazon cloud services. It provides built-in matchmaking, session management, and server health monitoring, which is tailored for the needs of real-time multiplayer games, as well as analytics, SDKs, and more. Amazon Game Lift Servers support 100 million concurrent players in a single game, and 100,000 player adds per second (AWS n.d.). It also supports game streaming at up to 1080p resolution and 60 frames-per-second to any device with a browser.

Thanks to the autoscaling feature, Amazon GameLift automatically scales game capacity up or down based on the gamer's demand. Previously, scaling would require a dedicated engineer to manually order more CPU in case the game involved more players.

Also, the service is specifically designed to support game engines like Unity and Unreal Engine and provide game-centric analytics to ensure stable and secure gaming environments.

Another exemplary service, Azure PlayFab, hosted, managed, and scaled on the Microsoft Azure cloud platform, helps game developers launch and operate online games completely on the cloud.

Azure PlayFab is a backend platform for games, which features managed game services, real-time analytics, and live operations management capabilities (Microsoft 2025).

As a back-end-as-a-service platform, Azure Play Fab removes the challenges of building and managing multiplayer servers as it comes with ready solutions.

The platform takes care of such features as multiplayer services, networking, matchmaking, leaderboards, and cross-platform identity (Microsoft n.d.-a). It means that it supports features like automating scaling to deliver low-latency infrastructure to multiple players (following the principle "more players—more resources"), helping players with peer-to-peer communication and finding new friends and competitors, tracking success and providing means to link accounts on platforms like Xbox, PSN, Nintendo, and beyond.

Such a system helps developers a lot: once the game mechanics are developed on tools like Unity or Unreal Engine, the game can be transferred to the PlayFab cloud for backend services with a lot of features prebuilt and not requiring coding from scratch.

The network of cloud gaming solutions increases. Google Cloud's Gaming Services, Pragma, Nakama, Beamable, and AccelByte offer similar solutions with variations in the game's budget, specific needs, and technologies used.

Data Compression for Low-bandwidth Gaming

Modern games offer players immersive visual experiences, yet complex graphics and architecture require more size to store. This makes gaming in low-bandwidth connections difficult while gamers experience issues such as lag and input delays, while actions take longer to register, the gameplay feels unresponsive. Another sort of issue connected with low connectivity is rubberbanding, which presupposes characters moving back to previous positions due to delayed position updates. In multiplayer games, players often experience desynchronization when players see different states of the game or the hits are not registered. Connection drops and timeouts can disrupt game sessions completely.

To solve the issues described, various data compression technologies have been used to lower latency and improve the gaming experience.

Generally, data compression is the reduction in the number of bits needed to represent the data. This reduction can be achieved through different methods and approaches that constitute data compression technologies and services.

Data compression technologies reduce bandwidth consumption, thereby minimizing the likelihood that a player will experience gameplay issues due to bandwidth limitations (Crocetti and Sliwa 2022).

Compression is performed by specialized programs that utilize algorithms to identify data strings that can be minimized and replaced with shorter code. For example, when there is a sequence of colors inside the game, with each color represented by a separate bit, the algorithm turns this sequence into a group coded as a separate bit, thus saving memory.

In terms of gaming, data compression can take the form of texture compression, delta compression, or network compression.

Texture compression in games refers to the technique used to reduce the size of texture files. Texture files contain images that define how objects appear in the game, providing visual information such as color, patterns, and surface properties. Every pixel of the image occupies several bits of code, and the amount of storage required for a single texture pixel is counted in bits per pixel (BPP) (Unity documentation n.d.-b). Textures with lower BPP will occupy less memory but will also have lower image quality.

Delta compression allows developers to avoid sending the complete game state and proposes sending only the changes from the previous state, also called deltas. In delta compression, the algorithm utilizes the previous block of bytes as a reference in the compression process for subsequent blocks (Tommy et al. 2023). This method is especially useful in large games, where instead of sending full asset files for every update, only the changes (deltas) between different versions of game assets (textures, models, etc.) are sent. In multiplayer games, delta compression allows the synchronization of game state between clients and servers by transmitting only the changes in player positions, health, or environmental data.

Network compression refers to various techniques used to reduce the size of data transmitted over a network. In contrast to delta compression, which reduces the size of the game by only sending the differences between states, network compression focuses on the transmission of all the data transmitted through the network.

Services that allow game developers to compress game size include Photon Fusion, Unity's Netcode for GameObjects, Mirror, Nakama, and Unity Relay.

Photon's fusion is a new high-performance state synchronization networking library for Unity, offering advanced features like data compression, client-side prediction, and lag compensation (Photon Engine n.d.-a).

Fusion relies on a state-of-the-art compression algorithm, which allows the reduction of bandwidth requirements with minimal CPU overhead. The platform used both network compression and delta compression, depending on the game settings.

Photon, both the platform and its products, are based on the binary protocol, which reduces the overall size of messages sent over the network, a form of network compression (Photon Engine n.d.-b). In a game, these messages represent player position updates, health changes, or weapon firing events, and with the help of compression, this data is transmitted more efficiently.

Photon also supports delta compression by allowing game developers to configure this option through custom serialization. Therefore, the developer can configure the game to send only the changed parts of the game, rather than the full data. In terms of a game, instead of sending the full position of a player, delta compression allows sending only the change in position since the last update. This enhances the performance of the game's fast-paced elements, such as aiming, hit detection, and shooting.

Besides compression, gaming quality can be enhanced thanks to the relay networks. A relay network is a type of network that works as an intermediary between two devices, such as a server and a gamer's computer.

Relay servers deliver messages between connected players using low-latency data exchange between game clients. Eventually, no two players ever connect directly to each other (Unity n.d.-e). Relay servers function as public endpoints, enabling gamers to connect to the relay server rather than directly to each other. This is helpful in real-world situations where the server and the gamer's computer are separated geographically or when game data must bypass numerous firewalls or NATs, which block direct connections.

Relay servers are helpful in such situations due to several architectural tweaks.

Relay networks route data around NAT and firewalls. NAT, or Network Address Translation, is a service that routes and tracks connections within the local network (e.g., all devices connected to a single internet provider or home devices connected to a Wi-Fi hotspot). When a gamer from outside these networks attempts to connect to a computer inside this network, NAT may not recognize their IP address and drop the data. It is comparable to dropping a call from an unknown caller.

Additionally, in multiplayer games, when multiple gamers with different devices attempt to connect to a game port, or the NAT doesn't have an entry for the connection, the connection is interrupted.

Relay networks help route data around NAT and firewalls, acting as intermediaries between game devices, which connect to the relay server outbound, which NAT allows. This way, different computers get connected to the relay server and send information through it.

Also, relay networks use optimized routing mechanisms to determine the best paths for mage data and distribute traffic evenly to avoid network congestion. For example, when a player connects to a game, their traffic gets routed through the nearest or the least-loaded relay server. Instead of connecting directly to other servers or gamers, creating network congestion, game data travels through the relay network more efficiently. This reduces bottlenecks that could slow down connections.

It is important to mention that relay servers are also placed closer to gamers geographically. This way, data has to travel shorter physical distances and get fewer obstacles.

One of the key relay server providers in the gaming market is Unity Relay. Unity Relay is a relay-as-a-service product offering focused on gaming. It enables peer-to-peer, listen-server UDP communication between players.

This service provides a way for game developers to securely offer increased connectivity between players by using a join code-style workflow, eliminating the need to maintain dedicated game servers and simplifying the network complexities of a peer-to-peer game (Unity Relay n.d.-c).

The service consists of two parts: relay servers and allocation services. While relay servers connect players and game servers as intermediaries, the allocation services enable the allocation of the host player and joining players for the game session and also match players with nearby relay servers for smoother gameplay.

Glossary of Terms

Adaptive Gameplay Game mechanics that dynamically adjust difficulty, pacing, or content based on a player's performance or emotional state.

Artificial Intelligence (AI) Computer systems that mimic human cognitive functions such as learning, decision-making, and pattern recognition and used in games for adaptive environments, intelligent NPCs, and content generation.

Augmented Reality (AR) Technology that overlays digital information onto the physical world via devices like smartphones or AR glasses.

Blockchain A decentralized digital ledger technology that records transactions across multiple computers in a secure, transparent, and immutable way. It underpins many Web3 technologies.

Brain–Computer Interface (BCI) Technology that enables direct communication between the brain and a computer or digital device, allowing mental commands to control software or hardware.

Creator Economy A digital economic system where individuals create, distribute, and monetize content, assets, or experiences—often via platforms that support NFTs or user-generated content.

DAO (Decentralized Autonomous Organization) A blockchain-based community structure governed by smart contracts, where decisions are made collectively by token holders without centralized leadership.

Dark Patterns User interface designs intended to trick or manipulate users into taking actions they might not otherwise choose (e.g., overspending or excessive screen time).

Decentralized Finance (DeFi) Blockchain-based financial services that operate without central banks or intermediaries, enabling peer-to-peer transactions and lending.

Digital Assets Virtual items or rights represented in digital form and often stored on a blockchain—includes tokens, avatars, virtual land, and NFTs.

Digital Inclusion The effort to ensure all people, especially in underserved regions, have access to digital technologies and opportunities.

Esports Organized competitive video gaming, often involving professional players, teams, and spectators across global tournaments and streaming platforms.

GameFi (Gaming Finance) The integration of gaming and financial services, allowing players to earn, trade, and invest through in-game assets and tokenized economies.

Generative AI AI systems that create new content—text, images, sound, or game environments—based on user input or learned patterns.

Guilds Blockchain-based gaming communities or cooperatives that invest in in-game assets and share profits among player-members.

Immersive Technology Technologies such as VR, AR, and haptic feedback that create deeply engaging digital experiences.

Interoperability The ability for digital assets, identities, or data to move seamlessly across different platforms, games, or virtual environments.

Metaverse An interconnected digital universe of persistent, immersive virtual worlds where users can interact, socialize, work, and play.

Mobile-First Gaming Games designed primarily for smartphones, common in emerging markets where mobile is the dominant mode of internet access.

NFT (Non-Fungible Token) A unique digital token that represents ownership of a specific asset—commonly used in gaming for skins, avatars, land, and digital collectibles.

Non-player Character A character within a video game or virtual environment that is not controlled by a human player, but instead operates according to scripted behavior or artificial intelligence (AI).

Player-to-Earn (P2E) A gaming model where players earn digital assets or tokens with real-world value through in-game activities.

Procedural Content Generation The use of algorithms to automatically generate game environments, levels, or characters instead of hand-designing them.

Smart Contract Self-executing code on a blockchain that carries out transactions or agreements once certain conditions are met.

Tokenization The process of converting real-world or digital assets into blockchain-based tokens that can be traded, owned, or programmed with conditions.

User-generated content (UGC) Digital material, such as text, images, videos, audio, or interactive media, created and published by end users rather than by professional producers or official content creators.

Virtual Reality (VR) Computer-generated simulation of a three-dimensional environment that users can interact with via headsets and motion tracking technology.

Web3 The next evolution of the internet, emphasizing decentralization, user ownership of data, and blockchain-enabled applications and economies.

Web4 (Symbiotic Web) A conceptual evolution of the web where humans and machines interact in real time through sensors, AI, and neural interfaces. Web4 envisions continuous connectivity between digital and physical realities, enabling predictive, context-aware experiences.

Web5 (Decentralized Web + Personal Sovereignty) A proposed future web model blending Web2 and Web3, focused on user control over identity and data. Spearheaded by TBD (a Block company), Web5 emphasizes self-sovereign identity, offline capability, and peer-to-peer communication, building a user-centric internet beyond platform dependency.

References

Adobe. (n.d.). Substance 3D Painter product page. Retrieved from https://www.adobe.com/products/substance3d/apps/painter.html

Announcing ethers.js: A Web3 alternative. (2017, October 24). Medium. Retrieved from https://medium.com/l4-media/announcing-ethersjs-a-web3-alternative-6f134fdd06f3

Aragon Association. (n.d.). Aragon: Decentralized governance tools. Retrieved from https://www.aragon.org/

Arweave. (n.d.). Arweave: Permanent data storage. Retrieved from https://arweave.org/

Autodesk. (n.d.). Maya documentation. Retrieved from https://help.autodesk.com/view/MAYACRE/…

AWS. (n.d.). Amazon GameLift Servers overview. Retrieved from https://aws.amazon.com/gamelift/#…

Baker, R.L. (2023). Deep Dive. Wiley. Retrieved from https://www.google.com.ua/books/edition/Deep_Dive/SOa3EAAAQBAJ?hl=en&gbpv=0

Benetollo, L., Crafa, S., Bugliesi, M., Pinna, A. (2024). Smart contract languages: A comparative analysis [PDF]. Retrieved from https://www.researchgate.net/publication/380192112_Smart_Contract_Languages_a_comparative_analysis

Blender Foundation. (n.d.). Blender features overview. Retrieved from https://www.blender.org/features/#…

BuildBox. (n.d.). BuildBox product signup (BB2). Retrieved from https://signup.buildbox.com/product/bb2

Building with the YGG Guild Protocol [Blog post]. (2024). Medium. Retrieved from https://medium.com/yield-guild-games/building-on-theygg-guild-protocol-d90e89e03463

Buterin, V. (2022). *Ethereum and the Merge*. Ethereum Foundation. Retrieved from https://ethereum.org/en/upgrades/merge/

Ceramic (n.d.) How Ceramic Works. Retrieved from https://ceramic.network/how-it-works

Ceramic Documentation (n.d.). Accounts. Retrieved from https://developers.ceramic.network/docs/protocol/js-ceramic/accounts/accountsindex

Ceramic Roadmap. (n.d.). Ceramic network. Retrieved from https://github.com/ceramicnetwork/.github/issues/19?utm_source

Chainalysis. (n.d.-a). Company overview. Retrieved from https://www.chainalysis.com/company/

Chainalysis. (n.d.-b). Full node documentation search. Retrieved from https://www.chainalysis.com/?s=full+node

Chainalysis Products (n.d.). Chainanalysis. Retrieved from https://www.chainalysis.com/?s=full+node

Circle Reserve Fund. (2024). BlackRock. Retrieved from https://www.blackrock.com/cash/en-us/stream-document?stream=reg&product=LCIRRF&shareClass=Institutional&documentId=2041739%7E2041738&iframeUrlOverride=%2Fcash%2Fliterature%2Fprospectus%2Fprocrf-us.pdf

Coinbase. (n.d.-a). CDP documentation. Retrieved from https://docs.cdp.coinbase.com/

Coinbase. (n.d.-b). Coinbase Wallet SDK documentation. Retrieved from https://www.coinbase.com/ru/developer-platform/products/wallet-sdk

Coinbase Commerce. (n.d.). Coinbase Commerce products. Retrieved from https://www.coinbase.com/commerce

CoinMarketCap. (n.d.-a). *Blockchain rankings*. Retrieved from https://coinmarketcap.com

CoinMarketCap. (n.d.-b). CoinMarketCap: Cryptocurrency market cap rankings [Web resource]. Retrieved from https://coinmarketcap.com/coins/

Common.xyz. (n.d.). Common.xyz product features. Retrieved from https://landing.common.xyz/product-features

Crocetti, P., Sliwa, C. (2022, December 8). Data compression. TechTarget. Retrieved from https://www.techtarget.com/searchstorage/definition/compression

DAOhaus. (n.d.). DAOhaus documentation. Retrieved from https://docs.daohaus.club/

Decentralized Identifiers (DIDs) v1.0. (2019). W3C. Retrieved from https://www.w3.org/TR/did-1.0/

Developer Survey. (2023). *Stack Overflow Developer Survey 2023*. Stack Overflow. Retrieved from https://survey.stackoverflow.co/2023

Egliston, B. (2025). Cryptogaming: Blockchain and the financialization of videogames. Palgrave Macmillan. Retrieved from https://www.google.com.ua/books/edition/Cryptogaming/B75HEQAAQBAJ?hl=en&gbpv=0

ENS Support. (n.d.). What is ENS? Retrieved from https://support.ens.domains/en/articles/7900404-what-is-ens

Entriken, W., Shirley, D., Evans, D., Sachs, N. (2018) ERC-721: Non-Fungible Token Standard. Retrieved from https://eips.ethereum.org/EIPS/eip-721

Epic Games. (n.d.). Real benefits of C# in Unreal Engine. Retrieved from https://dev.epicgames.com/community/learning/tutorials/waZ/real-benefits-of-c?locale=ru-ru

Ethereum (2025) ERC-1155 Multi-Token Standard. (2025, April 14). Retrieved from https://ethereum.org/en/developers/docs/standards/tokens/erc-1155/

Ethereum Foundation. (n.d.-a). EIP-1155: Multi-token standard. Retrieved from https://ethereum.org/en/developers/docs/standards/tokens/erc-1155/

Ethereum Foundation. (n.d.-b). Ethers.js documentation (v6). Retrieved from https://docs.ethers.org/v6/...

Ethereum Foundation. (n.d.-c). web3.js documentation. Retrieved from https://docs.web3js.org/

Ethereum Improvement Proposals (n.d.) ERC Retrieved from https://eips.ethereum.org/erc

Etherscan. (n.d.). Etherscan: Ethereum blockchain explorer [Web resource]. Retrieved from https://etherscan.io/

Finzer, D. (2018). OpenSea raises $2 million to make true digital ownership more accessible [Blog post]. OpenSea. Retrieved from https://opensea.io/blog/articles/opensea-raises-2-million

Flinders, M., Smalley, I. (2024, February 20). What is 5G?. IBM. Retrieved from https://www.ibm.com/think/topics/5g

Flutter. (n.d.). Flutter games overview. Retrieved from https://flutter.dev/games

Franklin Tan, O. (2021, November 4). Announcing the $100M Efinity Metaverse Fund [Blog post]. Retrieved from https://enjin.io/blog/100m-efinity-metaverse-fund

Geig, M. (2022, February 10). Get Started with Unity. InformIT. Retrieved from https://www.informit.com/articles/article.aspx?p=3129466

Godot Engine. (n.d.). Godot features overview. Retrieved from https://godotengine.org/features/

Green, A. (2025). DAO Governance. Publifye AS. Retrieved from https://www.google.com.ua/books/edition/DAO_Governance/p3JLEQAAQBAJ?hl=en&gbpv=0

References

Griffin, C. (2022). Mastering NFT. Top Notch International LTD. Retrieved from https://www.google.com.ua/books/edition/Mastering_NFT/sOqJEAAAQBAJ?hl=en&gbpv=0

Guild Protocol: The Era of Onchain GuildsYield Guild Games [Concept paper]. (2024). Retrieved from https://storage.googleapis.com/external_communication/YGG-GuildProtocol-ConceptPaper-2024Sept.pdf

Hardhat Developers. (n.d.). Hardhat development peer environment. Retrieved from https://hardhat.org/

Identifiers. (n.d.). Ceramic Documentation. Retrieved from https://developers.ceramic.network/docs/protocol/jsceramic/accounts/decentralized-identifiers#pkh-did

Immutable. (2024). More games signed in 2024 than in all prior years combined [Blog]. Retrieved from https://www.immutable.com/blog/immutable-announces-more-games-signed-in-2024-than-in-all-prior-years-combined#:…

Immutable X. (n.d.). Immutable X product page. Retrieved from https://www.immutable.com/products/immutable-x

IPFS Project. (n.d.). IPFS: Peer-to-peer hypermedia protocol. Retrieved from https://ipfs.tech/

Johnson, R. (2025). Building Web3 Applications with Moralis: Definitive Reference for Developers. NOBTREX, LCC. Retrieved from https://books.google.com.ua/books?id=8dBmEQAAQBAJ&...

Jones, B. (2024). Smart contracts and the rise of dApps. *Web3 Insights Journal, 10*(2), 50–66.

Joo, R., Proorocu, A.G., Krivosheev, S. (2023). NFT Gold Rush. Walter de Gruyter GmbH. Retrieved from https://www.google.com.ua/books/edition/NFT_Gold_Rush/zgevEAAAQBAJ?hl=en&gbpv=0

Ko-fi. (n.d.). Ko-fi vs. Patreon alternative overview. Retrieved from https://more.ko-fi.com/patreon-alternative?…

Krishnan, V. (2023). The Essential Guide to Web3. Packt Publishing. Retrieved from https://www.google.com.ua/books/edition/The_Essential_Guide_to_Web3/EGnmEAAAQBAJ?hl=en&gbpv=0

Lacity, M. C. (2020). *A manager's guide to blockchains for business*. SB Publishing.

Lawton, G. (2025, February 25). What are diffusion models? TechTarget. Retrieved from https://www.techtarget.com/searchenterpriseai/definition/diffusion-model

LayerZero Labs. (n.d.). What is LayerZero? Retrieved from https://docs.layerzero.network/v2/concepts/getting-started/what-is-layerzero#:…

Lebrun, J., Malghem, T., Thizy, K., Falempin, L., Boudjemaa, A. (2021). ERC-3643: TREX—Token for Regulated Exchanges. Ethereum Improvement Proposals. Retrieved from https://eips.ethereum.org/EIPS/eip-3643

Microsoft (2025) What is Azure PlayFab? (2025, May 21). Retrieved from https://learn.microsoft.com/en-us/gaming/playfab/getstarted/what-is-playfab

Microsoft (n.d.-a) Azure PlayFab. Microsoft. Retrieved from https://azure.microsoft.com/en-us/products/playfab

Microsoft. (n.d.-b). What is cloud gaming? Retrieved from https://www.microsoft.com/.../learning-center/what-is-cloud-gaming

Microsoft (n.d.-c) What is edge computing? Retrieved from https://azure.microsoft.com/en-ca/resources/cloud-computingdictionary/what-is-edge-computing

Moralis. (n.d.). Moralis FAQ: What is Moralis? Retrieved from https://developers.moralis.com/faq/what-is-moralis/#…

Nair, R., Merino, T., Togelius, J. (2025). God's Innovation Project: Empowering the player with generative AI [PDF]. ResearchGate. Retrieved from https://www.researchgate.net/publication/390989998_God's_Innovation_Project_%2D%2D_Empowering_The_Player_With_Generative_AI

Nakamoto, S. (2008a). *Bitcoin: A peer-to-peer electronic cash system*. Retrieved from https://bitcoin.org/bitcoin.pdf

Nakamoto, S. (2008b). Bitcoin: A peer-to-peer electronic cash system [White paper]. Retrieved from https://bitcoin.org/bitcoin.pdf

OpenSea IPO overview. (2022). ForgeGlobal. Retrieved from https://forgeglobal.com/opensea_ipo/

Patreon. (n.d.). Patreon platform. Retrieved from https://www.patreon.com/
Patreon Support. (n.d.). Patreon documentation: Introduction. Retrieved from https://docs.patreon.com/#introduction
Photon Engine (n.d.-a) Fusion 2 Introduction. Retrieved from https://doc.photonengine.com/fusion/current/fusion-intro
Photon Engine. (n.d.-b). Photon PUN binary protocol reference. Retrieved from https://doc.photonengine.com/pun/current/reference/binary-protocol
Plugin: OpenSea SDK by EzCode [Online forum post] (2021). Bubble Forum. Retrieved from https://forum.bubble.io/t/plugin-openseasdk-by-ezcode/176778
Project OpenSea (n.d.-a) OpenSea JS advanced use cases. Retrieved from https://github.com/ProjectOpenSea/openseajs/blob/main/developerDocs/advanced-use-cases.md
Project OpenSea. (n.d.-b). OpenSea JS developer docs: Getting started. Retrieved from https://github.com/ProjectOpenSea/opensea-js/blob/main/developerDocs/getting-started.md
Quantum Risk. (n.d.). *Security vulnerabilities in Ethereum smart contracts*. Retrieved from https://quantumrisk.org/reports
Rarible Help Center. (n.d.). What is Rarible Protocol? Retrieved from https://help.rarible.com/hc/en-us/articles/16899172465549-What-is-Rarible-Protocol
Reiff, N., and Team. (2024). Polygon: How it works and benefits. *Investopedia*. Retrieved from https://www.investopedia.com
Reijers, W., Wuisman, I., Mannan, M., De Filipi, P. (2018). Now the code runs itself: On-chain and off-chain governance of blockchain technologies [PDF]. Retrieved from https://www.researchgate.net/publication/331853151_Now_the_Code_Runs_Itself_On-Chain_and_Off-Chain_Governance_of_Blockchain_Technologies
Sabry, A. (2025). NFT inclusion and Web3 on Polygon. *Web3 Policy Reports*.
Sharma, A. (2024). Comparative smart contract languages. *Blockchain Dev Journal, 12*(3), 34–49.
Snapshot Labs. (n.d.). Snapshot documentation: Getting started. Retrieved from https://docs.snapshot.box/faq/getting-started
Snow, P. (2023). Learning Web3 Development. IT Campus Academy. Retrieved from https://www.google.com.ua/books/edition/Learning_Web3_Development/W4DZEAAAQBAJ?hl=en&gbpv=0
Solidity Team. (n.d.). *Solidity documentation*. Retrieved from https://soliditylang.org
Solscan. (n.d.). Solscan: The primary Solana blockchain explorer [Web resource]. Retrieved from https://solscan.io/
Statt, N. (2022, September 15). Ethereum completes 'The Merge' and joins proof-of-stake era. The New York Times. Retrieved from http://nytimes.com/2022/09/15/technology/merge-ethereum-crypto.html
Storj Labs. (n.d.). Storj: Decentralized cloud storage. Retrieved from https://www.storj.io/
Stripe. (n.d.). Stripe API documentation. Retrieved from https://docs.stripe.com/api
TechTarget. (2019, August 15). Low-Earth Orbit (LEO) satellite definition. Retrieved from https://www.techtarget.com/.../definition/low-earth-orbit-LEO-satellite#:...
The Move Book Team. (n.d.). *The Move programming language*. Retrieved from https://move-language.github.io/move
Themistocleous, M. (Ed). (2025). Handbook of Blockchain Technology. Edward Elgar Publishing. Retrieved from https://www.google.com.ua/books/edition/Handbook_of_Blockchain_Technology/9KFHEQAAQBAJ?hl=en&gbpv=0
Theta Token. (n.d.). Theta network site. Retrieved from https://www.thetatoken.org/
T. Tommy, F. Riza, R. Siregar, M. Yeni, A. M. Elhanafi, and R. Nurmadi (2023). Base-Delta Dynamic Block Length and Optimization on File Compression. Journal of Computer Networks, Architecture and High Performance Computing, 5(1), 229–240. Retrieved from https://jurnal.itscience.org/index.php/CNAPC/article/view/1993
TRM Labs. (n.d.). About TRM Labs. Retrieved from https://www.trmlabs.com/about
Twitch Developer. (n.d.-a). Drops documentation. Retrieved from https://dev.twitch.tv/docs/drops/

References

Twitch Developer. (n.d.-b). EventSub documentation. Retrieved from https://dev.twitch.tv/docs/eventsub/

Twitch Developer. (n.d.-c). Twitch API documentation. Retrieved from https://dev.twitch.tv/docs/api/

Unity. (n.d.-a). IL2CPP scripting backend documentation. Retrieved from https://docs.unity3d.com/6000.1/…

Unity. (n.d.-b). Rigidbody class reference documentation. Retrieved from https://docs.unity3d.com/Manual/class-Rigidbody.html

Unity. (n.d.-c). UGS Relay introduction. Retrieved from https://docs.unity.com/ugs/en-us/manual/relay/manual/introduction

Unity. (n.d.-d). Unity feature sets documentation. Retrieved from https://docs.unity3d.com/Manual/FeatureSets.html

Unity. (n.d.-e). Unity UGS Relay servers documentation. Retrieved from https://docs.unity.com/ugs/manual/relay/manual/relay-servers

Unity Documentation (n.d.-a) Level of Detail. Retrieved from https://docs.unity3d.com/530/Documentation/Manual/LevelOfDetail.html

Unity documentation (n.d.-b) GPU texture format fundamentals. Retrieved from https://docs.unity3d.com/Manual/texture-compressionfundamentals.html

Unreal Engine (n.d.-a) Epic releases $17,000,000 of paragon content for free. Retrieved from https://www.unrealengine.com/en-US/paragon

Unreal Engine (n.d.-b) Patreon for game devs. Patreon. Retrieved from https://docs.patreon.com/#introduction

Unreal Engine (n.d.-c) Blueprints Visual Scripting Overview. Retrieved from https://dev.epicgames.com/documentation/en-us/unrealengine/overview-of-blueprints-visual-scripting-in-unreal-engine

Verifiable Credentials Data Model. (2021). W3C. Retrieved from https://www.w3.org/TR/vc-data-model/

WalletConnect. (n.d.). WalletConnect: Decentralized connection protocol. Retrieved from https://walletconnect.network/

Williams, B. (2025). Decentralized Identities: Exploring Blockchain Solutions for Secure Authentication. Barrett Williams. Retrieved from https://www.google.com.ua/books/edition/Decentralized_Identities/Uz9CEQAAQBAJ?hl=en&gbpv=0

Woodrum, R. (2024). Decoding Tomorrow's Currency: An In-Depth Tokenization. Randy Woodrum. Retrieved from https://www.google.com.ua/books/edition/Decoding_Tomorrow_s_Currency_An_In_Depth/MxZSEQAAQBAJ?hl=en&gbpv=0

xDAO. (n.d.). xDAO supported blockchains architecture. Retrieved from https://docs.xdao.app/architecture/supported-blockchains

Yakovenko, A. (2018). *Solana: A new architecture for a high performance blockchain*. Solana Whitepaper. Retrieved from https://solana.com/solana-whitepaper.pdf

You42 Inc. (n.d.). Token project page. Retrieved from https://www.you42inc.com/token/

YoYo Games. (n.d.). GameMaker Language (GML) Visual Reference. Retrieved from http://manual.gamemaker.io/lts/en/GameMaker_Language.htm…

Zora. (n.d.). NFT docs overview. Retrieved from https://NFT-docs.zora.co/

Zora Labs. (n.d.). Coins SDK documentation. Retrieved from https://docs.zora.co/coins/sdk

ZoraOS Devs. (n.d.). ZoraOS ZDK documentation. Retrieved from https://ourzora.gitbook.io/zoraos/dev/zdk

MIX
Papier aus verantwortungsvollen Quellen
Paper from responsible sources
FSC® C105338

If you have any concerns about our products,
you can contact us on
ProductSafety@springernature.com

In case Publisher is established outside the EU,
the EU authorized representative is:
**Springer Nature Customer Service Center GmbH
Europaplatz 3, 69115 Heidelberg, Germany**

Printed by Libri Plureos GmbH
in Hamburg, Germany